The Miranda Affair

Margaret R. Davis

Published by Sand Hill Review Press, LLC
All rights reserved
www.sandhillreviewpress.com,
P.O. Box 1275, San Mateo, CA 94401
(415) 297-3571

ISBN: 978-1-937818-52-4 paperback
ISBN: 978-1-937818-53-1 case laminate
ISBN: 978-1-937818-66-1 ebook
Library of Congress Control Number: 2017940091
© 2017 Margaret R. Davis

Cover art by Dreamstime
Graphics by Backspace Ink
Art Direction by Tory Hartmann

The Miranda Affair is a work of fiction. Its characters, scenes and locales are the product of the author's imagination or are used fictitiously. Any similarity of fictional characters to people living or dead is purely coincidental.

SHRP
Sand Hill Review Press

For Ray, with love

Note to Readers

The action of this story takes place in San Francisco in 1989-90. In the minds of many San Franciscans, 1989 is most closely associated with the deadly Loma Prieta Earthquake of October 17. But there was a lot more happening in corporate America in the 1980's and 1990's that was in its own way as earthshaking as the Quake. For this was the time that many large companies in this country were starting to face up to the dysfunctional fattening of American corporations following the huge post-World War II corporate boom.

In this story, we see a fictional large corporation in 1989. Typical of many workplaces in the city, the digital revolution was in its infancy; the company was heavy with staff departments that supported the company rather than the customers. Then came the uneasy realization that maybe America needed to get rid of some of the bloat. "Lean and mean" became a popular catchphrase.

Another difference from the present day is in the role of women in the corporation. Although women were not excluded from management ranks entirely, it was typically men who determined what their positions would be. This state of affairs was largely accepted as "just the way things are," rather than something to be fought against—even by ambitious women like the heroine of this story.

The Redwood Power Corporation portrayed here is based on the bare skeleton of a real company but that skeleton is fleshed out with fictional characters and fictional places.

The Miranda Affair

Margaret R. Davis

Flash Forward

"Get out. You make me sick."

Katie Carlisle stood frozen until he repeated, "I said, get out." And then she did—out of his office and down the hall to hers.

The anger in his voice told her he had come to the end of his patience in dealing with her. This could only mean that she could say goodbye to her dream of shortly replacing him as department manager. True, the last few months had been unexpectedly difficult—with some near misses in her attempts to hold onto her job. But somehow she had felt she would eventually prevail—until today. Had she made one misstep too many?

Once seated at her desk, Katie swiveled her chair toward the window, past the jade plant on the sill—*oh, jade plant of happier days!*—toward the view up Market Street. Now, she must clear her head and make sense of what had just happened.

She knew the exact date everything had started to go wrong. It was on Friday, January 27, 1989—her 39th birthday.

Katie's World

ON JANUARY 27, 1989, Katie awoke with the alarm clock at five-fifteen. She pushed aside the still-sleeping figures of her two Russian blues and struggled out of bed. Then she walked to the mirror over her dresser and gave her reflection a long, hard look. Wide, gray eyes, dark, overly curly hair, bumpy nose—half-way between pretty and plain. Or so she'd long ago decided.

She'd done this mirror-reflecting several times over the past year, ever since Alan—for seven years her lover and best friend—had walked out of her life. At the time, it had felt like a vast chasm had opened beneath her. On top of the heartache his desertion had caused her was a more practical concern: she really had been looking forward to a conventional marriage and family with Alan. Not that she had ever pushed him toward commitment. Indeed, she'd treasured the special laid-back relationship the two of them shared and was certain that he'd never abandon her. Man, had she been wrong!

Today, though, she felt better about things. True, thirty-nine was pushing the limits for motherhood, but thirty-nine was a perfect age for something else she really cared about: her career. Katie felt herself to be creative and ambitious. Ever since she had joined Redwood Power Corporation (RPC) five years ago, she had worked hard to make herself indispensable to just about everyone in the company who counted, all the way up to the chief executive officer. She intended to climb that corporate ladder just as high as any glass ceiling would permit.

The past year, she'd allowed her resolve to be weakened somewhat by her aching heart, but today, her birthday, she planned to get back on track—starting at eight o'clock this morning during her weekly one-on-one with her department manager, Chuck Browne. She'd surprise him by stating, "It's my birthday today, Chuck, and as a present I'd like to take over the agenda for our meeting." He'd look amused, then bemused, then say, "Ooo-kay."

And then she'd tell him what she had in mind.

SO MUCH FOR the plans of people who want desperately to be on time. Today, there'd been horrific traffic delays and it was well past eight o'clock when Katie's commute bus pulled into its downtown terminal. She pushed her way off the bus and ran—one block to the left and two blocks to the right—to the crosswalk that would take her to her destination. The light turned red.

"Damn!" She paced in place to keep warm and stared across the street toward the headquarters of the Redwood Power Corporation. RPC's downtown headquarters occupied an entire block in San Francisco's financial district. Most of the block was occupied by a majestic forty-story skyscraper known as the Tower Building. At this time of the morning, the sun's rays sparkled on the top floors of the glass and chrome high-rise. To Katie's eye, the building looked like a giant silver and blue ice sculpture.

The light turned green and Katie started running again, not toward the giant Tower but to her left, toward an eight-story redbrick building squeezed into the southwest corner of the block. This was the Annex Building. With its elaborate stone parapets and gargoyles, it was as historic as the Tower was futuristic—a perfect exemplar of the city that had arisen from the ashes of the 1909 earthquake.

Katie crossed the old building's oak-paneled lobby, the gleaming brass fixtures and huge chandeliers, and dashed into the elevator. She alighted on the eighth floor, which housed the executive support services department. As always, her spirits rose as she stepped into the cheerful bustle of the floor and the chorus of *Good Mornings* from everyone she met. In her office, she hung up her raincoat and took a broad-toothed comb from her purse.

A tap at the door and the smiling, bespectacled face of her colleague Terence Lynch peeked in at her. "Gotta minute?" He waved a copy of their company's daily news-sheet, *The Redwood Rover*, as he spoke.

"No, I don't." Katie tugged at her hair with the comb. "God, this comb is useless. You don't have a hairbrush on you, do you?"

He grinned at this crack about his thinning hair. "Not today, kiddo. This should thrill you though. Hot news from Beresford Division. It seems some joker's come up with an invention that could put the whole company out of business."

"Oo, that's scary." Katie pulled a document from her briefcase and tucked it under her arm together with a notepad. "Sorry, Terry, I'm in a huge rush. I had some really important stuff to discuss with Chuck this morning. Now I'm running so late practically all my time is gone."

He called after her as she pushed past him. "Good luck. Seriously, Katie, this article is worth a look. I'll leave it on your reading pile."

Katie and Chuck

SEATED AT HIS DESK, Chuck smiled at Katie as she hurried into his office and slid into her customary chair opposite him. "Latie-Katie," he teased. She smiled back at the plump, middle-aged figure. Permanent frown lines, combined with a ready smile, gave him an expression that was simultaneously welcoming and anxious.

The department that Chuck managed--executive support services, known throughout the company as ESS—handled a number of traditional human resource functions like employee surveys and training of employees and management. Katie's official title was supervisor of management development. In practice, however, the company's CEO used the department manager as his personal staff person, charged with conducting confidential investigations of top executives and their departments. Increasingly, Chuck had called on Katie to assist him in these efforts and had recently given her the additional title of "special projects consultant."

Now, a breathless Katie said, "I'm so sorry I'm late, Chuck. Traffic was terrible."

Chuck handed a sheet of paper across the desk toward her. "Look at this. An invitation from Worthington to attend the executive committee meeting at eleven o'clock." As she took the paper, he added, "God knows what this is all about."

Katie skimmed the lines. "He's saying he won't be at the meeting himself but Barry Bryce will be there to announce some program that will be critical to the future success of RPC." She looked up to meet his eyes. *"Barry Bryce.* Holy cow!"

"Exactly!"

Barry Bryce had been recruited last summer from outside the company. Katie had never met him in person but knew of him by reputation and had seen him at a distance. Photographs of him in the *Redwood Rover* showed him to be a lean, wiry looking man, with close-cropped dark hair and stern expression. Handsome in a serious, almost sinister way.

Bryce had been given the new-to-the-company title of advisor to the chief executive officer on classified projects. The title itself may have been vague but the meaning of what he actually did quickly became all too clear in that every time Bryce was assigned a "classified project," slashed budgets and employee layoffs resulted. In other words, BB was a hatchet man.

After a few moments of glum silence, Katie said. "Until now, Bryce has focused exclusively on field offices and power plants. Do you think he's planning to enlarge his mandate to include head office staff departments?"

"Who knows? Truthfully, we both know, don't we, Katie, that even head office departments could do with the odd hatchet man or two?"

Katie jumped as she realized this was her opening. "Chuck, this brings me to the main issue I wanted to see you about this morning." She glanced at the clock, painfully aware of how little time there was left for this meeting. "Remember, I was working on some ideas for changing the direction of our department? A sort of blueprint for the future to make our department and the company more competitive? Well, *ta da!"* She pushed the manuscript she'd been holding toward him.

Chuck raised his eyebrows and read the title page aloud. *"Blueprint for the Future of the Executive Support Services Department—a Manifesto for the '90s.* Hmm!" He flicked quickly through the first few pages. "Manifesto, huh?"

"A bit dramatic, I guess. Basically it's an action plan for revising our department's strategy so that we can help turn RPC into what our beloved CEO keeps saying it should be—i.e., 'a lean mean machine' to meet the challenges of the nineties." She smiled, hoping to coax an answering smile from him.

It didn't work. He pushed the document back toward her and turned his head to gaze out the window.

Katie sat forward. "Chuck, I really think this is important. You know our company's facing an uncertain future, like all utility companies these days. To survive, we'll have to make major changes in the lackadaisical way we operate."

He turned back to face her. "And you propose our department do what about it?"

"Well, you know how we've always done whatever top management asks of us. We carry out all their requests in knee-jerk fashion. What I propose here..." she pointed at her document. "...is that we move from reactive to proactive. We take the lead in determining what areas of the company need to be studied and changed."

Chuck screwed up his face in disgust. "My God! You want our department to turn into some sort of departmental equivalent of Barry Bryce?"

The intercom buzzed. It was Chuck's secretary Dorothy with a reminder of his nine o'clock appointment. He said to Katie, "We'll have to continue this some other time." As she stood to leave, he added, "You do realize, don't you, that if men like Bryce get their way, our department could well be revised right out of existence? In fact, by noon today your manifesto may not have any relevance one way or another."

Katie reached over and retrieved her document before leaving. Walking back to her office, she felt more angry than discouraged. It was true she owed a lot to Chuck. He'd been her staunch friend and mentor ever since she'd worked for him. But at times like this, he did show his stripes. He was supportive and cooperative to the hilt to their department's internal corporate clients but cowardly in pushing them to consider actions they didn't like. His approach might have worked in the past but these days their company just had to make changes its executives didn't like if it were to survive.

Oh, well! It was foolish of her to have raised the issue this morning when they'd started their meeting so late. She'd have to catch him at a better time and make him see the truth. Now, she couldn't help worrying about the other issue he'd raised—the committee meeting this morning. As Chuck had said, maybe by noon today all her plans for her career at RPC would be moot.

Back in her office, Katie slid the pages of the manifesto into the bottom drawer of her desk. The drawer slammed shut, her reading pile teetered, and *The Redwood Rover* fell into the wastebasket below. Katie reached out to rescue it, but then changed her mind. She had more than enough stuff to read. Besides, for the life of her, she couldn't remember what it was Terry had wanted her to see.

3

Introducing Miranda

AT EIGHT-THIRTY on the same January morning, Everett Worthington, chief executive officer of Redwood Power Corporation, sat at an impressive burled-walnut desk in his huge corner office on the fortieth floor of the Tower Building. As the CEO of one of the state's largest corporations, he was among the city's most powerful business leaders. Most would agree he looked the part: over six and a half feet tall, bushy white hair and a ruddy complexion.

In a corner of the office, Barry Bryce stood glaring down the forty floors to the street below. He and Worthington had just engaged in a sharp exchange of words over a last-minute assignment Worthington was attempting to foist on him. There was a tap at the door and Worthington called out, "Come in, come in." To Barry, he murmured, "Here she is."

Barry turned as a woman entered the room. Worthington beamed. "Barry, this is Miranda Peabody. *Doctor* Miranda Peabody. Miranda, this is Barry Bryce, my chief advisor on classified projects."

The sight of Miranda momentarily removed Barry's scowl. She was a slender but shapely woman, probably in her early thirties, with shoulder-length auburn hair and dressed in a green linen suit. She walked over to him, her arm extended. "Barry," she said, brown eyes sparkling. "I'm so happy to meet you. I hear that you and I will jointly present my Corporate Values Program to the executive committee this morning."

In spite of the friendly voice, Barry's scowl returned at the reminder. Hastily, Worthington cut in. "Please, have a seat, you two."

As she sat down, Miranda turned to Barry again. "So, Barry, Everett tells me you've studied my proposal. What do you think?"

Barry chose his words with care. "About the Corporate Values Program? I've just skimmed over the details. It sounds... interesting."

"Oh, good." Miranda sat back and crossed one willowy leg over the other. Barry noted her shoes were dyed the same green shade as her suit.

Barry said, "The problem is I personally have no experience with programs like this. I'm really not sure that I'm the right person to introduce you...."

Worthington said sharply, "Okay, Barry, we don't need to go through that again. Miranda, I'm really sorry that I can't be there myself but, as I said before, I've had a last-minute summons to the mayor's office in City Hall this morning." To Barry, he added, "All you have to do this morning is introduce Miranda. She can spell out the details about the goals of the program and how it will be run."

Miranda's smile was tentative as she looked from one man to the other. Worthington said to her, "Barry's hesitation is no reflection on your very fine program, my dear. The fact is, he's known in the company as a hardline, trimming-the-fat kind of guy. That's why I hired him. Our company's coming under increasing pressure..."

Miranda said, "Yes, you told me. Cutting costs, streamlining, and all that. But, Barry," she swiveled in her chair to face him. "You know, my program gets hard results too. My aim is to make sure employees understand the company's values and can help to achieve them. When that happens, the streamlining pretty well automatically follows. Why, I have proof."

Worthington said, "Yes, Miranda has had great results with other companies."

Barry suppressed a sigh. Not only would his reputation as an efficiency guru be compromised by associating himself with a "touchy-feely" enterprise like

Miranda's but he felt the program might actually harm the company. RPC had spent far too much time and money in past years on programs like the Corporate Values Program, which ended up costing a lot of money and producing little benefit. In other words, the opposite of what this wasteful monolith needed.

But Barry knew he had little choice but to go along with this charade. Worthington wanted to hire Miranda. Both men were keenly aware of the rumors that floated around the company about Worthington's reputation with the ladies. It was obviously not politically expedient for him to be seen as her primary promoter, by introducing her at the meeting this morning, Barry would take some of the heat off.

Barry said, "All right. I'll do my best. But, remember, Everett, I'm shortly leaving town on assignment to the Shell Bay Power Plant. I'll be there for some months so there's no way I can support Miranda through this effort. And she will need staff support."

"Right, right. I did think of that. In fact, I sent over a note to Chuck Browne inviting him to attend the committee meeting this morning." He turned to Miranda. "Chuck is the manager of the executive support services department. *ESS,* we call it in the company. His department handles exactly this kind of program. In fact, there's this woman on his staff who'll probably be assigned to work on this. Katie Carlisle. Ever meet her, Barry?"

Barry shook his head. He was about to say more but the attention of both men was diverted by Miranda. She had uncrossed her legs and moved to the edge of her chair as Worthington spoke. Now, she frantically waved an arm at them. "Please, we need to get things clear here. Ev, you assured me I'd report directly to you on this project. I don't want it handed over to some other department. It's my program and I will be managing it. All of it."

Worthington gave an indulgent laugh. "Of course, of course. The mission of executive support is to—guess what?—support executives, which in this case includes you. Of course, it will be your project. But you can't do it alone and ESS will provide the staff support."

Miranda slumped back in her chair, eyes downcast.

Worthington said, "Right. Time for us to get down to business. The three of us need to map out what the two of you will say this morning. Miranda will handle the details but you, Barry, must be sure to impress on all committee members just how critical Miranda's program is to the future success of RPC."

He turned to Miranda and smiled. "Incidentally, I'm afraid I may not be back in time to take you to lunch today, as I'd promised. However, I'm sure Barry will be able to handle that chore too." He chuckled. "Some chore, huh, Barry?"

4

Back Ribs for Katie and Terry

SHORTLY BEFORE NOON, Terry tapped on Katie's door. "Ready for lunch?" Terry was treating Katie to a birthday lunch at one of their favorite eateries, Rory's Ribs.

"Sure am." Katie gathered her purse and jacket and they were walking out her door when suddenly Chuck rushed past them on the way to his office. He said nothing.

Terry muttered, "Wow, did you see his expression?" Katie had indeed seen it. "Looks ominous, huh? I wonder what happened in the executive committee meeting!"

"Let's go ask him."

They both followed Chuck down the hall. Katie had a sudden fear that today even Rory's Ribs would lose their appeal. They stopped at the entrance to Chuck's office. He was putting papers into a drawer and then turned to get his raincoat from the stand in the corner. He glanced at the two of them but still said nothing.

Katie asked, "Is it that bad, Chuck? Are we all going to be laid off?"

Pulling on his raincoat, he snapped, "Nope. Not at this time anyhow."

Terry spoke. "So what was all the fuss about? The big new program that's going to make the company more...whatever?"

Chuck paused and looked them both in the eye. He spoke slowly. "The big new program is called the Corporate Values Program. Worthington has hired a consulting firm, Miranda Peabody and Associates, to administer it. It consists of countless workshops to be conducted throughout the whole company over the next year or two, with everyone creating action plans that will..." He paused. "Sound familiar? Been there, done that?"

Of course, it did sound familiar. Their own department had conducted several other similar-sounding company-wide initiatives, all at the request of their CEO. In just the past three years, there'd been Total Quality Management (TQM), Employee Empowerment (EE), Market Oriented Organization (MOO)—all long on workshops and action plans, much expenditure of time and money, and short on measurement of results. Just the sort of thing Katie was proposing the company do less of in her manifesto.

Katie asked, "And this program was actually proposed by Barry Bryce?" The idea seemed preposterous.

"Oh, I have no idea. Come to think of it, Bryce didn't look all that enthusiastic. Miranda Peabody did most of the talking."

Katie was relieved by Chuck's news but still puzzled by his seeming anger. As he passed her on his way out the door, she said quietly, "I guess this really caught you off guard, Chuck? Worthington didn't consult you ahead of time about this program?"

He glared at her. "You're wrong. He most certainly did."

OVER LUNCH, KATIE said to Terry, "Well, I'm not sure why Chuck isn't cheering but at least we can relax and enjoy our lunch now." She frowned. "Miranda Peabody. Have you ever heard of her?"

Terry chuckled, "Only just. But I know what happened. I was talking to my buddy on the fortieth floor late this morning."

"Oh, yes?" Terry's friend was one of the administrative assistants who worked on the fortieth floor and had extensive knowledge of the activities of the company's top executives.

"He told me that Worthington discovered Miranda recently at a conference and she persuaded him to hire her for a year. So she's definitely *his* protégée, not Barry's. But today Worthington was called away at the last minute to a meeting in City Hall so he corralled Barry to introduce her in his place. BB was probably pretty annoyed about that."

"Hmm. And I suppose it goes without saying that the lady is, shall we say, good-looking?"

Terry laughed. "Positively steamy, I hear! Okay, so let's order. Baby back ribs as usual, Katie?"

A while later as they were eating—delicious thick barbecue sauce coating ribs, utensils, napkins, hands, and faces—Terry commented, "I'm surprised Chuck forgot your birthday." The thought had occurred to Katie too; last year, Chuck had thrown her a party with the whole department invited.

She said, "Probably getting forgetful in his old age."

WHEN SHE GOT BACK to her office after lunch, two surprises awaited Katie. One was a big jade plant sitting on her desk. It was wrapped in shiny green paper with a yellow bow and there was a card attached.

"Katie, sorry I forgot your birthday—getting forgetful in my old age. Hope this makes up for it. Chuck."

Katie smiled. Chuck had given her a jade plant for her birthday every year for the past three years. Somehow, she always managed to kill the things by the time her next birthday rolled around. One of the secretaries had told her, "You water them too much, that's the problem. Wait until they fall down and beg."

The other was a phone message from her oldest and dearest friend, Lorraine. "Hey, Katie. Remember party tomorrow. Peter's bringing along a colleague from work. Unattached, fortyish, literate even. How's that for a birthday present?" Lorraine threw a party for Katie every year. And Lorraine and her significant other Peter were always trying to fix her up with men. Katie chuckled. Some people just never give up.

5

Barry and Miranda Get Acquainted

BARRY SELECTED THE REGENCY GRILL for lunch. It was popular and flashy—a bright, noisy spot with décor he suspected would appeal to Miranda. There were mirrors on every internal surface, and windowed glass doors along one entire wall opened onto sidewalk tables. Miranda's face lit up as they walked in and were seated at a table beside the window. "Wow, what a fantastic place." Her eyes roamed the neighboring tables. "Do a lot of famous people come here?"

"We're here, aren't we?"

She giggled as she took the giant menu from the waiter. "Ooo, what's good to eat?"

As he studied the menu, Barry tried to quell his anger at the whole stupid situation he'd found himself in. A few days ago, he had been appalled when Worthington had first told him about meeting Miranda Peabody at a conference. It seemed that after a few drinks and other friendly activities, she had persuaded the old man that RPC could benefit from a Corporate Values Program that she was touting.

In vain, Barry had argued with Worthington that in the present environment—with customers and regulators alike putting the squeeze on their bloated corporation—a program like Miranda's was the last thing they needed. Worthington had countered, "Oh, for God's sake, Barry, relax. It's only going to cost a hundred thousand for her one-year contract. And that can come right out of my personal slush fund."

Barry conceded this was true enough. But, of course, the biggest source of his irritation was the fact that he didn't want anyone in the company to think that he, Barry, was in any way endorsing a program like this.

Hence, his annoyance at having been obliged to introduce her to the executive committee this morning.

Barry closed his menu and looked at Miranda. She was muttering to herself over the choices, "Seared chicken taco sounds good. But I'm always choosing chicken. Pretty soon, I'll start clucking. Oh, well, I'll make it salad Niçoise." She shut the menu and smiled across the table at him. Her large brown eyes were friendly and innocent as a child's. He couldn't resist smiling back. Disapproving as he felt about people like Miranda, he had to admit the old man sure knew how to pick 'em.

Miranda said, "So what are the next steps?"

"First, I have to get hold of Chuck Browne."

She frowned. But now the waiter approached them. As soon as he'd left with their orders, she said, "Again, who's Chuck Browne?"

"He's the manager of executive support services. They carry out all the employee training and indoctrination programs in the company. And Chuck's right-hand woman Katie Carlisle is the in-house expert on this."

Miranda's frown deepened. She raised an arm. "Now, wait a minute. Remember, I said...."

"Yes, I know. It's your program and you'll be running it. But I'll be out of town over the next few months, and you must have staff support."

She said, "Well, maybe a secretary."

Barry thought that she hadn't a clue as to the kind of pushback she was likely to get from local managers throughout the corporation while they tried to squeeze her workshops into their already crowded schedules. But all he said was, "Let's talk about it after lunch."

A while later, as they ate, Barry—in a needling mood—asked, "So you're a good friend of Everett's, huh?"

She put down her fork and gave a sly smile. "Yes, but that's not why he hired me—in case you thought that. Aha, I can tell by your blush you did."

"Blush? Miranda, you have an active imagination."

"Not that active. No, seriously, Everett is really sold on the Values Program for its own sake. Of course, he's also a wonderful person for advancing the cause of women in the corporate world."

"So I've been told." Barry couldn't resist adding, "In fact, I hear that a couple of years ago, he promoted one woman from secretary to vice president in less than a year."

Miranda enthused, "You see? That's what I mean."

He laughed.

She leaned toward him. "Barry, tell me about yourself. Are you married?"

"Yes, I am."

"That's right, I remember. Everett was telling me about your wife. He said that she's a good friend of his. And that's why he hired you?"

This time, Barry did feel the warmth come to his face. "My wife Lila is a partner in a firm of financial advisors. Everett is one of her clients. In fact, the company is one of her clients. And, yes, Everett was looking to create a new position to handle certain special projects and Lila recommended me."

She smiled, tucking her head on one side. "Everett thinks very highly of you, Barry. He was telling me you're going to make vice president one day."

"Yes, well... that would be nice." He put down his fork and looked across the table at her. "And how about you? Are you married?"

She took another forkful of food before replying. "Yes, to a much older man." Her expression had suddenly become mournful. "A couple of years ago, he had to have heart surgery, and now he can only work part time. So I became the chief wage earner." The big eyes facing him looked wider than ever.

He said, "I see."

AT ONE-THIRTY, they arrived back at the Tower Building. On the fortieth floor, Barry guided Miranda to his office, which was down the hall from Worthington's. As they sat across from each other at his desk, she surveyed the bamboo wallpaper, cherry-wood bookshelves, lush maroon carpeting. "What a beautiful office. Not as big as Ev's, of course, but beautiful. So this will be my office?"

"No," he said. "It will be my office. As it is now."

"Oh." Her face fell. "I'm sorry, I didn't mean to imply I was pushing you out of it. Ev said you were leaving town soon so I thought..."

"That's okay. Now, Miranda, we do have some business matters to settle. First, it's important we get your references. You said there are several other companies that have had great results from your program? Can you give me the names of some people to contact?" He picked a pencil out of a holder on his desk and poised it over a pad of paper.

"Mmm. I don't have those on me right now. But, you know, I'm sure I've given them to Ev already."

"So he's checked them out? He didn't tell me that."

"Well, I think he has. Or, at least, I think someone has."

Barry hesitated, then put the pencil down. It would probably be a good idea to check with Everett first before arguing about it. Miranda looked around again. "You know, even if I don't get this office, I'll probably get one like it, won't I? I mean, on this floor they must all be pretty nice."

"Yes, on this floor, they are. But only company officers and their immediate staff are housed on the fortieth floor. Your office will most likely be somewhere else. Probably in another building. Before we go any further, let me call Chuck Browne and ask him to meet us."

She wheeled her chair back and to the side so there was room for her to cross her legs. Out of the corner of his eye, he noted again the green pumps. She said, "You know, Barry, I really won't be needing much in the way of staff support. I've always done the workshops alone."

"Yes, but you need people to introduce you to company officers and managers to get their permission..."

"Permission? Why do I need their permission when the CEO himself has authorized the program?"

Once again, Barry reveled in his own good luck at having an out-of-town assignment. Poor Chuck Browne. "You know, I'm sure Chuck can explain things to you about how the company works. You'll enjoy working with him."

He reached for the phone. At the same time, she uncrossed her legs and leaned forward. He jumped as her soft hand came down on top of his.

"Barry."

"Yes."

"Make it clear to Chuck that I report to Everett, not to him."

Barry withdrew his hand from the phone and from her fingers. "I'm not sure that will be the case, Miranda."

"What!"

"Well, okay, maybe you'll report to both of them. To Everett, because he hired you—and to Chuck on everyday operational matters. We'll work out the details with Chuck."

"And make it clear..." He could see her hand wandering back across the desk and hastily put his own hands in his lap. "Make it very clear that it is my program from start to finish. I'm not handing it over to Chuck or anyone else."

"Yes, I'll make it very clear." He reached again for the phone.

On the phone, Chuck's tone was curt but he did agree to meet with them. When Barry hung up, he said, "Chuck will be coming over at three." He thought of something else. "You know what, if we go over to the window, I can point out where Chuck's office is and where your new home is likely to be."

Miranda followed him as he walked to the windows. From this fortieth story vantage point, there was a colorful panorama of San Francisco Bay with the City waterfront and Bay Bridge in the foreground, and, farther away, the islands—Yerba Buena, Treasure Island, and Alcatraz, and the distant East Bay hills swathed in haze. She drew a breath. "Incredible view!"

Barry said, "Now, look down. See that building, in the opposite corner of the courtyard over there?"

She squinted. "You mean that ugly brick building?"

"That's the Annex Building. All human resource departments are located there. It's only eight stories high but it's pretty historic. Dates back to...oh, I can't quite remember, but a long time. It has all these Old Barbary Coast touches—you know, chandeliers and paneled offices and things."

"Oh, Lord! Well, at least it's probably safer."

"Why do you say that?"

"Because it's not very high. It wouldn't shake near as much in an earthquake as this skyscraper would."

She had her back to him so didn't see his expression. He decided not to pursue the issue.

Katie Takes Stock

ON SUNDAY MORNING, January 29, Katie lay awake in the only bedroom of her small fifty-year old house in the island city of Alameda, located across the Bay from San Francisco. Five years ago, she'd been left sole inheritor of her parents' estate and the purchase of this house was one of the few happy outcomes resulting from the loss of two people she loved dearly.

Katie had grown up in a modest but respectable suburb in Orange County with parents who doted on their only child. Her parents had married late in life and had approved of her "having some fun before settling down"—with the understanding that one day she would settle down and provide them with a grandchild or two. Then, tragically, both her mother and father died in a car crash without ever seeing the grandchildren they had so looked forward to.

At eight o'clock, she got out of bed, pulled on her robe and slippers, and made her way to the kitchen. Her two cats, Kit and Kat, struggled out from under the comforter and followed, winding silky legs and tails around her ankles as she filled their bowls.

While the cats munched, Katie poured herself some orange juice and thought about Lorraine's party. Lorraine and Peter were both faculty members at the University of California, Berkeley. They regularly held bashes in their large, untidy apartment to which they invited assorted faculty members, students, neighbors— even the occasional street person.

Last night's event was typical: disorganized and cheerful. Katie's lingering irritation this morning was over the man they'd described as a great date for her. Yes, the man had been unattached and fortyish, as

Lorraine had promised. In some ways, he'd been reminiscent of Alan: skinny, untidy facial hair, quick with a quip. But what still rankled this morning was his reaction to her.

As soon as they had been introduced, he took her hand, looked her up and down as though appraising a prize heifer, and finally said, "Happy fortieth."

"Thirty-ninth," Peter and Lorraine chorused in unison.

He said, "Thirty-nine, forty, whatever. Over the hill no matter how you look at it, huh, Katie?"

Katie had ignored him for the rest of the evening. Later, she'd had a moment alone with Lorraine in the kitchen. Lorraine said, "So you don't care for our birthday present, darlin'!"

"Lorraine, honey, I know you mean well but maybe from now on you should leave it to me to find my own men."

Lorraine, a faded blonde whose pretty face was overpowered by her chubby body, looked at her with concern. "Yeah, I'm sorry, I don't know where Peter dug up that SOB. But, be honest, Katie, there hasn't been much action since Alan left, has there? What is it, two, three years now? We need to get you out of the house, girl."

"Closer to one year," Katie corrected her. "Look, that slob reminds me of how overrated the business of having a man is. When I find one, I'll find one. Until then..."

"Sure," Lorraine said blithely. "We'll butt out."

Katie was afraid she didn't mean this for a moment.

NOW, ON THIS SUNDAY MORNING, Katie rested her forehead against the cool glass of the kitchen window, and surveyed her small backyard. January was not yet over but already there were signs of spring. Golden blossoms trailed from the acacia trees along the back fence. In the flower borders, delicate green shoots poked up through the earth, forerunners of the sweet-smelling narcissus and hyacinths she had planted there.

Her eyes drifted upward to a less pleasant sight—the eaves, where large flakes of paint curled downward like miniature stalactites. She had to get this house repainted soon.

But it was a lovely day. A time to forget about peeling paint and oafish blind dates. She decided to take the one-mile walk to Benji's Bakery on Constitution Avenue and treat herself to breakfast.

ABOUT NINE-THIRTY, she set out along Alara Way, where she lived, in the direction of Constitution Avenue. In the driveway next door, her elderly neighbor, Mildred, was giving instructions to the young handyman she employed to do various chores for her. They both looked around as Katie walked by. The handyman, whose name was Dan, nodded politely to Katie. Mildred called out a cheery, "Good morning. Out for your constitutional?" This was Mildred's little joke, a question she asked every time she saw Katie headed in the direction of Constitution Avenue. Katie smiled and waved.

When she reached the bakery, Katie bought coffee and a bagel and carried them to a table in the sun. On weekends, Benji's was bustling with young singles and the occasional family with children. Katie spread a dollop of cream cheese on her bagel, and glanced around—not that any of the men there had even a glance for her.

This was not surprising. Since Alan's departure, she'd rather let herself go. Her mind flipped to her conversation with Terry during their lunch on Friday. They'd talked about career women, like Miranda Peabody. Terry had commented, "You'd wonder what someone like her could see in our paunchy CEO but I guess looks aren't that important to women. Not that I'd know, of course."

"On the contrary," she had told him. "You're often surprisingly perceptive when it comes to man-woman issues."

"Surprising, you mean, for a gay man?" he'd snickered. "No, seriously, Katie, have you ever noticed no one really seems to care what the men in our company's top ranks look like, but all our women executives are trim and smart?"

Now, glancing down at her far from trim sweatpants, Katie wondered if this remark had been a gentle dig at her. A career required a sharp appearance. It was time she paid attention.

Walking home, Katie plotted. First, she'd check out Weight Watchers; she badly needed to lose ten pounds. Next, the Y, only a couple of blocks from work, had lunchtime sessions that could help her tone up her muscles and improve her posture. Then she'd find a good hair stylist to shape her unruly mane.

Close to home, head up and mind awash with images of her new stunning self, Katie found herself flying through the air. She had tripped over a leg extending onto the sidewalk outside her neighbor's house. Just in time, she grabbed the fence and righted herself. The leg belonged to Dan the handyman who was sprawled on the ground, struggling to remove a rusted hinge from Mildred's garden gate.

"Oops," Katie said.

Dan said, "Sorry," and pulled his leg back in.

Katie walked on toward her own front path. Toward her peeling eaves. She stopped and retraced her steps. "Dan, do you paint houses?" He continued working for a few seconds in silence. Then, screwdriver in hand, he squinted up at her. Katie looked back at him. As she had observed on previous sightings of Dan, he was disarmingly handsome. Strong, chiseled features, dark blond hair—a little on the long side—bright blue eyes. "Mildred's always saying you do excellent work, and my place badly needs painting."

His stunning eyes met hers and she fell silent, feeling flustered at the blankness of his expression. After a moment, with seeming reluctance, he pulled himself to his feet and turned to stare at Katie's house.

He said, "How much work is involved?"

"Well, it's just the outside of the house. As you can see, it's not very big."

"No, but a lot depends on how much scraping and sanding it'd need." He crouched down again to resume working on the gate. "Mildred wants me to put new hinges on this gate. When I finish, I'll come over and take a closer look at your place."

"Fine. Of course, if you're not interested, I'll get someone else."

But he was already engrossed in his struggle with the gate and didn't respond.

A couple of hours later, he came over. Katie saw him as she stood by the kitchen counter, fixing herself a cup of tea. He didn't see her, or pretended not to, as he wandered around outside the house looking up at the eaves with a morose expression. She thought, "Oh, the hell with him!"

When he knocked at the door a few minutes later, she opened it, fully expecting a rejection. But he said, "Okay, I'll do it for fifteen hundred. It should move along pretty quick if I spray it."

Katie considered this while he rested his lanky body against the door frame and waited for her reply. She didn't care for the idea of spraying; she'd heard a roller and brush did a much better job. But she'd been procrastinating on this painting job for so long and it wasn't a bad price. "Fine. Why don't you go ahead?"

Quickly, he said, "I can't right now. Maybe in a coupla months?"

"Oh."

So this was his game. He clearly wasn't interested in this job and had agreed to do it in case he ran out of work at some future date. She said, "All right, but please let me know if you change your mind. Don't leave me dangling. Oh, and may I have your card please? That is, if you have such a thing."

Her tone was probably sharper than she'd intended because he took a step back and hesitated before reaching into his pocket for a grubby card. She took the card and noted his last name was Erickson.

He said, "If you gimme your phone number, I'll call when I can start."

Katie got her purse from the hall table, took out a business card, and wrote her home number on it. He studied the card as he took it from her, and read aloud, "Katherine Carlisle, Supervisor of Management Development and Special Projects Consultant, Executive Support Services Department, Redwood Power Corporation." He said in a deadpan voice, "Gee whiz, that's a mouthful."

Katie deadpanned back. "Yes, it is."

He glanced up at her. "But what do you *do*?"

Katie said, "Beats me."

This time, he grinned, his sparkling eyes looking right into hers. Katie's heart thumped. Then he was all business again. "Right. I'll phone when I'm ready to start. Meantime, you decide what you want. Colors and stuff."

Katie said, "I already know what I want."

She watched him as he walked down the path. Did she really know what she wanted? Certainly, not him. He was decades too young for her. Bound to be conceited, like all handsome men. And, for heaven's sake, only a handyman. She shut the door.

7

Katie Gets an Assignment

AT WORK ON MONDAY MORNING, Katie had just poured her first cup of coffee when Chuck stuck his head around the break room door. "'Morning, Katie," he said. "Can you spare a minute?"

"Absolutely."

She followed him as he hurried down the hall, his shoulders hunched forward as though he were walking into a wind. In his office, he waved her to a chair. He said, "On Friday afternoon, I had a meeting with Barry Bryce and *Doctor* Miranda Peabody."

"Oh, right. The Corporate Values Program." She'd hardly given a thought to the Values Program since Friday but remembered her surprise at Chuck's anger at hearing about it. "You said you already knew about that."

He frowned and turned to stare out the window. "I sure did. As soon as Worthington got back from that conference—the one where he met Miranda Peabody—he sent me a copy of her proposal and asked me to look into it."

Chuck's chair squeaked as he rocked back and forth. "Well, I looked into it. Read her proposal. Checked her references—huh!—all two of them. The woman is a charlatan, Katie. A bald-faced liar, to boot."

Katie was startled. Not only at his news, but at his vituperative tone. Chuck was normally diplomatic to a fault when it came to criticizing individuals.

Chuck went on, "I checked both her references. The people she named were astonished she'd given them as references. She'd made a presentation to one company and they'd said, 'No, thanks.' The other actually hired her, but terminated her services after a couple of months."

"Did they say why?"

"Well, for one thing, her so-called values are a one-size-fits-all affair. She personally developed a list of values that all companies should have, according to her. Apparently, she thinks it's a waste of time to get employees involved in coming up with company values. Much cheaper in the long run, she says, to simply tell everyone what their values should be."

"And you told Worthington what you'd found out?"

"Of course I did. And then he went ahead and hired her anyway."

Chuck's face was flushed, his forehead shiny. Katie said, "But, Chuck, you'll get the last laugh, won't you? The old man is going to wish he'd listened to you all along."

Chuck sighed. "You know, I could care less about her. We all know how Everett takes a shine to attractive women, and I daresay she has a persuasive line. It'll serve him right to be taken for the old fool he is."

He rocked some more. Squeak, squeak.

"No, what's so unsettling in this case is that when he decided he didn't like my advice, he must have turned to Barry Bryce. Then Bryce—for whatever reason, probably to spite me—supported him in his decision to hire her."

A despondent Chuck hung his head. "Katie, this might be the beginning of the end for me. If Everett no longer values my opinion, pretty soon no one else in the company will have any use for me either."

"I'm sure things will work out okay." Katie's sympathy was genuine, but she felt a tremor of excitement. This was the perfect time to remind him of her manifesto. "Remember, Chuck, what I was proposing the other day—that maybe our department should seriously think about adopting a new strategy? Become more proactive in deciding what services the company could benefit from rather than simply reacting to management requests?"

Chuck snapped back. "But that's the reason our department was created. To be reactive, as you put it. If top management no longer calls on us, we're history."

Katie longed to argue but this was clearly not the time. She sat back and crossed her legs. After a long pause, she asked, "So what happened at your meeting with them?"

He sighed and turned to a folder on his desk. "Right. The meeting. Well, we went over a whole bunch of stuff on the Corporate Values Program. Miranda has prepared workshops, which she proposes delivering throughout the entire company over the next year or so. I suggested it would be best if we first tried it out in just one division. That way, we could iron out the bugs before proceeding. Bryce agreed with me."

"See, Chuck, they do value your advice."

Chuck harrumphed. "Seeking advice is not what Bryce does. He gives orders and everyone salutes. As for Miranda, I'm not sure what she does other than flutter her big brown eyes and make a lot of inane remarks."

Katie smiled. "I suppose she and her company are planning to conduct the workshops? Or is she just a one-woman outfit?"

"You got it. This is the other part of what we discussed. Worthington wants her to have an entire department to back her up, and guess what? Our hapless department has been chosen for that purpose."

"Well, I guess that makes sense seeing our department would normally handle a program like this. I suppose we can bring in a temporary secretary for her. But we don't have a private office available. Do you think she'll be content with a cubicle?"

"Fat chance. Also, there's more. Worthington wants to have a company insider assigned to work closely with her in scheduling the workshops and dealing with company people to avoid her from 'treading on toes,' as he puts it."

Katie said playfully, "From what I've heard about Miranda, I don't imagine you'll find it too difficult to work with her, will you?"

An awkward expression crossed his face. "Actually, Katie, I volunteered you for that job. I can't imagine anyone better suited."

"SO WHAT EXACTLY does he have in mind?" a sympathetic Terry asked at lunchtime. They were sitting outdoors beside a sheltered wall facing the sun, eating sandwiches from the ground floor deli.

"You know, I was so angry I couldn't be bothered to press for details." Katie was still angry. She sputtered, "He knows I'm up to my ears in work right now. Even if I weren't busy, how dare he sign me up for babysitting Miranda without checking with me first?"

Terry chuckled softly. "Hey, Katie, I've often seen you mad, but not usually at old Chuckie. Look, it'll all be over soon. Worthington will find himself another pretty face and Miranda will be outta here before you know it. Right?"

Thoughtfully, Katie drank some milk. "You know, Terry, Chuck was saying how the thing he most fears is having Barry Bryce supplant him as Worthington's number one advisor."

"Oh, for heavens' sakes."

"No, he's right. I see signs it's already happening. One executive told me recently that Chuck's advice has become increasingly unimaginative. Safe to the point of being dangerous."

"Who said that?"

"I'd rather not say right now. But think about it. We're in a downward spiral of rising rates and increasingly unhappy customers. We desperately need new ideas and people willing to make tough decisions." She turned to look at Terry and said slowly, "When was the last time Chuck had a new idea? Let alone urged a tough decision about anything?"

Terry's eyes widened. "I had no idea you thought that way about Chuck."

"Oh, don't get me wrong. I love the guy. But, you know, if he were to take early retirement..." She paused.

"Yes?"

"Well, I think that's one job I would go all out to get. Terry, I'm just busting with ideas to shake up this old department. I think I might I'd be more than a match for any Barry Bryce."

Understanding dawned on Terry's face. "Really? You'd like Chuck to leave so you can get his job?"

"Of course, I'd never wish ill for Chuck." Katie crumpled up her empty sandwich packet. "So tell me about your weekend. Did you and Stefano get to the Monet exhibition?" Stefano was Terry's partner.

Terry's face clouded. "No, Stefano decided he wasn't up to it. I almost called you on Sunday to see if you'd like to go with me. Then I remembered it was your birthday weekend, and I was sure you'd have plans, you swinging single, you."

"Hey, what can I tell you? Actually, one thing I did do this swinging weekend was to find someone to paint my house."

"Finally! So when's this happening?"

Katie frowned. "Unfortunately, he no sooner said he'd do it than he said he couldn't start for a while."

"So pick someone else. But I suppose this guy had the lowest bid? You did get at least three quotes?"

"Well, no, but I sort of know the guy. He's my neighbor's handyman."

Terry gasped. "*Handyman*? Look, Katie, at a minimum, you should get at least three bids, and then insist on references before you pick anyone. And check up on those references. Too many people don't bother to check."

"Yes, Daddy."

"I'm serious. Did I tell you about those people Stefano knew who got half their house painted and then the painters skipped town?"

Katie gave an exaggerated moan. "Yes, you did."

AT FIVE O'CLOCK that evening, Katie got her raincoat from the hook behind the door. As she put it on, her eye caught her reflection in the darkened window. What were all those resolutions she'd made on Sunday about dieting and exercise? She hadn't given them a thought since. And there was the other thing that had been hovering in the back of her mind since lunchtime. House painting.

Terry was a bit of an old woman with his insistence on multiple bids and references, but he was right. Having her house messily painted would be worse than not having it painted at all. She really ought to look through the Yellow Pages tonight.

As she reached for her purse, she looked again at her reflection and smiled. The wavering image reflected her own wavering state of mind.

On an impulse, she opened her purse and drew out a quarter. She would toss it one time. If it came down heads, she'd follow Terry's advice and check the Yellow Pages. Tails, she'd leave things as they were with Dan. She gripped the coin between her thumb and forefinger, held it over her desk and tossed it a little way into the air. It landed on its edge on the blotter, teetered a moment, and fell flat.

Heads.

Katie put the quarter back into her purse, turned off the lights, and left the office, locking the door behind her. Funny, she thought, how something as simple as a coin toss could make it so clear what she really wanted to do.

8

Miranda Gets an Office

THE NEXT MORNING, there was another traffic tie-up on the way to work and Katie was again late getting to the office. On her desk, she found a sheet of paper headed "Corporate Values Statement," together with a note saying that Dr. Miranda Peabody would be addressing all department employees at eight o'clock. Five minutes ago. Katie put away her coat and purse and set off toward the departmental conference room. To her surprise, the door was locked.

The only sounds she could hear came from a storeroom down the next hall and she made her way there. Sure enough, the room was full of employees squeezed in among boxes and shelves of supplies. Katie slid into a spot by the door, next to Terry who made a face at her. There was no sign of Chuck.

At the far end of the room, a slender redheaded woman was reading aloud from a sheet of paper. "Underlying Redwood Power Corporation's activities is a set of enduring values that guide our decisions and actions."

So this was Miranda. Miranda had a soft, husky voice. As she spoke, she rested her willowy body against the table behind her, looking totally relaxed. Katie admired the woman's composure in this crowded room of restless strangers. They were restless because there was standing room only in this confined space and already it was becoming uncomfortably warm. Why had this meeting not taken place in their regular conference room?

Miranda said, "Note the first value." She read from the sheet, "We value our customers and are committed to supplying their needs at the lowest possible prices."

Then, she paused and looked up. With a deliberate gesture, she pushed back a sleeve of the oatmeal-colored raw silk dress she was wearing and glanced at her wristwatch. "You know, I've been told not to take up too much of your time, so maybe I should leave you to study this sheet by yourselves. Let me move on and describe the process we'll be using to carry out the program."

For the next fifteen minutes, Miranda talked while everyone else in the room fidgeted. "Every employee will have to attend a five-day workshop to learn the corporate values. In these workshops, each employee will draw up an action plan to show how he or she will incorporate each value into daily work activities."

She beamed a sweet smile around the room. "I will, of course, help you in developing those action plans. That's in year one. In year two, we'll have another series of workshops so that people can report results of their action plans."

Katie exchanged glances with Terry who rolled his eyes at the ceiling. She knew what he meant: *same-ole, same-ole.* At last, the meeting broke up. Terry whispered, "Thank God. I was about to faint."

As he and Katie hurried to leave, she heard a dulcet voice calling, "Is Katie Carlisle here?"

Katie turned against the tide of outgoing employees to face in Miranda's direction. "I'm Katie."

"Oh, good." Miranda said, "We need to talk for a few minutes."

"Well, actually," Katie checked her watch. "I do have an appointment."

"Don't we all?" Unfazed, Miranda continued to gather up her notes.

Chuck's secretary walked past. Katie grabbed her sleeve and said loudly enough for Miranda to hear, "Dorothy, the regional sales manager from Change Management Systems will be waiting for me in my office. Would you stick your head in and say I'll be a couple of minutes late?"

Miranda joined her. "Let's go to my office." Katie followed her with interest, wondering where Miranda would lead her. On their floor, there were few private offices and these were all occupied. Had someone now been displaced?

Outside the conference room—their department's real conference room—Miranda stopped, pulled a key from her pocket, and opened the door. Katie's mouth dropped open with astonishment as she looked inside. The usually neat room was a shambles. Chairs were stacked on top of one another; the large oval table was covered with taped cardboard boxes.

Miranda pulled a couple of chairs from a stack on the side of the room and arranged them at one end of the table. "Please take a seat. This used to be a conference room or something. They're going to put all this stuff in storage and get me some proper furniture."

Bemused, Katie sat down. "So this is your office?" This room was even larger than Chuck's office. Chuck had long ago told them he'd made it a conference room because its views of the bay alone made it too choice to be anyone's private office. But, Katie realized, there was no way he could have put Miranda in a cubicle, so he had to give her the only private space available on the floor.

"Mmm," Miranda murmured. Her tapered fingers shuffled through a stack of folders on the table. Close up, Katie thought, Miranda was not as movie-star glamorous as she'd seemed at a distance, but she certainly was attractive. She had small, even features in an oval face, and she was all color—auburn hair, creamy skin with pink cheeks, and a smattering of freckles. The soft full mouth and large milk-chocolate eyes gave her a friendly, innocent look.

Or maybe it was an insincere, vacuous look. Katie found herself both drawn to the woman and wary of her.

Finally, Miranda drew a folder from the stack, and held it open on the table in front of her. Peering, Katie saw that the folder was her own confidential personnel file. The brown eyes looked up at her. "Katie, I've been so looking forward to meeting you. Thank you so much for agreeing to be my personal assistant."

Katie's initial indignation dissolved into a snort of laughter. "Miranda, I'm not going to be your personal assistant. I already have a more than full-time job."

Miranda glanced at Katie's file. "You're the management development supervisor?"

"That's only part of my job. I also assist Chuck on sensitive investigations, and that takes a lot of my time."

Miranda's eyes widened. In a friendly way, she asked, "Sensitive investigations? What are those?"

Katie hesitated. She didn't want to violate any confidences but she also wanted it established that she was too high-level an employee to be anyone's personal assistant.

She said, "Well, we carry out many special projects for Worthington and other executives—things like investigating poor performance or malfeasance in the higher echelons."

Miranda didn't look impressed so much as puzzled. With furrowed brow, she said, "But that's the kind of work Barry Bryce does."

Katie tried not to sound defensive. "Well, our aim is different. Barry focuses on things like cutting costs and reducing staff. Chuck and I have broader goals. We try to come up with win-win solutions that work out well for everyone."

Miranda said, "You mean, so you don't have to fire anyone? I'm with Barry here. In the long run, you're better off getting rid of poor performers instead of coddling them."

Katie swallowed. This childlike outsider, with her overly long eyelashes—false, no doubt—had come painfully close to the mark. In fact, Katie's manifesto, still languishing in her bottom drawer, contained a whole section on the value of an occasional win-lose. But she wasn't about to admit that to Miranda.

Miranda was now reviewing some notes on a piece of paper. Katie got to her feet. "Miranda, I'm sorry but

I've got to go. I can't leave my visitor waiting for me any longer. He's flown in from Chicago just to meet with me."

"Oh, okay. But I have a favor to ask of you. We're about to select a field division to be the test site for our Values Program. What can you tell me about Beresford Division? The manager is..." She looked again at the piece of paper she was holding.

"Mike Weston," Katie offered. She'd never met Weston but knew the names of all division officers. Also, she vaguely remembered there was some scandal that had been associated with Weston in the past.

"You're right." Miranda said happily. "You see, you're invaluable to me already."

Katie headed toward the door. The uncomfortable drag in the pit of her stomach reminded her she hadn't even had her first cup of coffee this morning.

"Katie."

What now? Katie half-turned.

"Don't worry about trying to get your other work done. Chuck understands the situation. He'll make sure you're relieved of all that other stuff. The Corporate Values Program has priority over everything else."

"Sure." Katie kept going out the door. The woman still didn't get it.

As she headed down the hall toward the coffee room, a fleeting thought crossed Katie's mind. Maybe she was the one who didn't get it.

IT WAS FIVE O'CLOCK and Katie was about to go home when Chuck stopped by her office. "So how's it going with Miranda?"

"Just the man I want to see. Chuck, what gave Miranda the idea that I was to be her personal assistant? Did you tell her that?"

He screwed up his face. "Miranda believes what she wants to believe." That was not an answer, Katie decided. Chuck went on quickly. "Perhaps she told you we've decided on Beresford Division as the site for the three-month pilot study. I've put together some notes on that division and its manager, Mike Weston." He tapped a slim folder he was carrying and placed it on her desk.

Katie shook her head. "You know what's going to happen, don't you? There isn't a field division in this whole company that will be willing to go along with this test site business. Not after that fiasco with the MOO program last fall."

Chuck said, "Oh, I think Weston will go along."

"Really? Because he owes you one?"

"You could say that," he said and winked.

After he left, Katie remembered where else the name of Beresford Division had come up lately. It was in that *Redwood Rover* article that Terry had wanted her to read—about some invention that might put the company out of business.

But now Katie looked down with annoyance at the folder Chuck had handed her. Why had he given this to her and not to Miranda?

9

Sherman Granger, Inventor

LESS THAN A HUNDRED MILES from San Francisco, in the heart of California's Central Valley, is the city of Beresford (population 300,000). RPC's Beresford Division headquarters were located in the city center in the six-story Cooper Building, the tallest building in town.

At a quarter to twelve on Tuesday, Sherman Granger walked into the lobby of the Cooper Building. Sherman—a stocky man with a wide, heavily jowled face and a ready smile—was a regular visitor. Joe, the security guard, greeted him with a wave. "Hey, Mr. Granger. You gonna see Mike? They're all in a big meeting in the conference room. Should be through by noon though."

"Thanks, Joe. I'll go up and wait in his office." Sherman took the elevator to the top floor. The doors opened onto a large room that housed the division's administrative employees. Desks, computers, chairs, and file cabinets were scattered across the area in clusters that approximated cubicles but without cubicle walls.

Sherman made his way to the manager's office, a large glassed-in section in one corner of the floor, where he sat down in one of the chairs arranged in a semi-circle around a big desk. He put his briefcase on the floor and leaned back, looking around the familiar room. Faux walnut furniture, potted plants, framed certificates from local service organizations. And, of course, on the wall behind the desk, the large acrylic and oil painting Weston was so proud of. Boats in the harbor at Gloucester, Massachusetts.

Sherman sighed. He and Mike had grown up together. Right out of high school, Mike had gone to work for RPC and was now looking forward to a comfortable retirement. But, from the age of eighteen, Sherman had wanted to make his own way by marketing his inventions. It had been an uneven road, to put it mildly, and today he was eking out a living as a sales representative for a struggling company called Sierra Enterprises. He had little money in the bank, hated his job and was too old to get another. His latest invention was his only hope.

Right at noon, a hubbub erupted at the far end of the floor. Through the glass door, Sherman could see Mike's lanky frame towering above the other employees spilling into the general office from the conference room. Mike called out in response to someone's question, "We'll deal with it as best we can. Same as we do with all the other BS head office slings at us."

Sherman smiled. He knew that Mike had little patience for "those staff people" in San Francisco who, in his words, made it their mission in life to screw up the real work of the company which was, in Mike's opinion, done in the field divisions like Beresford.

Mike beamed happily when he reached his office. "Sherm. Great to see you." The two men shook hands and Mike took his seat in his big swivel chair. "So, what's cookin'?"

Sherman chuckled. "Our lunch today?" He had deliberately not called to remind Mike because that might have given his slippery friend an excuse to cancel out. And obviously Mike had forgotten.

"Oh, right, right." Mike ran the fingers of one hand through his hair, while riffling through a stack of message slips with the other. "Gee, Sherm, this place gets more like a zoo every day. And the animals sure are jumpy. Did I tell you the latest? Head Office just came up with another damn-fool program."

"The Corporate Values Program? Yeah, you told me the other day when I called to make our lunch date. Always something, huh?"

"This one is particularly bad for us. I learned this morning they're going to start by doing a pilot program in one location for three months." Mike thumped his elbows onto the desk. "And guess what location they've chosen for this pilot program?"

Sherman said, "Not Beresford?"

"Give the man a prize. Beresford Division it is."

"Jeez, Mike, that's too bad." Sherman meant this with all his heart. This was terrible news. It meant he was about to become the farthest thing from Mike's mind for at least three months.

"Darn tootin' it's too bad. I just had all our management team in a meeting..." he waved toward the conference room, "...to figure out how the hell we're going to deal with it. Three months of disruption. Employees pulled off the job to go to idiotic workshops. It makes me so mad I could spit."

Now, both Mike's hands were running through his hair. He moaned, "Do you know how many major—and I do mean major—construction projects this is going to interfere with? We'll end up blowing all kinds of target completion dates. And there goes my bonus for the year." He leaned forward, directing a gloomy stare at Sherman.

Sherman clucked sympathetically. "Well, I was planning to take you to lunch and tell you about my good news. I finally have the patent for my mini-cogenerator invention. And I have a demo all set to go. But I suppose you're going to be too swamped for a time..."

Suddenly Mike's eyes lit up. "Hold on. I just thoughta something. You know what they say about an ill wind... doing something? Anyway, from your point of view, this dumb project might turn out to be a lucky break. You see, the person at HO in charge of running it is someone called Chuck Browne. His department does all the touchy-feely management training and stuff."

There was a tap at the door. Mike's secretary Maisie slid her thin body around the doorframe. "Sorry to interrupt, but the crew foreman called again. They really want you out at the site. Like, a coupla hours ago."

"Ah, shoot." Mike told her. "Tell him on I'm on my way." He turned back to Sherman and grinned. "Right after I have lunch with my good friend Sherman." He jumped to his feet and shouted over Maisie's squeals of protest. "Hey, I gotta eat, don' I? Come on, Sherm. It'll have to be a quick one."

He muttered out of the corner of his mouth as they made their way out. "I get fed up with that damned woman pushing me around."

As the elevator doors closed behind them, Mike continued, "So what was I saying? Oh, yes, Chuck Browne. A year or so ago, he and I worked together on some... er... stuff. Now that man is smart, sympathetic to people in the field. And, best of all, he has a whole lot of influence with just about everyone at HO from the CEO down. If there's any one person in this company who can help move things along with your invention, it's Chuck."

Sherman was almost afraid to question Mike further. Sherman knew that his old friend frequently exaggerated. Yet he so much wanted to believe that something good could finally be coming his way.

Sherman had decided to take Mike to Daisy's Tavern for lunch. Daisy's had good food, dark oak paneled walls, and crypt-like lighting. When they sat down, Mike squinted at the tables around them. "What's this, Hernando's Hideaway?"

Sherman let this pass. He knew the muted ambiance of Daisy's was conducive to serious conversation—not for noisy exchanges of greetings across the room with local businessmen, table-hopping, shoulder slapping—exchanges that division managers like Mike actively sought in noontime forays out of the office.

After they'd placed their orders, Mike immediately launched into a spirited exposition on a topic uppermost in his mind—some battle looming over a right of way the company was trying to get. Sherman sipped iced tea and listened patiently. At last, their salads arrived. Mike started to eat, and Sherman seized his chance.

"So," he said, "this man, Chuck? You said he might be able to help get the company interested in my cogen unit?"

A munching Mike looked up. "You bet. Ole Chuckie can tell you exactly how to proceed, who at head office you should contact, what your pitch should be, how they'll react, how they part their hair." He gave a triumphant burst of laughter. "I don't know why I didn't think of him before."

Sherman tried not to feel too excited. He asked, "So you'd be willing to talk to this man about me?"

"Ha," Mike almost shouted. "Better than that. You can talk to him yourself. You see, he left me a phone message this morning. He'll be here in Beresford on Friday. He asked me to set up a meeting with my department heads for nine o'clock so's he can brief us on the pilot project. After the meeting, I plan to whisk him off for lunch. Just the two of us." He snickered. "Unless, of course, my good friend Sherman Granger happens to stop by—in which case it will be the three of us."

Sherman worried. "But if he's coming to see you about this pilot project, won't he be annoyed if I start talking about my cogen invention?"

"No way. I won't tell him ahead of time so he won't have time to think about it. But he knows I'll be taking him to lunch, and if you happened to stop by my office at noon, he can hardly tell me not to invite you too."

Sherman drew a breath. "Of course, this Chuck guy may not think my unit will be of any interest to your company. It's a compact unit, small enough even for private homes. Your company usually deals with very large users of energy."

Mike's eyes were on the large platter the waiter had set before him. Mint-glazed double lamb chops with garlic-mashed potatoes. "Smells great. Look, Sherm, ol' buddy, quit agonizing over it. Your device is the single most sensational PR tool that's come down the pike since I've been manager of this division. It aims right at the heart of all the little guys—all those customers who've been up in arms of late. This would prove to them we really care about helping them save money."

Sherman put down his fork and gripped his water glass.

Mike continued, "Your invention is right on the cutting edge of technology. I can see our company wanting to set up a separate subsidiary company just to make and sell these babies. Sherman Granger, President, Compact Cogen Subsidiary of RPC. How about that?" He guffawed and slapped the table. Then, his face serious again, he wagged a finger in front of Sherman's nose.

"No kidding, Sherm. This is worth pursuing. Most of our company's subsidiaries are linked into our benefit programs. Pensions, savings fund plans, health insurance, all that good stuff." He leaned forward and looked into Sherman's eyes. "Judy, bless her soul, would have been thrilled, huh?"

Sherman winced. His wife had died almost five years ago. She'd stuck with him for over two decades, through thick and thin. Mostly thin, he reminisced bitterly, including one particularly disastrous business venture that had driven them to the brink of bankruptcy. How much dear Judy would have welcomed his having a decent job with benefits.

Mike placed his hand on Sherman's arm. "Now you have a chance to do her memory proud. Anyway, like I said, Chuck Browne is the nicest guy you could hope to meet. And he has a real thing about innovation. He'd be real excited to meet a brain like you."

"Thanks, Mike. So I'll just turn up at your office on Friday at noon?"

"If you're free, of course. Do you need to check your calendar?"

"No, I'm free." No matter what was on his calendar, Sherman knew he'd be free for this particular lunch.

10.

Miranda Gets Her Way

ON THURSDAY MORNING, Katie and Miranda sat at the big conference table in Miranda's office. Tomorrow, Chuck and Miranda were to visit Beresford to meet with the manager and his department heads. This morning, Katie was giving Miranda background information to prepare her.

Miranda asked, "How many employees in Beresford Division, Katie?"

"Almost two thousand."

"Hmm," said Miranda, "Maybe I'd better check with Barry to be sure." She picked up the receiver and punched in the number for Barry Bryce. As she did so, she primped—smoothing her hair, adjusting her collar— as though she thought he'd be able to see her. Then she purred into the telephone, "Barry, it's me. I'm sorry to bother you again, but do you know how many employees there are in Beresford Division?"

Katie uncrossed and recrossed her legs. There was a time she would have felt indignant at Miranda's seeming lack of confidence in her knowledge, but after even this short time of working with Miranda, Katie had begun to realize that the woman's frequent calls to Bryce were motivated less by a need for facts than by a desire to hear his voice.

Miranda said, "About two thousand. Yes, that's what I thought." She nodded at Katie as if to reassure her that her estimate had been confirmed by an expert. But getting an answer to her question was not sufficient reason for Miranda to end the call, and she continued, "So how's everything going? Are you all set for Shell Bay?"

Katie settled back in her chair. This could take a while. Next week, Barry was leaving on assignment to the Shell Bay power plant, located on the California coast 200 miles south of San Francisco. His mission, it was rumored, was to determine why the plant had failed to meet its budget and production goals over the past two years, and to recommend changes needed to correct this sorry state of affairs. No doubt, Katie thought, heads would soon roll at Shell Bay.

"Oh, Barry, I'm going to miss you." Miranda said. "How long do you think you'll be gone?" A pause. Then she wailed, "Several months!"

Thank goodness, Katie thought. *With Barry out of the way, Miranda might finally knuckle down to work on the values pilot.*

Miranda wound her legs around the base of her chair and leaned forward on her elbows, caressing the receiver in both hands as though she were about to kiss it. "Barry," she cooed. "Will I be able to visit you at the power plant?" She made a pouty face as she listened to his reply. "I know," she said, "but I would really like to visit a power plant, Barry. Surely, it's a key part of my getting to know the company."

Her expression evolved from disappointed to determined as she listened to his response. "But, Barry, you said you were flying down to the plant this Friday, just for the day. Couldn't I come with you then?"

You had to hand it to the woman, Katie thought. Not many people would be so pestily persistent. She listened for a while longer, but when Miranda wailed, "Oh, Barry, pretty please," Katie suddenly felt embarrassed on her behalf.

Mouthing, "Back in a minute," she got up and left the room.

Down the hall, she stopped at the entrance to Terry's cubicle. Terry was working at his computer, head down and fingers flying over the keyboard, but he must have seen her out of the corner of his eye because he started humming the "K-k-k-Katie" song. After a moment, he pushed the Save button and swung around to face her with his usual grin. "Has Miranda let you come out to play?"

"She's in one of her endless telephone tête-à-têtes with Bair-eeee." Katie rolled her eyes at the ceiling and slumped into a chair opposite Terry. "What with the cooing, flirting, wiggling, whining—I thought I'd better leave before I puked."

He laughed. "And we used to think it was Worthington she was aiming to please. It seems it's Barry she's trying to get her hooks into."

"Like getting your hooks into a concrete slab, I should think."

Terry rocked back in his chair. "So how are things going with the pilot project?"

"Tomorrow, Chuck's going to Beresford to meet with the division manager and his department heads. Miranda's supposed to go with him but I wouldn't be surprised if she wiggles out of it." She grinned. "It's rumored that Mike Weston practically had a stroke when he heard Beresford had been chosen for the pilot."

"And he couldn't get out of it?"

"Well, it seems that a couple of years ago, Chuck got him out of a big jam of some sort, and now he feels he owes Chuck one."

Terry raised his eyebrows, waiting for more, but Katie decided she'd said enough. The folder Chuck had handed her two weeks ago had reminded her of the Beresford scandal. Mike Weston had been caught taking kickbacks from contractors in a big undergrounding project. Chuck had been dispensed by Worthington to smooth things out, and had done so. Katie wasn't sure how.

Katie said, "Anyway, if all goes well at that meeting, Miranda will be scheduling her workshops for the whole division." She looked at her watch. "I'd better get back. If the creature's still emoting, I'll leave again."

Miranda wasn't still emoting. She was off the phone and complained to Katie, "You were gone a long time."

But then her face lit up and she said, "I'm going to the power plant with Barry tomorrow. We're taking the company plane down first thing in the morning."

Wow! Katie thought. Miranda had managed to wangle herself into something she wanted to do and out of something she didn't want to do. Katie said, "So you won't be going to Beresford with Chuck?"

Miranda picked up a pen and pulled a pad of paper toward her. She said, "I forgot about that Beresford trip. But I'd probably just be in the way when Chuck's trying to explain things to those division people."

She scribbled hard with her ballpoint pen to get the ink to flow, and muttered, "I need to do some planning here." Then she looked up at Katie, her face bright. "Katie, what sort of clothes do you think I should wear to the power plant?"

Katie regarded the willowy figure seated across from her. Today, Miranda wore a bouclé jacket in a magenta shade accompanied by a black turtleneck sweater and slim black skirt. Who would think a redhead could look so stunning in magenta? But then Miranda would look stunning in anything. She said, "Pantsuit or even jeans. No skirts. Comfortable shoes."

Miranda stuck one foot out to the side of the table and cast an appraising glance at her shoe, a black patent leather pump with a slim high heel.

"No, Miranda," Katie said, "Don't even think about those. Flatties for a power plant, preferably with rubber soles."

Miranda made a face, put her leg down and said, "That means I'll have to go shopping."

THAT AFTERNOON, Chuck phoned a few minutes before five o'clock. "Katie, would you stop by?"

Katie said, "Sure," and glanced at the clock. She hoped this wouldn't take long. Tonight she was in a hurry to leave. She had to go home, feed the cats, change her clothes, and fight the traffic the ten or so miles to Berkeley where she was to meet Lorraine at seven. After a quick bite to eat, they'd be off to see the Kirov Ballet at Berkeley's Zellerbach Hall. She'd looked forward to this event for weeks.

Chuck was at his desk when she walked into his office. He waved her to a chair and said in a flat voice that suggested his mind was on something else, "Ah, Katie, how's everything going?"

"Fine." She sat down. Chuck had a folder on the desk in front of him. She could read the words "Beresford Pilot" on it.

"Katie, I want to ask a big favor of you."

"What's that?"

Chuck said, "Tomorrow, Worthington is giving a speech at the annual meeting of the Human Resources Council. They've asked him to talk about what companies like ours are doing to assess employee satisfaction. Needless to say, I wrote the speech for him."

He smiled at her and she smiled back. "Anyway, he just called to say he'd like me to be there to help field questions from the audience." He paused. "So, Katie, are you doing anything important tomorrow?"

"No."

She felt a happy tingle of anticipation. She knew that Chuck couldn't go to the council meeting tomorrow because he had to be in Beresford. This meant that he was going to ask her to accompany Worthington. This was quite an honor. Mentally, she started to frame a reply. "I'd be happy to go...."

She stopped framing as Chuck went on. "You know what the old man's like. It doesn't matter how reasonable your explanation, he just hears you say no and thinks you're being uncooperative. So I'll have to go with him. That means I can't make the trip to Beresford."

Now what's he saying? Her stomach tightened.

Chuck leaned forward and looked hard into her face. "Katie, I know this is a lot to ask of you, especially at the last moment like this. But I know you can handle things with Mike Weston and his people. You're really good at...."

Katie heard a high-pitched voice—her own—interrupting him. "You want me to go? How about Miranda?" She swallowed and lowered her voice. "Miranda's the project manager, isn't she? She should be going with you tomorrow anyway."

"Miranda can't make it tomorrow."

Katie couldn't hide her disgust. "Yes, I know all about the trip to Shell Bay with Barry Bryce. Chuck, don't let her fool you into thinking it's some kind of command performance. I overheard her conversation with him and, believe me, it was all Miranda's idea. She was hammering away at him for all she was worth trying to persuade him to take her."

But Chuck shook his head. "It's no good," he said. "She's adamant about going on this trip with Barry and, frankly, I need to pick my battles with Miranda carefully. We're always at odds and if I keep crossing her Worthington will accuse me of not being a team player." He pleaded, "Besides, you're by far the better person to meet with the Beresford people. You know the company well. You're tactful, perceptive, intelligent."

"Oh, Chuck, what shameless sweet talk."

But Katie knew she was stuck. She put out her hand for the folder Chuck held and opened it. The folder contained a sheaf of lined yellow sheets covered in Chuck's handwriting. Chuck said, "These are my notes on what I'd planned to say at the meeting with Weston. Call me tonight if you have questions. Oh, and here's your ticket."

Katie glanced at the itinerary attached to the ticket. "Holy cow! I have to be at the airport at six-thirty in the morning!" She got to her feet, "Chuck, you owe me big on this one."

"You're a trooper, lady." As she hurried out the door, she barely heard his last words. "By the way, I tried to call Weston to tell him you'd be taking my place but he wasn't in this afternoon. His secretary says she'll make sure he gets the message first thing in the morning."

Katie waved a hand without turning and walked back to her office.

One thing was for sure: she was not going to spend this evening deciphering Chuck's bad handwriting or phoning him with questions. Tonight she would eat, drink, and be merry with Lorraine and the glorious Kirov ballet. Tomorrow would have to take care of itself.

11

Barry and Lila at Home

THAT SAME THURSDAY EVENING, Barry Bryce was in the kitchen of his house in the upscale St. Francis Wood neighborhood of San Francisco. His wife Lila was working late tonight so Barry had stopped off at the fish market on his way home to pick up a piece of fresh halibut and a loaf of French bread.

Now he sipped a glass of Chardonnay and grunted with contented concentration as he measured out herbs and spices to sprinkle over the fish. Lila had left a message to say she'd be home at seven. At a quarter to the hour, Barry poured the remains of his glass of wine over the fish and put the dish in the oven. While it baked, he prepared vegetables for steaming and set aside ingredients for a salad on a cutting board. Lila liked to make the salads herself.

Shortly after seven, he heard the sound of the front door opening and called out a greeting. Lila shouted back a breathless "Hi" before going into their bedroom upstairs. Their house, like many others built on hilly terrain, had an unconventional floor plan. The entrance hall and bedrooms were on street level, while the kitchen and other living areas were downstairs.

After a few minutes, Lila came into the kitchen. He said, "Hi, babe." She walked over to him and he turned his head to exchange a brief kiss.

She sniffed the air. "Mmm. Something smells good."

Barry watched her as she sat down at the counter. Lila's silky blonde hair was pulled back in a chignon. She had delicate features and a pale complexion that gave her an ethereal look. This evening, Barry thought, she looked more fragile than usual. There were lines of weariness around her eyes and her thin shoulders slumped forward as she started to prepare the salad.

He asked, "Tiring day?"

"Sort of. I'm glad to be home."

Barry poured a glass of wine and carried it over to her. He slid an arm around her shoulders but withdrew it when he felt her tense up. Lila didn't always like to be touched when she was feeling tired. He said, "Why don't you stretch out on the couch, take a load off your feet? I'll fix the salad."

She shot back, "Oh, no, you don't. Trying to rob me of my salad-fixing exclusive." Her smile was affectionate.

While they continued preparing dinner, Lila talked about her day at work. The investment management firm in which she was a partner handled the portfolios of some of the city's biggest corporations and most influential individuals. Barry listened carefully while she talked for news related to two of her clients, RPC and its CEO. Although Barry had Worthington's ear on most important matters, there were times Lila passed on useful tidbits of information he hadn't heard elsewhere.

When the food was ready, they sat at the kitchen table to eat. Lila picked up her fork and looked down at her plate—halibut, cauliflower and broccoli covered in a fragrant bubbling sauce. She exclaimed. "Barry, this looks delicious." Taking a bite, she added, "You must be the world's best cook. I'm sure going to miss you when you go down to Shell Bay."

"I'll try to get back at weekends." He ate a mouthful of fish. "You're right, lady, this is superb." Lila made a lip-smacking noise. He said, "I don't mind doing the cooking, but you know, darlin', you work too long and too hard. Isn't there some way you can ease up?"

"Things are kind of crazy with tax season in full swing. But tomorrow I plan to come home early. In fact, Barry, I have a great idea." She put down her fork. "As you know, the Worthingtons have season tickets to the symphony. Everett said they hardly ever use the ones on Friday nights. Maybe we can scrounge a couple of tickets for tomorrow. That would be a great way to end the week, wouldn't it?"

Barry said, "I'm going to the power plant tomorrow." Her expression was blank. "Shell Bay, remember? By the time I get home, it'll be after eight. We'll have to make it another time."

Her face fell but Barry felt too annoyed to be sympathetic. Lila was always forgetting about his work plans. Just because she earned three times as much as he did was no excuse for her to treat his job as though it were a hobby.

"I'm sorry. I forgot. I guess I'm still not sure why you have to go tomorrow. I thought your assignment didn't start till Monday."

"As I explained the other day, their monthly safety meeting is tomorrow. With their abysmal safety record, I want to be in on that. Also they've just shut down one of the units for maintenance and I'd like to see how they're handling that process. It seems something's very wrong with the way they—"

The phone rang. Barry stopped talking and took a mouthful of food. Lila raised her eyebrows. "You expecting a call?"

He shook his head and continued. "Also, most of the workers aren't expecting me to be there until next week, so it'll be a good opportunity to do some quiet snooping around on my own."

The answering machine whirred and clicked. Barry paused again. Then he froze as a familiar voice, at once sultry and childlike, came from the recorder.

"Barry, it's me again. I'm so sorry to bother you at home but you know something? I don't know where I'm supposed to be meeting you tomorrow morning. I know you said the company hangar at the Oakland Airport, but I have no idea how to get there. So *help*!"

The voice went on, relaying a phone number and more apologies. Furious, Barry continued to eat. How dare the stupid woman call him at home! Any number of people in Chuck's office could have given her directions to the hangar. The machine clicked off.

Lila broke the silence that followed. She said, mimicking the caller, *"Barry, it's me again."* She added, "What 'me' would that be, I wonder? Sexpot me? Whatsername?" Barry was silent and she asked, "What is her name again?"

Lila had met Miranda only once—at one of Worthington's periodic wine-and-cheese do's—but Barry couldn't imagine that his wife with her needle-sharp memory would truly have forgotten the "sexpot's" name. He took a sip of wine before answering. "Miranda."

"Miranda. Right. The corporate values lady. You didn't tell me *she* was going to Shell Bay with you tomorrow." A pause. "That is where you're going tomorrow, isn't it?"

"Oh, cut it out," Barry snapped. "Miranda is a giant pain in the butt. The main reason I'll be glad to move down to Shell Bay for a while is to put some distance between me and Miranda. The damned woman won't stop bugging me. Every five minutes, she calls with some niggling thing."

"Surely you can easily fix that. Tell her to get lost."

"How can I do that? She's Worthington's protégée. You don't want me to upset him now, do you?"

Lila slammed down her fork and glared at him. For a moment, she struggled to find her voice. Then she said, "Barry, I've just about had it up to here with your snide comments about Everett. I persuaded him to give you this job because I thought both you and the company could benefit."

With a trembling hand, she pushed her plate away and stood up. Breathlessly, she continued. "You seem to think you're doing me a favor by working at RPC. Well, think again. I don't care if you upset Everett. It isn't going to affect my relationship with him in any way. If you hate the place so much, why don't you quit? Go find yourself your own lousy job."

Barry started, "I didn't say I hated...." But Lila didn't stop to listen. She marched out of the kitchen, down the hall, and up the stairs. He heard her overhead, opening and slamming the door of her office.

He poured himself some more wine and reflected on the demon inside him that got such a kick out of needling Lila. There was a time their verbal sparring had lent a touch of spice to their relationship. But these days, Lila was not as resilient as she used to be. She was easily upset, looked tired a lot, and withdrew from the fray too readily. He'd have to learn how to control that little demon, especially since he really did owe her a lot.

BARRY'S LAST JOB before joining RPC had been the superintendent of operations at a local steel mill. He'd done an excellent job of running the mill, trimming costs and producing the most efficient operation the company had known in its history. But then there'd been a series of labor disputes that resulted in a costly strike. Barry had taken the heat for what people saw as his hard-nosed and unsympathetic approach toward the workers. Ultimately, despite Barry's strong recommendations to the contrary, management had given way to the workers' demands and Barry had left the company under a cloud.

Finding a new job had proved difficult, in part because Lila was unwilling to move out of the area. So she had asked her long-time and exceedingly valuable client, Everett Worthington, to create a special position for her husband at RPC.

AFTER A WHILE, Barry stirred. It was time to make up. He made a pot of coffee, filled two mugs, and carried them to the coffee table in the living room. Then he went upstairs and tapped on Lila's office door. Opening it a crack, he murmured, "Would Madame like coffee in the drawing room?" Lila, seated at her desk, looked up. Her smile was strained, but she rose and followed him down to the living room. There, they sat at opposite ends of the couch and looked solemnly at each other for a moment. Then he moved closer to her, putting an arm along the back of the couch and letting his hand fall onto her shoulder.

He said, "Sweetheart, I'm sorry I distressed you. Everett has always treated me well and I didn't mean to imply otherwise. This job is the best opportunity anyone has ever given me and I am truly grateful."

Her face softened and she slid closer to him. "I understand. You're such an independent person, it must really gall you to feel obligated to me or to Everett."

Amen! Barry thought, but he said, "No, it's not that. It's just that I get so frustrated with RPC sometimes. It's such an archaic company. And the place is so full of deadwood it's a wonder it doesn't burst into flames. Everett's always asking me, 'What can we do to become more competitive?' The answer is obvious but when I tell him, what does he do? He decides we need Dr. Miranda Peabody and her Corporate Values Program." He made a face.

Lila smiled and moved her face still closer till her cheek was resting on his. He went on, "I'm sorry I didn't tell you earlier about Miranda going with me tomorrow. To be truthful, I've felt so annoyed about it I kind of blotted it out of my mind. Anyway, when we get there, I'll fob her off on some junior clerk and tell him to give her a long, detailed plant tour. She'll be so bored she'll never pull this stunt again."

Lila rubbed a finger across his chin. "And I'm sorry I got so huffy. You see..." She laughed. "I've always thought of Miranda as Ev's bit of stuff. I didn't think you and he would be sharing."

He laughed too and brushed his lips lightly across her mouth. "Lila, she's just a two-bit tramp." He felt a pang as he spoke. He didn't really think Miranda was a tramp; she was just a silly little girl, both annoying and endearing. But he knew Lila needed double reassurance when it came to Miranda because Barry wasn't the only man his wife felt possessive about.

Lila and Everett had known each other since long before Barry had entered her life. Worthington made no secret of his admiration and affection for her, describing her as having "the features of a Greek goddess" and being "the most astute businesswoman" he had ever known. And, long ago, Barry had realized that Worthington's extra-marital dalliances were unsettling not only to the long-suffering Mrs. Worthington but—though she vehemently denied this—to Lila too. Barry even wondered whether at some time in the past Lila herself had been one of Everett's "bits of stuff."

Lila said, "Tramp she may be. An attractive one though, you must admit."

"Okay, I admit it. Now how about some coffee?" He picked up the mugs on the table and handed one to her. As she took it, the corners of her mouth turned up in a cat-like smile.

"Now don't forget to call her back. And give her the wrong directions."

He whispered, "Shush," and kissed her nose.

12

Katie Catches Flack at Beresford

ON FRIDAY MORNING, Katie shivered as she climbed down the steps from the United shuttle at the Beresford Airport. It was cold and foggy and it had been a bumpy flight. She walked across the tarmac toward the arrivals lounge, hoping the division had sent someone to meet her.

Inside the terminal, she was relieved to see Mike Weston staring out through the windows at the airfield. She walked over to him. "Mike?" He glanced at her without recognition. This wasn't surprising. He'd been pointed out to her at a couple of company meetings but they'd never been introduced. She said, "I'm Katie Carlisle. From Chuck Browne's office?"

He nodded but then turned his attention back to the passengers still walking toward them from the plane. When the last straggler had walked into the terminal, West turned to her and said, "Where's Chuck?"

"Chuck isn't coming. Didn't you get the message?"

From the way his mouth dropped open, it was obvious he hadn't. Katie said, "Mr. Worthington needed Chuck to be with him this morning. Chuck did leave you a message."

She stopped. The astonished look on his face had been replaced with one of fury. He exploded, "I don't believe this. You mean he's not coming after he insisted I get all my department heads assembled to meet with him? Do you people have a clue how difficult it is to arrange something like this? And now you're telling me the whole thing's off."

Katie said, "No, of course it isn't off. That's why I'm here."

His mouth snapped shut and he swung around and marched toward the exit. Katie, half-running to keep up, mumbled to his back, "I don't understand why you didn't get the message."

Weston stormed out through the door ahead of her and over to a large late-model American car parked by the curb. He went to the driver's door, opened it and climbed in. Katie walked up to the car, half-expecting him to drive away without her. But he didn't and she opened the door and got into the front seat beside him. As he pulled away from the curb, he muttered, "Do you realize it's past nine already? This meeting is supposed to start at nine. They'll all be sitting there, right now, waiting for us."

"I'm sorry. The plane was over an hour late taking off—because of the fog in Beresford, they said. Will it take us long to get to the office?"

He didn't answer.

Katie leaned back against the headrest and stretched her limbs in an attempt to relax her tense muscles. This was an unfortunate start to the day, but she told herself not to worry about it too much. All she had to do this morning was to explain the workshops and get Mike and his supervisors to approve the workshop schedule.

There wasn't much to see during the ride into town. The expressway was straight and flat, lined by sound walls for much of the way. Fog obscured most of whatever lay beyond.

After a while, in a calm but still angry voice, Weston said, "I know none of this is your fault but, I tell you, this whole business makes me mad. When you get back to the city, tell your boss that next time something like this happens, he should have the courtesy to reschedule the meeting. It would do us all a favor."

Katie said, "But, Mike, we didn't want to postpone the meeting. I'm hoping to answer everyone's questions about the program and get the workshop schedule set today. We'd really like to get the whole thing done as soon as possible."

He snorted, "So would I."

IT WAS ALMOST TEN by the time they reached the Cooper Building. As soon as they left the elevator on the sixth floor, Weston was assailed by a thin, flat-chested, young woman. "Mike, I've been frantic trying to get hold of you. Why didn't you return my calls?" She looked at Katie and said, "At least you found each other okay."

Mike ignored her and strode across the room. Katie followed. The woman fell in step with Katie and complained, loudly enough for Mike to hear, "He didn't come into the office this morning. I left two messages at his home and tried to get him on his beeper several times, but he didn't call me back. He's always doing this kind of thing." She waved her hands.

Katie didn't respond for by now she had followed Mike into a large corner office where several men sat in chairs arranged around a walnut desk. They were drinking coffee from Styrofoam cups and some were helping themselves to doughnuts from a pink cardboard box on the desk.

Mike walked around the desk and sat down. Katie couldn't see anywhere for her to sit so she stood in the middle of the room, clutching her purse and briefcase. Mike jerked a hand in Katie's direction and announced, "She's come to talk to us about this values project."

They all turned to stare at Katie as they continued to slurp and munch. Someone asked what had happened to "that Chuck guy." Mike said, "Oh, he couldn't make it because something more important came up." Restless murmurs followed. Mike shrugged his shoulders. One man scraped back his chair and said, "I might as well get back to the yard then."

Mike waved him to sit down. "Not yet. I told you, *she's* going to talk to us."

At this point, there was a squeaking sound as the beanpole woman entered the room wheeling what looked like a typist's chair. She pushed it over to Katie. "I figured you don't want to stand for the rest of the meeting." She glared around at the men as she spoke, and said to Katie. "You could probably use a cup of coffee too."

Katie accepted, feeling a bit overwhelmed at such civility. Mike broke in crossly, "I'd kinda like a cup myself, you know. And it looks like these guys have eaten all the good doughnuts." An argument erupted concerning whether or not his accusation was justified. The beanpole woman shook her head at Katie and left the room.

No one offered Katie a doughnut, but Mike found one that was apparently satisfactory to him. He took a bite and said to Katie, "Why don't you get started? Chuck's not the only one's got more important things to do this morning."

Katie pulled her chair as close to the desk as she could and placed her briefcase on it. Then she took out a notepad and the folder with Chuck's notes. As she struggled to balance the papers on her knees and search in her purse for a pen, she said, "Well, for a start, some introductions. My name is Katie Carlisle. I work for Chuck Browne who's the manager of the executive support services department."

Someone growled, "This ain't gonna take long, I hope." Katie looked up. The speaker was a big man with a dated military crew cut. She glanced at the rest of the group. Most looked like outdoor workers with ruddy complexions and heavy denim clothing. Only two of them besides Mike wore business attire.

The skinny woman reentered the room with two large mugs of coffee, which she handed to Mike and Katie. She then reached into the pocket of her jacket and produced a handful of packets and wooden sticks, dropping them in the middle of the desk. She whispered to Katie, "Cream and sugar, if you want."

Mike said, "Thanks, Maisie. Close the door on the way out, would you."

The coffee smelled enticing. Katie did want cream and sugar and wistfully eyed the packets. But they were out of her reach and the crew-cut man was muttering again so she turned instead to the folder on her lap. She said, "Let's see. Next week, we hope to start our workshops on the Values Program and I should point out that the person giving them will be Miranda Peabody."

A balding, freckle-faced man interrupted, "What program is that?"

"The Corporate Values Program." Katie glanced around the room as she spoke. She was met with blank expressions all round. She turned to Mike who was busy tearing open a sugar packet.

"Take no notice. They all know about it."

Katie took another breath. "Okay. As you know, Beresford Division is the site of a pilot for this program."

"And whose fool idea was that?" The speaker this time was a wizened little man with a shock of white hair. His question sparked noisy speculation in the group as to why their division had been selected for the pilot.

Katie sat upright and said in her firmest voice. "Listen, all that's been settled. Today, I want to tell you about the workshops. Over the next couple of months, Miranda Peabody..."

The crew-cut man interrupted. "Miranda who? Pee what?" There were snickers all round.

Katie took a breath. "Doctor Miranda Peabody is an outside consultant whom Mr. Worthington has hired to conduct this program. She's..."

"A sexy broad, so we hear." More snickers.

Mike said, "Yeah, okay." To Katie, he said, "Keep going."

"Okay. To repeat, I want to tell you about the workshops. Over the next couple of months, all Beresford Division employees will be taking a five-day workshop on corporate values."

Her words brought cries of outrage. She heard, "Over my dead body" and "Not my people."

Again, Katie turned to Mike who was now leaning back in his chair, sipping his coffee, a smug expression on his face. He looked, Katie thought, like an indulgent parent who is thoroughly enjoying the havoc being wreaked by his unruly children. Sharply, she asked, "Are your staff meetings usually like this?" He nodded, as though acknowledging the rebuke, put down his cup, and called for order. Thereupon, order was restored but, as a rueful Katie later related to Terry, "only for about two minutes."

Shortly before noon, Mike said to Katie, "Are you about finished? It's lunchtime."

"Well, we still haven't settled the workshop schedule. Maybe we could spend a few more minutes reviewing it."

As she pulled the schedule out of her briefcase, the folder of Chuck's notes that was balanced on her lap fell to the floor—the yellow lined sheets splaying around her chair like autumn leaves. Everyone seemed to regard this as a signal that the meeting was over. A general hubbub ensued as the men rose and broke into conversation with each other on their way out of the room.

Katie sighed but, in truth, she felt this was a fitting end to a ridiculous morning. In the past two hours, her attempts to get Mike and his people engaged in a serious discussion on the workshops had been deflected. Instead, she had heard all she could stomach about what "us division people" think of head office people and their "dumb programs." Maybe these men were deluding themselves that if they raised enough of a ruckus, head office could be persuaded to call off the whole thing.

Weston too was making his way to the door, interrupted every step of the way by one or other of his men who wanted to bend his ear. But, finally, they all left and Katie heard him say to someone outside his office, "Hi, Sherm. I'll be right there." Then he returned to stand beside Katie who was kneeling on the floor, gathering up her papers.

She looked up and said, "Mike, we must get these workshops started next week. So this afternoon I'll try to get at least a couple of your people to okay the schedule.

Who do you think would be available to meet with me this afternoon?"

"This afternoon? No one. All these folks got work to do. We've tied up enough time on this stuff for one day." He gathered up the remaining sugar and creamer packets on his desk and tossed them into the empty doughnut box. He said, "You didn't drink your coffee."

Katie looked up at him again. She would have loved that coffee but just hadn't been able to get to it. Something in her expression must have touched him in some way because suddenly he smiled. He said, "Bet you're hungry. I'm having lunch with a friend. Why don't you join us?"

Katie's refusal was prompt. "Thank you, but no. If I can't interview anyone this afternoon, I might as well get back to the city. I'm booked on the five o'clock flight, but I'm sure there's something earlier than that, isn't there?"

"Nope, " he said cheerfully, "The five o'clock is the next one out. So you might as well have lunch with us, then I'll drive you to the airport."

It seemed she had no alternative. As she finished collecting her things, she saw Mike glancing over his shoulder at the large painting hanging on the wall behind his desk. Boats in a harbor. It had caught Katie's eye many times during the endless morning. He said, "You like boats?"

She felt too dispirited to be polite. "Not really."

Outside the office, Mike greeted his friend, a short, plump man with a friendly smile. "Katie, meet Sherman Granger." Sherman Granger said, "Good to meet you." Then—like Mike at the airport—Sherman peered into the empty office behind them as though expecting someone else to materialize.

Mike said, "Er, Katie, I'm sure you'd like to freshen up before lunch. I need to have a word with Sherman." He pointed down the hall. "Ladies' room thataway. Let's meet by the elevator in a few minutes."

Sherman Granger seemed a bit subdued when they met up again, but his smile was as friendly as ever. Mike talked and Sherman responded as they went downstairs and out to the parking lot. When Katie headed for the back door of Mike's car, Sherman hastened to open the door for her.

After they set off, Mike cleared his throat and looked up in the rear view mirror at Katie. He said, "I don't know if you're aware of it, Katie, but Sherm here has invented a great energy-saving device that we think RPC would be interested in. It's a cogeneration unit for small offices and private homes."

"Oh?" Something stirred in Katie's memory. "Oh, wait a minute. Was something written about that in our company news sheet a while ago?"

Sherman swung around to face her, his face eager. "Yes, that's right."

Katie recollected she'd thrown the paper in the trash without reading the article. She did recall that Terry had made some joke about the invention being something that would put them out of business. Mike went on, "I must confess, one reason I'd hoped Chuck would be here today was I wanted him to meet Sherman."

Sherman, who was watching her face, smiled at her. Again, she said, "Oh?"

"Yes. You see we thought that Chuck would be the ideal person to help Sherm make the right contacts at RPC."

Katie didn't know what to say. She couldn't imagine the company would be interested in a device that would reduce their revenues. From the silence that followed, it seemed she was expected to respond. Finally, she said, "I'm sorry. I'm really not up to speed on the subject."

Mike said, "Not the only subject you're not up to speed on, huh?" He snickered and said to Sherman, "Katie here sure was unprepared this morning. My guys just took over the meeting, didn't they, Katie? Wiped the floor with you." Grinning, he glanced at her in the rearview mirror.

Katie gasped. "Being prepared had nothing whatever to do with that fiasco of a meeting. In all my years at this company, I've never encountered such a disorderly and rude bunch of people. It's a wonder your division gets any work done at all with a management team like that."

She regretted her words instantly. They were unprofessional, childish, and, worst of all, likely to get back to Chuck.

Mike sounded amused. "Wait till I tell 'em that."

Sherman turned to look at her again. He said in a gentle, serious voice, "Sounds to me like you were set up, Katie. People in the division are always resentful of head office people. You were a scapegoat. And you, Mike," turning to his friend, "should be ashamed of yourself."

Mike gave a shout of laughter. Sherman's sympathy made Katie feel better, but she didn't think he spoke the full truth. She was sure those men would have behaved better with Chuck. They'd given her an especially bad time because she was a woman. She wondered how Miranda would have made out. Probably Miranda would have done just fine. Those sexist pigs would have been too busy drooling to interrupt.

As for the division manager—she glared at the back of Mike's head—Mike was an ill-mannered hick who'd done as little as possible to help her today. Sherman Granger, on the other hand—her eyes moved across to the man in the passenger seat—well, Sherman was a darling.

Mike drove them out of town, down a river road to a restaurant perched on stilts above the river. Willie's Watering Hole. From Sherman's admiring comments, Katie gathered the locals considered this somewhere special. They sat at a corner table and, at Mike's recommendation, ordered broiled swordfish.

Conversation immediately switched to Sherman's invention. Katie's mind drifted as the two men discussed a demo unit that Sherman had apparently built. She jumped when Sherman said, "So, Katie, do you think your boss would be interested in learning more about this?"

"I'm sorry, I wasn't following the conversation."

Sherman bent toward her earnestly. "But you have heard of cogeneration, haven't you, Katie?"

"Let's see. That's a process that reuses energy that's been produced by one process to generate energy by another process."

"That's right," Sherman continued. "Cogen is usually feasible only for very large users of energy. But my invention, which I call the compact cogenerator, will be small and cheap enough to be practical for places like offices, apartment buildings, even private homes."

"So it would save consumers lots of money on their energy bills?"

"It sure has that potential."

"But, Sherman, seeing our company makes money on selling energy, do you really think it would be interested in your invention?"

Sherman leaned back as the waiter brought their entrees. He looked over at Mike, as though seeking reassurance. Mike said, "If they don't, they're a bunch of idiots. Sherm's device is on the cutting edge of technology." He turned to Katie. "Katie, how about you approach Chuck about this? Sherm has some pamphlets printed up. Projected savings and all that good stuff. Maybe ask Chuck to talk to folks at head office—engineering, law, operations. He'd know how to proceed."

Katie looked at Sherman's anxious expression. "Sure, I'd be happy to follow up with Chuck." That was the least she could do for this courteous man.

TRAFFIC WAS LIGHT on the drive home from the airport. Katie had left her house long before dawn and was anxious to get back to Kit and Kat. Making the turn into Alara Way, she just missed a panel truck coming in the opposite direction. When the driver tooted, she thought at first he was irate because she'd cut the corner.

But then she realized that the tooter was Dan. Blue-eyed Dan, the erstwhile house painter. She still hadn't checked around for other painting contractors. She really ought to get going on that.

Eager feline yowls accompanied Katie's entrance into the house. Five minutes of kissing and cuddling later, she opened up a can of Mackerel Entree and spooned it into two bowls for the cats. She watched them as they ate, delighting in their lip-smacking contentment.

If only men were this lovable and this easy to keep happy! And, for that matter, this easy to get!

13

The Program is Killed

"Chuck has absolutely no free time this afternoon," Dorothy told Katie. It was the first Friday in May, almost two months after Katie's visit to Beresford Division. The pilot project was now almost over.

No sooner were the words out of Dorothy's mouth than Chuck walked past them on his way into his office. "A quick minute, Chuck?" Katie begged.

"For you, Katie, anything." Dorothy gave an exasperated sigh.

Katie closed his office door after them and waited until they'd both sat down before speaking. "I heard something rather disturbing yesterday, Chuck. You know, the values pilot at Beresford is almost over and Miranda tells me she's already leaning on Worthington to let her expand it to other sites. I reminded her we had to do an evaluation of the pilot first, but she seemed unconcerned."

Chuck smiled. "Don't worry about it."

"Why? Have you heard something?"

Chuck hesitated. " Katie, what I'm about to tell you isn't public knowledge yet. You must promise not to breathe a word of it to anyone. At least, not yet."

"Of course."

"Well, at the executive committee meeting this morning Worthington brought up the subject of the Corporate Values Program. And, guess what? The executive committee voted to terminate the program, effectively immediately. The Beresford pilot is terminated too, of course. That means no more workshops, no evaluation of results, nothing."

"For heaven's sake. Do you know the reasons for this decision?"

"I'm sure you can guess. For one thing, the manager at Beresford hasn't stopped complaining about the workshops. He says they disrupt division work. They prevent customers from getting served properly. He won't be able to meet his goals for the year. On and on. And you know Worthington. He loses interest pretty fast at the first sign of trouble."

For a few moments, they looked at each in silence. Chuck said, "Isn't this the day we've all been dreaming about?"

"Absolutely."

In fact, Katie had mixed feelings about the news. Of course, she was happy that Miranda and her program would soon be history. On the other hand, she felt uneasy about the abrupt manner in which the project was ending. There would inevitably be a finger-pointing postmortem, in which no one even remotely associated with the program would be safe.

The intercom buzzed. Dorothy said, "Chuck, your one o'clock."

"We're just finishing up here." As Katie walked toward the door, he said to her, "Smart outfit. Is it new?"

She beamed as she walked back to her office. She was sure his praise was as much a comment on her new svelte figure as her suit. In the past three months, she'd lost twelve pounds although no one in the office seemed to have noticed.

AT THE SHELL BAY POWER PLANT that day, Barry was in earnest discussion with the general foreman in the turbine building when a breathless secretary ran into the building. "Barry, it's Mr. Worthington on the phone for you." Barry excused himself and accompanied the secretary back across the yard to the main administration building. He wanted to take this call.

A couple of minutes later, he picked up the phone in the office. "Hi, Ev."

"*Barry.*" As it usually did, the CEO's loud voice caught him off-guard and he momentarily jerked the phone away from his ear. The voice boomed on. "Just read your report. Good work, good work."

"Thank you."

"Hmm, yes." From the paper-shuffling sound on the other end of the line, it seemed Worthington was looking through the report. "Yes, here it is. You recommend we start a search immediately for a permanent plant manager for Shell Bay. Should I assume then that you are not interested in applying for that job yourself?"

"That is correct, yes."

A few days after arriving at the Shell Bay Power Plant in February, Barry had persuaded the plant manager to take early retirement. It seemed, as Barry had reported to Worthington at the time, that the man had for too long been "letting the animals run the zoo," and this sad fact was at the root of the plant's abysmal performance. At the CEO's request, Barry had then taken on the role of acting manager until he had completed his initial assignment of getting things back on track at the plant. He had no intention, however, of making the acting position a permanent one for him. He said, "It's a good time to bring a new leader on board."

There was a pause. Worthington said, "And time for you to get back to Lila, right?"

"That, too."

Since he'd moved to Shell Bay, Barry had spent only a few weekends in the city with Lila. Power plants, as he'd told her, don't take the weekends off. And he hadn't once been able to persuade her to spend a weekend with him in what she called "the boonies."

"Okay. I guess the next step is to ask HR to rustle up a candidates' list."

"Yes, and I'll be happy to get that process going."

Worthington said, "Thanks, Barry. I must say it'll be good to see your handsome face around HO again." He chuckled.

A good segue, Barry thought, to what was on his mind right now. He said, "Everett, I guess this is as good a time as any to get back to this issue. When I return to head office, I would be really grateful if you could find a new position for me. Don't get me wrong. Being your chief of classified projects is both challenging and rewarding but...."

"Barry, Barry," the voice boomed, "you don't have to explain. Of course, you'd like to move on. I understand that. And I agree. We must see you get experience in a whole range of responsible positions. That's an essential part of grooming you for a vice-presidency. Believe me, I'm not forgetting about this." Again, he chuckled, "Your lovely wife won't let me."

Barry asked, "Do you have something specific in mind?"

Worthington ignored the question. "While I have you on the phone, there's something else I need to fill you in on. At the executive committee meeting this morning, we decided to kill the Corporate Values Program."

Surprised, Barry repeated, "Kill it? They haven't even finished the pilot yet, have they?"

"I'm not sure. But that's not the point. The point is the damned program just isn't going anywhere. Those workshops have been causing unbelievable pandemonium out in...what's that Valley place? Beresford. No evidence that productivity has improved or whatever all else Peabody claimed."

Barry resisted making an *I told you so* kind of comment. Instead, he said, "It's a bit soon to decide that, isn't it?"

But Worthington continued to talk. "This morning, at the meeting, I asked if anyone was interested in having these workshops conducted in their department or division. The answer was an emphatic *No*. So what the heck! It might be a great program for some companies, but it's not working for us. So we might as well cut our losses, eh?"

Barry thought about a phone call he'd received from Miranda a few days ago. "Know what, Barry?" she'd coo'ed. "I have an appointment with the old man on

Thursday and I'm going to lean on him to let us get moving on picking the next workshop site. We're almost finished at Beresford so it's time."

Barry had urged her to wait. First, he'd told her, she had to do at least a nominal evaluation of the Beresford pilot before expanding the program to other sites. ("*For Heaven's sake, Miranda, that's the whole point of doing a pilot.*") Also, he'd stressed that no matter what she wanted, she ought to go through the proper chain of command. That is, talk to Chuck Browne before approaching Worthington. Miranda had reacted to his advice with a sulky, "I'll think about it."

It seemed she had ignored his advice and had hastened the demise of the program as a result. But Miranda wasn't the only one acting rashly here.

Barry said, "You know, Ev, a neutral observer might get the impression that the committee's decision was pretty arbitrary. How do you think it would sit with the Board of Directors? Or anyone else who'd heard you propose this program as something that was going to revolutionize the company?"

Worthington sighed. "So what do you advise?"

"For a start, it's imperative we give the impression that the pilot project was well planned and carried out. And, most important of all, we must make it clear that the decision to kill the program was based on a careful evaluation of the pilot and nothing else."

A short silence before Worthington said, "You're suggesting we need a formal analysis of some kind? Before-and-after statistics, that kind of thing?"

Barry almost laughed out loud. Worthington had a hope if he thought Miranda had gathered data of that sort. He said, "There's no need for that. All we need is a carefully written report. If done properly, it'll read like a formal analysis, and we can make sure it conveys whatever message we want it to."

"Good idea." Worthington sounded relieved. "Barry, would you handle that for me please? Oh, and Miranda doesn't yet know about the committee decision. I'd appreciate your taking care of that too, if you would."

Barry compressed his mouth into a grim smile. To think he'd been lecturing Miranda to go through the chain of command. Worthington seemed to have forgotten that he, Barry, had no formal role at all in the values project. He asked, "Oh, one other thing. Miranda has a one-year contract with us. What do you have in mind for her? After she's finished the report, of course."

"Oh, there'll be no difficulty there, I'm sure. We'll be able to find her something to do to finish out the year. Don't you think?"

He didn't say, "*Would you take care of that for me, Barry,*" but Barry knew it would likely come to that anyway.

14

Katie's in Love

ON SATURDAY, Katie awoke feeling restless. She decided she needed some mood-uplifting activity to take the place of her usual weekend chores. Accordingly, after breakfast, she set off for the most mood-uplifting place she knew, Bernini's Nursery.

Bernini's was a feast for the eyes at any time of year, but it was especially beautiful in May with vibrant displays of roses, cyclamen, fuchsias, and azaleas. The Berninis had a penchant for Italian opera, and the strains of heart-tugging arias wafted from the speakers scattered throughout the nursery. For a while, Katie drifted up and down the aisles, her senses both heightened and soothed by the blissful mix of color and music.

Finally, she made her selection: six pots of zinnias in splashy reds, oranges, and yellows.

After arriving home, she parked in the driveway and removed the heavy box of plants from the trunk. As she struggled toward her back gate, she noticed the sheet of paper impaled on her door knocker. Katie put down the plants, climbed the steps to the front door, and retrieved the paper. It was a handwritten note. "I'm ready to start on your paint job. Will try to catch you later. Dan."

Both the tone and content of the note irritated Katie. She and Dan hadn't spoken a word to each other for over three months and here he was assuming that because he was ready, she would be ready too.

After she had had deposited her purchases in the backyard, she glanced at her watch. It was not yet eleven. Time to get changed and do a little gardening before lunch. She had no sooner let herself in through the back door than she heard the front door bell ring. Dan, no doubt. .

The bell rang again. And again. And again. As she reached the front door, it rang yet again. She opened the door and there stood Dan, with his thumb on the bell. He said, "I saw you come in so I kept trying." He held a large manila envelope, which he waved at her. "Paint chips."

Katie looked at his serious, handsome face. He still needed a haircut. She saw there were two tiny frown lines between his eyes that made him appear older than she'd thought he was. Today, she thought sardonically, he looked all of twenty-two.

"Um, Dan, I'm afraid I haven't given much thought to the house painting since I last spoke with you. I've been very busy."

"So what are you saying? Do you still want your house painted?"

"Well, yes."

Right away, he pulled open the flap of the envelope. "So let's take a look at these," he said. "Can we spread 'em out on a table somewhere?"

Not quite knowing what else to do, Katie led him into the kitchen where he seated himself at the table and tipped out the contents of the envelope. He arranged the colors in pairs. "One is for the siding, the other for the trim," he explained. "Now what I thought would be real good for your place would be this creamy-beige for the walls and for the trim..." He reached across her to pick up another chip, his bare forearm brushing against hers. "This brown here. See, there's just a hint of red in it."

Katie sat with her arms resting on the table, staring down at the colored squares. She tried to remember what was so all-fired important about getting three bids. Why shouldn't she just hire Dan? Wasn't it too late now to do anything else?

Dan said, "If you decide on the colors today, I'll buy the paint tonight and start work on Monday." He looked at her intently, the dark blue eyes searching her face. "I'm not trying to rush you, but I do have a window of time here. I can work on your place next week, but then I might get tied up again."

Katie sat back and moved her arms off the table, taking care not to bump that bare forearm. She said, "I agree with you. The cream and brown combination looks really nice."

"Great. Shall I go ahead then?"

Afterwards, she couldn't remember exactly what she'd responded, but it must have been in the affirmative because several minutes later Dan was walking around the outside of her house with a tape measure. When he went back to the kitchen to pick up his paint chips, Katie walked him to the front door. She asked, "How long do you think it will take? To do the house?"

"Not long. By next weekend, you'll have the smartest little house in the neighborhood." For the first time this morning, he smiled. A bright, friendly smile.

Katie gulped. Doing her best to sound businesslike, she asked, "Dan, have you painted any houses before?"

He seemed surprised. "Of course, I have. Did you think I was practicin' on you or something?"

"No, it was just... oh, never mind. Incidentally, I keep the house locked when I'm at work, but the garage side door is unlocked so you can store your things in there if you need to." He nodded but made no move to leave.

After a moment, she asked, "Is there anything else?"

"It would help if you could give me some cash for the paint."

"Oh, of course." Katie went to the bedroom for her purse and took out fifty dollars. She thought he might protest that fifty dollars was too much but when she handed him the money, he just said, "Thanks," and set off down the steps. As she closed the door, it occurred to her she should have had him confirm the price he'd originally quoted her. Terry would be disgusted at such laxness.

It was now almost noon. Katie decided to have lunch first and finish planting the zinnias afterwards. As she stood over the stove heating soup, one of those Italian arias kept going through her mind. There were English words to this tune too and Katie burst into song. "There's no tomorrow when you're in love."

Wonderful, she thought, what an effect an hour at Bernini's could have!

15

Money in the Bank

At midmorning on Monday, the phone rang. A male voice said, "Katie? This is Sherman Granger. Remember me?"

"Sherman. How's everything going? Did you manage to contact the two people I told you about?"

"Yeah." He sounded hesitant. "Your friend in Engineering said he'd get back to me, but he hasn't. As for the Law Department! Oh, man!"

"What did they say?"

Sherman laughed. "The attorney you referred me to told me he represents RPC and has no authority to discuss business with anyone outside the company without being instructed by someone inside the company. Lawyers! Phew!"

"I'm sorry. I guess I haven't been much help, have I? You know something, Sherman, I haven't yet spoken to my boss about your situation. He's been too swamped over the last couple of months. But things should be easing up now the Corporate Values Program is coming to an end. I'll check with him to see what ideas he has."

"That would be terrific, Katie."

Katie hung up, pleased to have an excuse to get on Chuck's calendar. He'd been hard to reach of late. She called Chuck's number and left a message describing Sherman's plight and asking to meet with him as soon as possible.

It was the next afternoon before Chuck called back. "Katie, would you stop by my office. There's something I need to discuss with you."

"I'll be right there."

Chuck greeted her with a smile and a distracted expression. To her surprise, his first words were, "Where to start?"

She prompted, "Something to do with the Values Program?"

Chuck swung his chair around to face the windows of his office and leaned back. He said slowly, "As you can imagine, there was fierce political infighting behind the decision to cancel that. Some members of the executive committee would be happy to see any initiative of Worthington's fall flat."

Katie knew what Chuck was referring to. More than one member of the executive committee was rumored to have aspirations to Worthington's job. And, lately, a member of the board—a certain Harry Bosworth—had been especially active in arguing that their CEO was simply not aggressive enough to handle his responsibilities.

But Katie found it hard to get excited about this infighting. There'd been three chief executive officers in her five years with RPC. It hadn't made much difference to her who'd been at the helm. Chuck had always managed to weave a protective cocoon around their department and it had thrived relatively untouched by corporate machinations.

Chuck turned to face Katie again. He said, "I got a call on Friday from Barry Bryce. It seems Worthington asked him to tell Miranda the program had ended. But he thought I was the appropriate person to tell her."

"Oh, my."

"Mind you, I agree with him, so I called her at home this weekend. Huh!" A wry smile crossed his face. "She was pretty..." He struggled to find the right adjective.

"Hysterical?" Katie suggested. "Livid? Enraged? Apoplectic?"

"All of the above. Screaming about how she expects payment for the full year, et cetera, et cetera. Anyway, that's not my concern. The Law Department can deal with her contract."

He picked up the yellow pad in front of him and studied his scribbled notes for a moment. Katie had noticed that Chuck had as much trouble deciphering his handwriting as did everyone else.

Chuck went on, "Another thing Barry said was that we need to have a report evaluating the pilot study. You know, the usual stuff. Why we adopted it in the first place, why we did a pilot, what happened, why we dropped it."

Katie could think of only one reason Chuck was telling her all this.

"Chuck, I hope you're not suggesting I write this report. I've deliberately had as little to do with Miranda and her program as possible."

Chuck removed his glasses and rubbed his eyes. "You're still an infinitely better person to write it than Miranda is. Look, you've done reports like this a zillion times. Do the usual thing. Send out a questionnaire to the people who went to Miranda's workshops, talk to the manager."

"Mike Weston? Oh, no. I draw the line there. Sure, I can send out questionnaires. But, Chuck, I can't imagine Barry Bryce would be happy to have me author this report."

"You're wrong. When he was talking to me, Barry expressed doubts about Miranda's ability to write this report. I suggested your name to him and he agreed."

"He agreed? I've never even met the man. He doesn't know me from a hole in the ground."

But Chuck said firmly, "He's heard reports of all your good work in the company. We need a well-written, formal report. And you're just the person to do it."

Katie said slowly, "Chuck, there's no way I feel like doing a snow job on this project so I'll want to tell it straight. But I don't want this to be career-ending for me. I'll do it on the condition that you carefully review every word of the draft before it goes to Worthington."

Chuck said breezily, "Thanks, Katie. I owe you one. Yet another one." He turned to his stack of messages.

As Katie walked toward the door, she reflected it didn't hurt to have Chuck feel indebted to her. Doing favors for people, she thought, is like putting money in the bank. It's there for you to draw out when you need it. She stopped and turned back toward him. "Chuck, I left you a message."

"About that inventor, yes." He spoke quickly. "You told me you'd already given the man the names of a couple of head office people to contact. I'm not sure what else you can, or should, do. How about referring him to Public Relations? It's part of their job to pacify troublemakers in the community."

Katie protested, "I wouldn't say Sherman was a troublemaker."

"Whatever. Katie, there's nothing to be gained by getting mixed up in issues like this. Let PR handle it." He picked up his phone. Katie left his office, frowning.

So much for money in the bank.

16

Katie Meets Barry

OVER THE NEXT two weeks, Katie collected information for her report from members of her staff who'd worked with Miranda on the pilot and from a questionnaire administered to Beresford Division employees. Then she spent the better part of two days reviewing the findings and writing a draft.

During this time, she didn't once hear from nor see Miranda who, Chuck said, was taking some time off. This suited Katie just fine. It was much easier to get the evaluation done without having Miranda hovering.

Early on Friday morning, June 2, Terry appeared at Katie's door. He cast an eye around her office. "You look awash with paper, as usual. Is that the fall class schedule that's oozing out of your printer?"

"No, this is the draft report on the Corporate Values Program pilot study."

"Aha," said Terry. "What we're all waiting for."

"You'll have to wait a bit longer, I'm afraid. In fact, I have something of a problem." She leaned back in her chair and wearily massaged her neck with both hands. "Worthington intends to present it on Monday at a special session of the executive committee. Chuck knows this and he knows he should review it before Worthington sees it. Then, for some unearthly reason, he decided not to come in today and Dorothy told me there's no way of getting in touch with him."

Terry perched himself on an arm of her guest chair. He said in a low voice, "Do you think something funny is going on with Chuck? Lately, I've found it impossible to get on his calendar."

"You're right." Katie pondered a moment. "Now that you mention it, he's been acting out of character in other ways too. For instance, that business with Sherman Granger. I told you about that, didn't I?"

"About how Chuck said you shouldn't get involved in trying to help Sherman? Yes, you did."

"Poor Sherman was so disappointed when I told him."

Katie thought back to that phone call. Sherman had, in fact, sounded devastated. Katie said, "I felt I had to give him some usable advice so I urged him to go straight to the top."

Terry looked puzzled. Katie explained, "I suggested he appeal directly to Worthington. Send him a 'what-how-why' type of letter that describes his invention, all its potential benefits to our customers, the ways he envisions RPC could work with him on this and why they should do so."

"Hmm! Do you think this guy is up to writing a letter like that?"

"We'll have to see."

In fact, Katie had serious doubts about Sherman's ability to compose such a letter. And so, as a personal favor, she'd offered to edit the letter. This was an offer Sherman had eagerly accepted.

As Terry stood to leave, he turned to face her. "Katie, I can't help but wonder. Why are you so eager to stick your neck out for Sherman?"

Katie stood also. She put an arm on his shoulder and steered him toward the door. "Well, it started as a really small favor for a kind, friendly man."

Terry said, "Then, as the opposition mounted, it became a point of honor and you dug your heels in? Until now, by golly, they'll have to fire you before you'll give up on good old Sherm."

Katie laughed nervously. It was beginning to feel like that.

MIDMORNING, the phone rang. It was Eileen, Worthington's secretary. "Katie," she said, "Everett would like to see that report you're writing on the

Corporate Values Program. Would you bring a copy up to his office today, please. He needs it before five."

Katie sighed. "I'm sorry, Eileen. All I have so far is a draft and Chuck has to review it before I can show it to Everett. Chuck should be in first thing on Monday."

Eileen said, "That'll be too late. The meeting on Monday starts at nine o'clock. But, you know, Katie, your draft will be fine. Ev doesn't need a polished final version by then."

Katie knew it was futile to argue further. If Worthington wanted her to send him something today, she'd have to send him something. Reluctantly, she said, "I'll do my best."

After hanging up, Katie placed the freshly printed draft report onto the desk in front of her. Then she went through it, page by page. She grimaced as she reviewed some of her conclusions, particularly those relating to Miranda's performance as program manager.

In spite of herself, Katie felt a smidgen of fondness for the ditzy woman, but there was no doubt that Miranda's shortcomings contributed greatly to the failure of the pilot project in Beresford. While she was thus musing, the phone rang. It was Eileen again. "Katie, Barry Bryce says maybe he can help you prepare the report for Worthington."

Katie's first reaction was surprise. She hadn't realized Barry had already returned to San Francisco from the Shell Bay Power Plant—where, she'd heard, his actions had already sparked several wrongful termination lawsuits.

Her second reaction was alarm. Barry was the last person in the world she'd want to show this report to without Chuck's okay. Anyway, Barry hadn't been involved in the Beresford pilot study, so how could he help?

She said firmly, "If he wants to give input, he should get hold of Chuck first thing Monday morning. I can't spare the time to talk to him today."

Eileen gave a nervous cough and said, "Here he is."

A male voice came on the line so quickly that Katie suspected Bryce had been on an extension phone all along. He said, "I'll try not to take up too much of your time."

Katie hastened to compose herself. She said, "I'm sorry. It's just that Everett's request has taken me by surprise. I'll have to scramble to get something ready by five o'clock."

The smooth voice said, "Yes, I know. That's why I think we should talk. Excuse me a moment." He exchanged words with someone at the other end of the line; then said to Katie, "I have to take another call. I'll get back to you in a few minutes."

"Okay."

Katie was longing for a cup of coffee but didn't want to leave the room in case she missed his call. She took a sip from the bottle of Calistoga on her desk and sat back, contemplating the true reason for his interest in her report. Probably he wanted to find out what she'd written about Miranda. It might be a good idea to let him think she hadn't yet written anything about Miranda. It really was none of his business.

She turned her chair toward the window and her eye lit on the sad spectacle of the jade plant on the ledge. She always feared over-watering it, but this poor thing appeared to be gasping. Katie reached across her desk with the bottle and sprinkled water over the leaves. She cooed, "There you go. Drink your little heart out."

A voice said, "I'm sure it welcomed that." Katie jumped and swung around. She was embarrassed to see that the voice came from a man in the doorway who could be none other than Barry Bryce.

"I thought you were going to phone me." Katie cast a reproachful look at her telephone as she spoke, as if it were somehow to blame for the mix-up.

He ignored the comment and walked into her office, extending a hand. "Barry Bryce."

His handshake was firm and she made sure to exert equal pressure with her own hand as she responded,

"Katie Carlisle. Please sit down." Both her guest chairs were piled high with papers but, without hesitation, he scooped up the papers on one chair and piled them onto the second chair. Then he sat down and gave her a long, steady look across the three feet of her desk that separated them.

In spite of her discomfort at this sudden intimacy, Katie couldn't resist staring back at him with the same frank curiosity he was exhibiting. He was about forty, she guessed, with hazel eyes and short brown hair, layered to fit his head. He looked vigorous, ready to tackle anything. The kind of person one should always try to stay the right side of. The kind of person she would like to be anywhere other than here. But, she comforted herself, he couldn't hurt her, the way he had those hapless people at the power plant.

Because only Chuck had the authority to fire her.

Barry finally stopped staring and looked down at the document spread out in front of her. "Is that the report?"

"No." But, as she attempted to gather up the loose pages and push them into a drawer, he leaned forward and read aloud from the title page, "*Draft Report, Corporate Values Program.*"

"What I mean is, this is a very rough draft. I'm not permitted to show it to anyone outside our department without Chuck's approval."

The corners of his eyes crinkled in amusement. "But Chuck isn't here today, is he? And you have to deliver something to Everett this afternoon." He put out a hand. "So why don't you let me look over that document? Perhaps I can give you some feedback."

Katie flushed and tightened her grip on the pages. His voice was polite, but there was no doubt he was putting the squeeze on her. And it didn't help that he seemed to be enjoying her discomfort. He said, "If Chuck objects to your showing it to me, I promise I'll take full responsibility."

Katie tightened her grip even more. How dare he imply she couldn't take responsibility for her own actions?

He said, "If it will ease your mind, Everett himself asked me to review this report before you give it to him."

Katie wasn't sure whether to believe this, but as he continued to stare her down, her resolve wavered. He put out his hand again and she allowed him to take the report from her.

Bryce skimmed over the first part of the report, which was a prosaic description of the program's goals and methodology. He slowed down, however, when he reached the more critical sections on findings and conclusions. For Chuck's edification, Katie had included a few verbatim comments from the workshop evaluation sheets and Barry gave a burst of laughter as he read aloud, "The project from hell!" But, as he read on, his brow furrowed.

Finally, Katie could stay silent no longer. She blurted, "I must stress we didn't intend for this to leave our office in its present state. It obviously needs to be reworked, softened. That's why it's essential that Chuck review it first."

Barry ignored her. When he reached the end, he gathered the pages together and tapped the edges to make a neat pile. He asked, "What were Chuck's instructions to you when he asked you to write this?"

"To describe honestly and frankly what occurred, what went right, what went wrong..."

He broke in, "What went right? I must have missed that part. Or did you decide nothing did?"

Katie met his eyes and blinked. Strange eyes, she thought. They changed color as the light struck them from different angles. A few minutes ago, they'd been golden-brown, now they were an opaque green. And they were strangely hypnotic, reminding her of a snake she'd read about—was it a cobra?—that mesmerizes its prey before striking.

Remember he can't fire you.

She said, "So little did go right, it was hardly worth mentioning."

As soon as she'd spoken, she realized she'd gone too far. His eyes narrowed and two spots of dark color appeared on his cheeks. He said in an icy voice, "That's quite an admission given that your department was responsible for carrying out the Corporate Values Program. Are you telling me you screwed up so badly that not one single thing went right?"

Katie retorted, "Excuse me, but I recall that Miranda Peabody was the person responsible for carrying out the Values Program. Wasn't she paid to be the project manager?" She felt her voice rising as she spoke.

His voice rose too as he responded. Slamming his fist down on the report, he said, "You've done quite a number on Miranda here, haven't you? Lambasting her for having poor organizing skills, not following company procedures, offending division management by not being sensitive to their schedules, on and on."

Katie's heart thumped. She opened her mouth and closed it without speaking. He said, "Miranda is an expert on giving workshops, for God's sake. She's not an expert on RPC's foibles. That's why your department was asked to provide support to her. As I recall, you personally were assigned to work closely with her. If you'd done your job, these problems may not have occurred."

Katie's palms were damp and she reached into the bottom drawer of her desk for a tissue. She said angrily, "As I explained to Miranda, I already had a heavy workload and it just wasn't possible for me to find the time to hold her hand. We all did the best we could."

"Evidently," he snapped, "no one explained to you that the Values Program had priority over whatever other work you were doing."

"And, evidently," Katie managed to say, before her throat ran dry, "you're not aware of how resistant to advice, let alone direction, Dr. Peabody is."

There was another silence while Katie defiantly returned his glare. This time, she thought she could detect the glimmer of a smile in the hypnotic eyes.

He was the first to break eye contact. Sounding condescending but also calmer, he said, "Katie, the whole point of writing this report is to provide helpful information to management. You should save this kind of hyperbole for your memoirs."

Tapping the report, he went on, "Criticisms of Miranda aside, your entire report is too negative. You need to assure management that the program is inherently a good one, that the pilot was well run, and that we decided not to go forward company-wide at this time because the timing was not ideal."

"The timing?"

Barry waved a hand to shush her. "Yes, after a careful evaluation of the pilot, we decided it wasn't the right time, workload in the division was extra heavy, or whatever. Make it clear that it's an excellent program we'd like to try out again as circumstances permit. Let's see. I need a piece of paper."

Katie watched, speechless, as Bryce searched around her desk. He found a lined pad, half-buried under a stack of interview notes, and helped himself to a pen from the holder on her desk. Then he bent his head over the pad and started to write, formulating his thoughts in a mutter from time to time.

When he reached the end of the page, he tore off the sheet and handed it to Katie. He said, "Don't bother to send Everett the report you've written. Just write up one page summarizing the major points he needs to have for the executive committee meeting on Monday. I've outlined them here for you."

With this, he stood up. Katie stood too. She realized her mistake as his eyes moved down to her waist and then quickly up again. When she'd stretched across her desk to water the plant, her skirt—already loose, thanks to another two pounds lost the past couple of weeks—

had twisted around and her blouse had slipped out of the waistband. What a slob she must look!

He said some kind of farewell and left, looking, Katie thought crossly, as tailored and crisp as if he'd just stepped out of a fashion plate.

Katie straightened her skirt, tucked her blouse back in, and sat down to study the sheet he'd handed her. Unlike Chuck's scribble, Barry's writing was bold and legible. But, as Katie's eyes ran down the sheet, she found herself torn between indignation and amusement at his sheer audacity. Clearly, he didn't believe any relationship to the truth was required. He wanted her to produce a whitewash job, something that would make everyone look good.

She folded the sheet of paper in half and dropped it into her wastebasket.

BY FOUR O'CLOCK, the draft report for Worthington was ready. Katie reviewed it one last time. She was pleased with her efforts. She had softened the wording of some particularly critical comments but had otherwise prepared a fair and truthful version of the facts. She put the document into an envelope addressed to Everett Worthington with the notation, "Confidential—For Eyes Only." This notation ensured that no one else, not even his secretary, was to open that envelope.

Then she went to Worthington's office on the fortieth floor of the Tower. His office door was closed. Eileen greeted her with a smile. "Oh, good. You got it done. Was Barry helpful?"

Katie said, "Very."

"Great," Eileen said. "Ev's in a meeting but I'll be sure to get it to him before he leaves for the day."

Katie returned to her office with a light heart. Work was over for the week and it was time to hurry home. Dan had promised the painting would be done by tonight. And Katie planned to celebrate by inviting him in to have a drink with her.

IN HIS OFFICE, Worthington was meeting with Joe Fenniman, the Vice President of Human Resources, and Barry Bryce. Their topic was one dear to Barry's heart: a new position for him at Head Office.

At five o'clock, Fenniman left. Worthington tapped the red position description folder in front of him and said to Barry, "You've made a good decision, Barry. This is an essential step on the way to a vice-presidency." He smiled. "But we sure will miss you on the fortieth floor."

Barry started to speak but stopped as Dorothy walked in with a large envelope that she handed to Worthington. "Katie brought this for you."

"Thanks, Dorothy. Close the door, would you?"

Worthington read from the envelope, "*'For eyes only'*? What's this?" He slit open the envelope and pulled out a sheaf of papers, clipped together with a handwritten note. He read the note aloud. "*'Everett: Please keep in mind this is a rough draft only. It would be best if Chuck could review it with you Monday morning before the executive committee meeting. Katie.'*" He asked Barry, "Did you talk to Katie about this?"

"I sure did."

"And you thought her draft was okay?"

"Not the way she'd originally written it. I made some suggestions for her to follow." Barry could see from where he sat that Katie had not followed his suggestion to condense the report to a one-page summary. He said, "May I see that?" Worthington handed over the report.

Barry looked quickly through the pages. Shaking his head, he said, "Can you believe it, she ignored my advice. You can't possibly present this to the executive committee. Let alone the board of directors."

Worthington sighed. "And this is because...?

"It's far too negative. If this gets out, you'd be lambasted for even adopting such a program."

"So what do we do?"

Barry pondered a moment. "How about if I take this home with me? I'll rework it over the weekend and have something for you at eight o'clock Monday."

"Mmm. That won't give me much time to absorb it before the nine o'clock meeting."

Barry said, as if he'd only just thought of the idea, "Know something, Ev? It might be a good idea if I come with you to the meeting. You can say you assigned me the task of reviewing the report. That way, we can let me do all the talking."

"That's a great idea, Barry. Trust you to come up with the perfect solution."

As Barry stood to leave, Worthington pointed to the red folder. "Don't forget the P.D. You'll be kept busy this weekend."

He would indeed, Barry thought, but it was all in a worthy cause.

17

Katie and Dan Get Acquainted

THAT EVENING, Katie stopped off on the way home to buy some cold beer. All she had in the house was red wine that, of course, no blue collar worker was likely to choose. She found Dan waiting for her.

"Come see," he said.

Together, they walked around the exterior of the house. She said, "It's lovely, Dan. I'm really pleased. Now, if you'll come inside, I'll get your check." As they walked into the house, she added, "This calls for a drink, don't you think?"

"Sounds good."

In the kitchen, they were assailed by the cats. Katie put away the drinks in the fridge before scooping up the two furry bodies for some mutual nuzzling. She said, "Just give me a minute to feed these guys and then I'll get you a beer." He hesitated. Katie asked, "Or wine?"

"I'd prefer wine. Red, if you have it."

Katie fixed two bowls of cat food and satisfied chomping sounds soon filled the air. Then she poured two glasses of burgundy and led Dan into the living room. There was a small couch and two easy chairs with a low glass coffee table between them. Katie sat on the couch and Dan, winding his long legs awkwardly around the table, settled in the chair opposite her. They lifted their glasses to mutual toasts of "Cheers!"

Dan took a sip of wine and cast his eyes around the room. "You got a nice little place here."

"Thank you. 'Little' is the operative word, isn't it?"

"It's great to own your own place, no matter what size."

Katie nodded and settled back into the couch. Dan, who was more relaxed than she'd seen him before, continued talking. About houses in the area, painting schemes. As he talked, Katie found herself unwinding into a sleepy state of contentment. She could think of no better antidote to the irritations of this stressful day than to be sitting here on her comfortable couch, sipping a glass of wine, and feasting her eyes on the blond Adonis in front of her.

After a while, he asked, "You must have a good job, huh? Real good pay?"

She smiled, remembering his reaction when he'd first seen her business card. "Yes, it is a great job. Things have been a bit topsy-turvy of late, but I think the future looks rosy." She fought an urge to cross her fingers. "How about you? Do you enjoy doing what you do?"

Gripping his glass in both hands, he said, "I used to be an electrician."

"Oh." After a moment, Katie said, "Electrician, huh? Did you like the work?"

"Yeah." He sounded morose.

Katie prompted, "But you decided you'd rather be a handyman?"

"I guess." His brusque tone sounded like a reprimand for her nosiness.

While they'd been talking, the two cats had finished eating and strutted into the living room to take up their favorite position with Katie on the couch. Katie laughed as Kit took a sniff of her silk blouse and wrinkled his nose. She explained to Dan, "He's disgusted that I haven't changed my clothes. Usually, I put on an old wool sweater when I get home and they both paw all over it."

She looked at his face and laughed again. "Dan, from that expression, I would guess that you don't much care for cats."

He looked sheepish. "You guess right. Now dogs I like, but cats always remind me of the batty old spinster lady who lived next door to us when I was a kid."

"Thanks a lot."

"No, no, she was nothing like you." He leaned forward earnestly. "This woman was really off the wall. She used to talk to her cats, just like they was people."

"No!" Katie exclaimed. "Why, some folks should be locked up."

With some amusement, she watched his expression as he tried to decide whether or not she was serious. Finally, he laughed, with a tinge of unease, and the conversation lapsed.

After a few moments, Dan asked, "Have you ever been married?"

"No." She wasn't sure what compelled her to add, "A couple of years ago, I came very close." She took a sip of wine and his next question caught her in mid-swallow.

"That was the guy who went to Japan?"

Katie gulped and sputtered, "What?"

Dan said, "Your neighbor..." jerking a hand in the direction of Mildred's house, "...told me how you was going with this guy for years and you thought you'd be gettin' married, but then he went off to Japan and it all fell through."

Katie was stunned. It was bad enough to learn that her love life was the topic of casual conversation among the local handymen. It was even worse to learn that it was motherly Mildred who had betrayed her confidence.

Dan said, "What was he doing in Japan?"

Katie found her voice. "He was a visiting lecturer at a Japanese university."

"And he's still there?"

So Mildred hadn't told him the full story.

KATIE AND ALAN had been a couple for some six years when he decided to accept the position in Kyoto. Katie had been sad, of course, about their upcoming separation but not worried. He'd suggested, and she agreed, it would be healthy for them to take a short break from each other before settling down to marriage.

When his appointment was reaching its end, Alan wrote to say he planned to stay on in Japan for a couple more months so that he could tour the country. Again, Katie was not worried.

She continued not to worry even when he stopped writing. He'd always been a poor letter-writer. But, two months after receiving his last letter, she'd had a chance meeting with a mutual acquaintance who'd heard a rumor that Alan had, in fact, already returned to the States. Katie's further inquiries of Alan's department in Berkeley revealed that he had resigned his position at UC and accepted an offer from a college in Missouri.

A month of agonizing uncertainty passed before Alan finally called her—from his new home in Missouri. He was sorry he hadn't called earlier, he said, but he hadn't wanted to upset her. "You see, Katie," he'd explained, "this tenure track position came up in a small women's college. It's just what I've been looking for and I felt I had to take it. But also I knew you would hate the thought of living in a backwoods place like this."

Katie had forced herself to be forgiving. She had to because she couldn't imagine life without him. "It's all right, honey," she'd told him. "I'm willing to give it a shot. Who knows, I might love small-town life. Why don't I take a week of vacation and come check it out?"

Alan had hesitated and then told her the rest of his news.

NOW KATIE SAID to Dan, "No, he came back. But while he was in Japan he met another woman and she came back with him."

To this day, Katie's face burned when she thought of how naïve she'd been. She focused her eyes on Kat, curled up on her lap, and tickled his tiny chin with one finger.

Dan said, "Life sure sucks sometimes."

She pulled herself up out of a slouch. "Enough of that. How about you? Have you ever been married?"

"I'm divorced. I have a little boy. He lives with his mother in Merced."

"Really? You look too young for all that. How old is your son?"

"Almost ten." Katie gave an audible gasp and he laughed. "I'm thirty-two."

"You're kidding. I thought you were about twenty." She was astonished but also pleased to know that he was over thirty. It made her feel—well, not quite so old. There followed an awkward silence while she wondered whether to tell him her age. Finally, she said, "It's been seven years since I was thirty-two."

He nodded without changing his expression, as though he already knew. Which he probably did, thanks to Mildred and her big mouth.

Katie asked, "Do you see your son often?"

Dan gazed up at the ceiling with a distant expression. "Once a month, I drive over to Merced and take him out for the day. I could see him more often only it's a long drive. Also..." He looked down and rubbed his leg self-consciously. "...I never know what to do with him exactly."

What a terrible admission, Katie thought. She couldn't imagine having a son—she pictured a miniature version of Dan—and visiting him so seldom.

"Is he happy, do you think?"

Dan responded with fervor, "He has a wonderful life. My wife's second husband is a real successful building contractor. You should see their home. It's in this great development outside of town. Minimum lot size is half an acre."

Dan continued with an enthusiastic description of all the ways in which the new husband was taking "great care" of Dan's former wife and child. Katie found it hard to concentrate. What, she wondered, had caused Dan and his wife to break up? How long ago had it happened?

But she wasn't about to find out today. Dan abruptly stopped talking, drained his glass, and stood. "I better get going."

"Of course. I'll get your check." She extricated herself from the cats and went to her bureau to get the check, which she'd already written. She said as she handed it to him, "Fifteen hundred, right?"

Without meeting her eye, he stuck the check in his pocket and made his way to the front door. Outside the door, he announced, "Hey, you have a visitor." Katie followed him out to take a look. Sure enough, there was Lorraine's battered green Chevy pulling into the driveway.

"That's my friend Lorraine." Katie told Dan. "She told me she'd be coming by this weekend to inspect my newly painted house."

Dan made a face. "She sure could use a new car."

Katie snorted. "You're a fine one to talk." She nodded in the direction of his faded red truck at the curb. "And I'll have you know Lorraine is an eminent woman of letters. She's an associate professor at the University of California in Berkeley. An expert in medieval history."

Her mock indignation dissolved into a grin at his disrespectful "Oh, that explains it." He ran down the steps with a cheerful, "See you around," and nodded to a bemused Lorraine as he passed her in the driveway.

Katie called from the front porch, "Lorraine, I wasn't expecting you until tomorrow." Then, waving one arm at the house, she said, "Ta, da! What do you think?"

But Lorraine wasn't paying attention to the house. As she left her car and climbed the steps toward Katie, she kept looking over her shoulder at the figure of Dan as he walked out to his truck.

"Who is *that*?"

Lorraine never could remember how much her voice carried. Katie shushed her and grabbed her arm to lead her into the house. Inside, she explained, "That was Dan, the guy who painted the house, which, incidentally, you haven't even commented on."

Lorraine grinned. "I got distracted. Katie, he's beautiful. Aren't you the sly one, keeping that up your sleeve?"

Katie went down the hall to the kitchen, but Lorraine detoured into the living room where she peered out the front window. She said, "Maybe I can get him to paint my house."

"The apartment building? But that was painted last year, wasn't it?"

"Darn. So it was."

Katie returned to the living room with the bottle of burgundy and an extra glass. She said, "When you're done spying on that poor man, how about some wine?"

"Alas, he's gone." Lorraine turned away from the window. Then her eyes fell on the two wine glasses already on the coffee table. "What's this? The two of you were having a drink together? Oo, Katie!" A dramatic hand-thumping-forehead gesture followed. "And I interrupted you. Oh, no...."

Laughing, Katie said, "Don't be ridiculous. Didn't you notice? He's only a child. Well, thirty-two, but still...."

"Katie," Lorraine chided her, "You are so pathetically out of touch. Don't you know it's absolutely the thing for women our age to dally with younger men, men much younger than that. Toy boys, they call 'em."

"You dirty old lady, you! But you know something? Even if I felt ready for a toy boy, I think I'd aim for someone a bit higher up the scale than Dan. He's only about two steps above an itinerant."

Lorraine cut in, "Oh, stop being such a snob." She settled herself into the chair lately vacated by Dan and poured herself a glass of wine. "These days it's all the rage for professional women to take up with blue-collar men. There's been all kinds of stuff written about it. In fact, one of our graduate students in the Psych Department did a paper on the subject. She called it 'The Brawn-and-Brains Connection' or something."

"Enough already. Let's have a toast." Katie lifted her glass. "To Lorraine, the world's most hopeless romantic." She sipped her wine. "So how have things been with you lately. Did you find a publisher for that article...?"

"I'm fine. No, I didn't." She added, "Nine years ago, at your thirtieth birthday party, I asked you what you wanted in a mate. Remember?"

Resigned at her failure to change the subject, Katie replied, "Let's see. As I recall, I said he had to be intelligent, well-educated, have a good sense of humor, be a cat-lover, not necessarily knock-'em-dead handsome."

Lorraine said, "And then you met him."

Realizing where this was going, Katie flinched. "Lorraine, please."

Lorraine wouldn't stop. "And look what your perfect man turned out to be. A lily-livered louse who pretended to agree with you about getting married and instead ran away to Japan. Who didn't have the courage to tell you he wanted to end your relationship. Who let you find out from other people that he'd taken a job in Mississippi and was living with another woman."

"Missouri." Katie corrected her.

In the silence that followed, Kit stood up on his hind legs and tried to climb onto Katie's lap. She helped him up. The cats—tiny kittens then—had been a gift from Lorraine to help mend Katie's broken heart after Alan left. She said, "Lorraine, I know Alan was a mistake, but that doesn't mean my criteria were poor criteria. The list wasn't complete, that's all. For example, I should have added 'honest, responsible....'"

Lorraine said, "And before long you'd end up with a list even a saint couldn't satisfy. I think you need to toss out your criteria altogether. I think the type of man you think is your type isn't your type at all. Hey, that sounds like a line from a Country-Western song."

They both giggled but then Lorraine looked earnest again. "I'm serious. Maybe you should stop focusing on intellectuals. Look what happened when we tried to fix you up with that egghead friend of Peter's on your last birthday. How about getting someone just to have fun with? Like you-know-who." She jerked her head in the direction of the front door. "Young, handsome, not a care in the world. You owe it to yourself, girl."

Katie shook her head. "This entire conversation is beside the point. It doesn't matter what I owe to myself. I mean, do you see *any* guys—young, old, cute, ugly, blue, white or pink collar—beating my door down for the opportunity to give me a fun time?" She poured herself more wine and added, "As for Dan, I had to twist his arm to get him to agree to the house-painting. And then it took three months for him to get around to it."

Lorraine put down her glass and sat back in the chair, examining her fingers and picking at the peeling polish on her nails. Finally, she said, "You say he's finished up here? What were his last words to you before he left tonight?"

Katie thought for a moment. "He said, 'See you around.'"

Lorraine looked up and her eyes met Katie's. "Not too encouraging," she said.

18

Chuck Has a Surprise

Katie got to the office at seven on Monday morning and immediately went in search of Chuck. He wasn't in yet. Nor, to her dismay. had he called in at the office over the weekend to pick up her draft report. She left a note for Dorothy. "I have to talk to Chuck before the executive committee meeting. Please let me know as soon as he gets here."

Katie went back to her own office to wait. It was eight-thirty before Dorothy called. "Hey, Katie. Chuck just phoned. He wants to take you to lunch. He said you should stop by about noon."

"But what about the executive committee meeting and my report? Did he say anything about any of that?"

"No, but, Katie, I wouldn't worry about it. He sounded really upbeat. I'm sure everything's okay."

AT TEN MINUTES of twelve, Katie presented herself at Chuck's office. He greeted her cheerfully. "Katie, lovely day, huh? Arturo's okay with you?" Arturo's Cafeteria on Mission Street was where Chuck frequently treated members of his staff to working lunches.

As they walked, Katie quizzed him. "Did you get a chance to look at my report?"

"Your report?"

Terry was right, Katie thought. Chuck really didn't seem to be on the ball these days. "My report on the Corporate Values pilot project, Chuck. The one Worthington was presenting to the executive committee today at nine."

"Oh, yes, right."

"I left two voice mail messages for you. I also left a copy of the report on your desk on Friday. I thought you might pick it up over the weekend."

"No. I didn't call in. So you got it done? Congratulations."

"Let me tell you the rest. Worthington's secretary called me on Friday morning to say Worthington wanted the report on his desk by five o'clock. I tried to explain you needed to review it first but she said he wanted it anyway." Chuck said nothing and Katie turned to look at him. "Remember, Chuck, you promised me you'd go over that report with a fine tooth comb before letting Worthington see it."

Katie couldn't keep the reproach out of her voice. It felt to her that Chuck had really let her down—and seemed not to care.

They reached the café and made their way through the door. Chuck said, "You grab a table while I order. What would you like? The usual?"

"Yes, please."

The "usual" consisted of a bowl of Arturo's delicious homemade soup-of-the-day and crusty French bread. While Chuck went to the counter to order, Katie found a table for two against a wall. She sat down, looked around, and found herself looking straight at Barry Bryce who was at a nearby table. He wasn't alone and didn't notice her. Katie hastily turned away.

When Chuck arrived with the food, he asked quietly, "Did you notice Miranda over there? With her good friend Barry?"

Katie muttered, "Sure did. I hope she doesn't see us. I don't know how I can ever face Miranda again."

"Why do you say that?"

"Because of my report. All my critical remarks about her performance as project manager. Barry's bound to have told her."

"Don't worry about it." He took a mouthful of soup. Then he put his spoon back in the bowl, leaned forward and said, "Katie, I have something to tell you."

Struck by his serious tone, she, too, put down her spoon and waited for him to continue.

"The fact is, I've just resigned from RPC."

"*What*? But why?"

He beamed. "I've found a new job. Vice president of human resources at Quali-Tech Industries in San Jose. I'll be starting on Monday."

"Chuck, I'm stunned. I don't know what to say."

"I'm sorry if I caught you off guard. I thought perhaps you'd already guessed something was up—with me being out of the office so much recently."

"No, I didn't have a clue."

Katie struggled with her emotions. For so long, she'd dreamed of the day when Chuck would retire and she'd have a chance to get his job. Yet now the time had apparently come, she found herself genuinely sad at the thought of his leaving—also rather frightened of the coming shakeup in her world. Besides, the timing felt odd.

"Chuck, of course I'm happy for you. But why now? The Values Program is over, Miranda Peabody is out of the picture, everything's about to go back to normal." She paused. "Isn't it?"

"You're absolutely right. Things should soon be back on track. At least for you. But, you know, it's different for me. As manager of ESS, it's critical I have the full confidence of our CEO. My relationship with Worthington started to fall apart when that damned Bryce came on board." His voice had lowered to a whisper and he glanced furtively across the restaurant at Barry as he spoke. "Bryce is always at Worthington's elbow, advising him and countermanding my recommendations."

She said, "Speaking of Barry, does he know your news?"

As soon as she asked the question, Katie was sure of the answer. Of course, Barry knew. That's why he'd been amused at her insistence that Chuck had to okay her draft report before anyone else could see it.

Chuck said, "I don't know what he knows, but you're the first person in our department I've told."

"Oh, Chuck," Katie wailed, "we'll all miss you so much."

He laughed. "You'll all be just fine. Especially you, Katie. You're a clever, capable person, well thought of throughout the company. In fact, I've suggested to HR that you be appointed acting manager of the department till they find a replacement for me."

He continued to spoon down his soup. Katie watched him for a few moments, summoning her courage to ask the big question. "Do you know who they're considering as a permanent replacement for you?"

He replied, "I've no idea." Abruptly, he stopped talking as two people approached their table. Miranda and Barry.

Miranda was all smiles. She bubbled, "Why, hullo there, you two." She said to Katie, "Bet you thought I'd deserted you."

"Well..." Katie looked at Barry, standing a couple of paces behind Miranda. Solemnly, he nodded, first to Katie, then to Chuck.

Miranda bubbled on, "I promise I'll be coming into the office soon. There must be a ton of paperwork from Beresford to clean up."

"Well, actually, I've already..."

But now the sparkling brown eyes were beaming at Chuck. "Chuck, I hear you have a fabulous new job. Congratulations!"

So Miranda knew the news also. Chuck mumbled something. Katie saw that Barry was studying Chuck with a hard-to-fathom expression. Was he envious, Katie wondered, of Chuck's new position or simply glad to know Chuck was leaving? Or perhaps he didn't care, one way or the other.

Miranda and Chuck exchanged some more pleasantries. Then Miranda smiled a gracious farewell and apologized for having interrupted their lunch.

After the two of them left, Katie met Chuck's eye and he winked. "They make a beautiful couple, don't they?" She laughed at his sarcastic tone. In truth, she was relieved that Miranda had, after all, been friendly. Barry must not have told her about the report.

Katie said, "Miranda really is something, isn't she? She doesn't seem in the least bit upset that she's now unemployed. Or maybe she's too dumb to realize it."

"She realizes it all right. Remember how hysterical she was when I told her they'd terminated the Values Program? I guess she's had time to regain her composure. Or maybe she's found another job."

Chuck took a stealthy glance at his watch. Katie knew he had many people to talk to about his upcoming departure. She said quickly, "Chuck, before we leave, have you heard anything about how things went at the executive committee meeting this morning? Did they even discuss the Values Project?"

"Yeah, I guess so." He pulled a single folded sheet of paper from his jacket pocket and handed it to her. "Worthington's secretary sent me this."

Katie unfolded the sheet and read, "Evaluation of Corporate Values Program—Talking Points for Executive Committee Meeting." Quickly, she ran her eye down the page. "Chuck, this is just the list of Barry's talking points that he gave me last Friday." She looked into Chuck's face; he avoided meeting her eye. "Chuck, these didn't come from my report. In fact, I tossed this list into the trash. Is this all that was presented this morning?"

"Mmm. It would seem so."

Katie fought to keep the hysteria out of her voice. "You're telling me Worthington ignored my report entirely? This is all he presented to the committee today?"

Chuck sighed as he took the sheet back. "I'm afraid the situation is worse than that. From what I understand, Worthington himself didn't present anything. Barry did all the presenting."

"Good Lord!"

There was a sudden sour taste in Katie's mouth. After a moment, she said slowly, "You know, Chuck, I have a feeling I'll soon be following you out of RPC. Think you might find a place for me in your new company?"

She tried to laugh but Chuck wasn't fooled. He leaned forward, lightly clasped both her shoulders in his hands, and said gently, "Now don't overreact. If Everett prefers to ignore your good work and lets Barry lead him by the nose, well, that's up to him."

He let go of Katie's shoulders and sipped his coffee, adding, "Now that I'm a lame duck, there's nothing much I can say or do to influence anything. But please don't worry about it, Katie. You did the job you were asked to do. The rest of it is out of our hands." He put down his coffee cup. "I'd better be getting back. I need to talk to Terry and Dorothy, and then the rest of the department."

As they walked back to the office, Katie felt despondent. Over the years, she'd received so many compliments from their CEO about her good work and good judgment. But, today, he'd apparently dismissed her report—the report she'd written with such care—and instead turned to Barry and his slick suggestions that were designed only to hide the truth.

And where was Chuck? He said he'd review her report before it left the department. A feeling of dread welled up inside. She couldn't trust anyone anymore.

LATER THAT AFTERNOON, Terry stopped by Katie's office. Katie said, "Things will never be the same without him." Terry nodded, staring out the window. She said, "We shouldn't really blame Chuck though. He obviously felt it was in his best interests to make a move."

Terry said, in a faraway voice, "Or someone else felt it was in their best interests to have him make a move." He looked thoughtfully at Katie. "Do you wonder, Katie, did he jump or was he pushed?"

"Surely he wasn't fired! That would be terrible. I never should have let that bastard Barry see my draft report on Friday. You should have heard him lecturing me about how the damned program would have been just fine if Chuck and I had done our jobs properly."

Terry pooh-poohed. "Oh, Katie, I'm sure it has nothing to do with you. All this got started long before last Friday. Of course, no doubt Miranda's been bitching about the lack of cooperation from our department." He wrinkled his nose. "Not without some justification, you must admit."

"I don't know about that. But I do know they had to find someone to blame for the collapse of the Values Program. Someone other than Miranda."

"Also, there's something else." Terry reached out and closed her office door. "There's a rumor going around that Chuck may have been pushed out because Worthington wanted to create a managerial vacancy at head office."

"Why?"

"Because there's someone he wants to make a manager."

Katie frowned. "What someone? Not Miranda, surely?"

Terry stood to leave. His hand on the doorknob, he said, "Worthington wouldn't be that dumb. Come on, Katie, guess again."

THE NEWS WAS formally announced the next morning. Katie picked up a copy of the *Redwood Rover* in the lobby and read the bulletin as she rode up on the elevator. It stated:

Effective July 1, Barry Bryce, currently Chief Advisor on Classified Projects, will become Manager of the Executive Support Services Department. He replaces Chuck Browne who has resigned from the company.

19

First Date and a Squabble

ON A SATURDAY MORNING a couple of weeks after Barry's appointment, Katie was in her backyard working on one of her least favorite jobs. Pruning the privet hedge. The hedge ran for some thirty feet alongside the fence that separated her property from Mildred's. Over the years, aided by Katie's neglect, the hedge had grown so tall she could no longer reach the top branches.

It was perfect weather for gardening. Later on, it would be too hot to work in comfort, but at this time of day a delicious coolness still lingered from the recently burned off early-morning mist. From next door came the summer sounds of Dan mowing Mildred's lawn.

After an hour or so, Katie had trimmed everything that she could easily reach. She paused to review the situation. One straggly tendril had grown so long it was tipping over to the other side of the fence. Standing on tiptoe, she stretched out and zeroed in on it. *Clip.* But the heavy shears dragged on her arms and distorted her aim. She missed. "Damn!" she said aloud.

Suddenly, the inverted V of another pair of shears rose like a conning tower from Mildred's side of the fence. The shears slid over the top of the hedge, and, *clip!* The offending growth was gone.

Katie grinned. "Dan to the rescue! Thank you, sir."

Dan called out, "Your hedge is way too tall. When it grows that high, it gets straggly and unhealthy looking."

She hardly needed any lectures on this topic but answered politely, "I know. The trouble is, it's almost impossible for me to reach those high branches."

"You shouldn't let it get so high in the first place."

She muttered, "Duh!"

He evidently heard this because he gave a burst of laughter. He said, "Would you like me to do the top of the hedge for you? I can come over when I'm done at Mildred's."

Katie thought quickly. No use kidding herself. She'd probably never get to it. She said, "That would be great, Dan."

When Dan arrived later in the morning, he surveyed the hedge with disapproval. "I noticed this hedge when I was painting your house and wondered if you ever paid any attention to it." Katie hung her head at the rebuke. As he clipped, he admonished her. "You don't need a dense hedge like this, not with a fence. In any case, this location's too shady for privet. You oughta dig it all out. Put in rhodies or somethin'."

His earnestness had a little-boy quality to it that made Katie smile. Did he really think she had the energy to dig up thirty feet of impenetrable thicket? No, he was probably hinting she hire him to do the job. Watching his muscled arms as he stretched and clipped, she thought it might not be a bad idea at that.

Dan leaned down to scrape together privet clippings with his shears. He said, "So how's the paint job holding up? Is it comin' off yet?"

There was a playfulness in his voice that triggered her to tease, "Well, now that you mention it, these big black streaks have appeared on the front of the house and the paint's all bubbling on the garage door."

"Aw, shucks!" he deadpanned. "Just when the guarantee's run out."

Katie giggled. On a flirtatious whim, she moved close to him and gave him a gentle shove with her shoulder. Dan turned to face her and moved back a step, seemingly startled by the contact. Then he laughed too and continued to scoop up the clippings.

Katie got a rake to help him. She wondered if she should offer to pay him for the hedge pruning. Would he be insulted if she brought it up? Or insulted if she didn't?

Then Dan said, "I'll be knocking off for lunch in a coupla minutes. Would you like to come along?"

Katie felt sure she had misheard him. "I'm sorry, what...?"

"Lunch. My treat. To make up for the paint streaking and all."

"Dan, I was only kidding."

"You don't say." He moved up beside her and gave her a playful push with his shoulder. Just like the one she'd given him. Katie felt herself blushing. He said, "Nothing fancy. McDonald's or Taco Bell."

Katie's mind was aflutter. She was touched by the invitation but concerned about what had prompted it. She hoped he wasn't overreacting to their silly repartee, her touching him like that.

She looked at the grubby figure standing before her. Dan was under-dressed, even for McDonald's. And one thing was for sure. She'd never live it down if anyone she knew saw her riding in that truck of his. Dan's truck, a sporty red in its youth, had suffered a lifetime of bumps, scrapes, sloppy repair jobs, and oxidized paint that had left it a patchwork of unappealing shades of pink.

Katie said, "Do you mind if we go in my car?"

"Fine," he said. He set off to collect his things from next door and Katie went into her house to get ready.

When he joined her a few minutes later, she was pleased to see he'd put on a long-sleeved blue shirt that covered up the work clothes. In fact, he looked respectable enough for Katie's favorite weekend haunt, Benji's Bakery.

She drove them there.

AT THE BAKERY, Katie accompanied Dan while he ordered at the counter. Torpedo sandwich for him and tuna on rye for her. He also ordered a chocolate milkshake and asked her, "How about you?"

"Just water, please."

She watched the counter clerk as he set to work on the milkshake, pouring foamy milk, ice cream, and dark syrup into a frosty shaker. In her mind, she could taste the cool, creamy concoction. Dan said, "Sure you wouldn't like one?" She shook her head but when he laughed she realized she was running her tongue around her lips. He said to the clerk, "Make that two milkshakes." They carried their lunch to a sidewalk table.

At first, Dan was too busy munching his torpedo to talk much. It was a comfortable silence, and Katie ate with relish, feeling grateful she'd allowed Dan to force the luscious milkshake on her.

After a while, Dan asked, "So, how's things?"

Katie, her mouth full, mumbled, "Fine." She swallowed and amended her answer. "Actually, not so fine. Since I talked to you last, there's been a truly terrible development at work."

His eyes widened. "No kiddin'? What happened?"

"My boss—who has always been my dear friend and mentor—is leaving the company. Worst of all, his replacement is a man I just hate."

His face relaxed. "Oh. I thought you was going to say you'd been fired."

"This is just as bad," Katie protested. "I don't see how I can possibly work for this new guy. If he doesn't fire me, I'll end up quitting anyway."

"Meantime, you can look for a new job, right? Which someone like you could get just like that." He snapped his fingers. "You probably have a college degree, don't you? Or some college anyway?"

She said quickly, "Of course, I do. In fact, I have a bachelor's and a master's degree. But that doesn't mean...."

"Well, there you go. There's millions of people who'd jump at the chance to trade places with someone like you."

Katie watched him as he slurped his milk shake. Of course, Dan didn't understand the unfairness, not to say danger, of her situation. Over the past couple of weeks, as she'd acted out her role of acting manager, her frustration at the way she'd been treated had grown. A replacement for Chuck had been chosen not on the basis of merit but for political reasons. And there was nothing she could do about it but hope she wouldn't be fired in the fallout.

Katie's eyes drifted to two little girls giggling together at an adjoining table. Dan looked, too. He asked, "Do you like kids?"

"I adore them."

"That much?" He chuckled. "Maybe you'd like to come with me one day when I visit my little guy. Help me entertain him."

Katie drew a breath. Dan was cram-full of surprises today. But this surprise wasn't a welcome one. Katie had discovered long ago that she wasn't that enamored of the children of divorced men friends. They all too often were whiny and demanding—and resentful of her.

He smiled as he waited for her reply. Stalling, she asked, "What's your son's name?"

Dan shuffled. "Same as me. We call him Danny." He went on quickly. "It wasn't my idea. I think it's kinda silly having two people in the family with the same name. But my wife—my ex-wife—wanted it. She said the baby should have the same name 'cause he looked so much like me."

He squashed the empty milkshake container in both hands and stared straight at Katie. He said, "I wasn't all that flattered at the time. I mean, here was this squalling blob with his red face and she was trying to tell me he looked..." he swallowed before finishing the sentence. "...like me."

Katie felt an ache in her throat as she wondered again at how and why the breakup with his wife had occurred. It obviously still caused him heartache. She felt guilty at not responding to his suggestion about visiting his son but hoped he wouldn't raise the issue again. He didn't. She finished her milkshake.

On the way back to Katie's car, Dan explained that he couldn't "stick around" because he had signed up for an electronics class that afternoon. They got into the car and started home.

Katie asked, "Are you planning a career in electronics?"

"I'm looking at different possibilities. I'd like to move beyond this handyman business." Katie nodded her approval. He went on, "What I'd really like to do is get into manufacturing. I like to make things. I have all kinds of electrical and mechanical experience. I thought it wouldn't hurt to learn electronics too."

She suggested, "Maybe you could start by getting a job in a business that could use your skills. A factory or machine shop?"

"I don't want to work for other people."

"Why not?"

"Employers are too nosy. Always poking their noses into what don't concern 'em."

"Hmm," Katie said. "It's hard to get a business of your own going though, isn't it? Raising money and all that?"

"It's not the money. What you need is a great product. If you have that, banks will fall over themselves to lend you money."

Katie suppressed a laugh. She said gently, "I don't think so, Dan. Banks don't loan money just on the basis of ideas; usually, they want collateral."

"Nah," Dan scoffed.

"No, not nah," she retorted. "There's this man I know who's got a fantastic invention which he's patented. It has the potential to reduce the amount of electricity everyone uses. There's no doubt there'd be a great market for it but first he has to find someone who's willing to back him. In fact, he's trying right now to interest RPC. It's not an easy sell."

As she drove and talked, Katie wondered fleetingly if she was violating Sherman's trust by talking about him to Dan. Surely, she decided, Dan was too far removed from Sherman's world for it to matter.

Dan listened quietly as she talked but when they pulled into Katie's driveway, his cocky manner returned. "I don't know what's the matter with your friend," he said. "Why's he bothering with your company? Why don't he just go ahead and make these things and sell them to anyone who'll buy 'em?"

Katie said, "That's what I'm trying to tell you. He needs capital to get the facilities and equipment and materials. He's hoping our company will back him because he can't get money from a bank without collateral."

"Phooey," said Dan, with an imperious toss of his head, "If his invention was any good, he'd have no trouble finding someone to lend him money."

Katie was filled with indignation on Sherman's behalf. As they got out of the car, she asked, "Dan, have you ever in your life attempted to get a business loan from a bank or anyone else?"

"No."

"So you've no idea what you're talking about. That's what I thought."

She'd intended it as a put-down but was still shocked at how cruel her words sounded. Looking into Dan's surprised face, it seemed to Katie that she could see his ego deflating like a pricked balloon in front of her eyes.

After an endless minute, he mumbled, "Well, I better get going."

Katie called to him as he started down the driveway, "Thank you very much for the lunch. The hedge too." The words sounded insincere.

Without turning around, he mumbled, "Sure."

Watching the defeated slump of his shoulders as he walked away, Katie felt she couldn't leave things like this. She said, "Dan, if you're serious about taking me with you to visit your son, I'd be willing to give it a shot."

He stopped and looked back at her for a moment. "Okay." His flat tone made it clear he hadn't forgiven her, but she imagined she saw his face brighten just a little.

Later that evening, reliving the scene, Katie decided she'd imagined his face brightening. Hell would freeze over before he accepted her offer. Which was just as well.

20.

The New Manager's First Day

ON JULY 5, Barry's first day as manager of ESS, he arrived at the office before seven. Dorothy, the department secretary, arrived shortly after. She cast an admiring glance at the small stack of books and two cardboard boxes that had been delivered to his office the previous evening. "My, you travel light," she commented.

"Yup," he agreed.

In fact, Barry had a basement full of work-related papers in his home. No one who had fired as many people as he had could afford not to keep meticulous records. He felt, however, there was no advantage to keeping those records in the office. Quite the contrary, with snooping secretaries always eager to pry and gossip.

Dorothy asked, "Can I help you unpack?"

"That's okay, thanks. A couple of things you can do for me though. One is to contact everyone in the department, reminding them that I'm now aboard. Also, please tell Katie and Terry to come to my office at eight o'clock."

"This morning?" Dorothy sounded startled. "Okay, I'll check when they get in and see if they're available."

Barry raised his eyebrows. "*If* they're available? For a meeting with their manager?"

Dorothy explained, "It is kind of short notice. They might have other meetings scheduled for that time. With clients...or something."

"Tell them I expect to see them at eight o'clock."

Dorothy pursed her lips. "Very well."

Barry sighed as he searched in the drawer for a paper knife to slit open his boxes. He knew he shouldn't bark out ultimatums like that. But, damn it, people in these staff departments had been allowed far too much leeway in how they spent their time. Some tightening up couldn't hurt.

The phone rang. He'd no sooner picked it up than he heard Miranda's cooing voice. "Ho, ho, ho, Mr. B. I made it, after all."

Barry smiled. "A miracle indeed. Come on over."

He and Miranda had had a playful argument about her ability to get to the office before eight o'clock.

A few minutes later, Barry heard Dorothy's surprised squeal outside his door. "Miranda. Long time, no see. Have you come to get your things?"

Miranda ignored the question. "I've come to see the boss. Big Bad Barry." She smiled cheerfully at Barry as he walked to his office door to greet her. Dorothy gave him a look that could only be described as smug. No doubt, Barry thought, she imagined she was witness to some kind of illicit rendezvous.

He said cheerfully, "Miranda! Bet you haven't had breakfast yet. Dorothy, how about you run down to the cafeteria and get us some coffee and muffins. Oh, and don't forget the butter."

Dorothy looked shocked. After a moment, she inquired in an icy tone, "And should I get the money from the petty cash?"

"Absolutely, yes."

Barry winked at Miranda as he ushered her into his office. In response, she made a wry face at his blasphemy. They both knew it was a no-no to ask secretaries to "run to the cafeteria" for coffee, let alone for muffins and butter—let alone to use the petty cash for that purpose.

AT EIGHT O'CLOCK, Katie arrived outside Barry's closed door. Hearing voices inside, she asked Dorothy, "Is someone with him?"

"Yes. Miranda."

"Miranda? She hasn't shown her face here for almost a month and now she turns up on Barry's first day as manager."

Dorothy nodded. She leaned toward Katie and whispered, "They've been in there with the door closed for over half an hour. *And* he sent me down to the cafeteria to get coffee and muffins for them." Before she could expound further on this managerial chauvinism, Barry flung open his office door. "Katie, come on in. Where's Terry?"

"He doesn't start work until nine," Katie told him.

She saw something flicker in his eyes but he said nothing. She followed him into his office. Miranda was sitting at the conference table by the window. She smiled at Katie in a bright way that suggested she was not only pleased to see Katie but was confident Katie was equally pleased to see her.

Barry said, "It's a nuisance Terry isn't here. I wanted to talk to you both at the same time. We'll have to do something about this flexible working hours policy. All of you need to be on the same timetable as me."

Katie glanced at Miranda. The flexible hours policy had been established only a few weeks ago as part of the department's efforts to incorporate "employee empowerment," one of the corporate values Miranda had been touting. It seemed that today, however, Miranda's mind was elsewhere. She sat upright, elbows on the table, her slender fingers shaped into a pyramid. She was looking at Barry. Katie, feeling uncomfortably like a voyeur, watched as Barry caught Miranda's eye and smiled.

Then, abruptly, he turned to Katie. "Well, I might as well tell you now. I'm sure you'll be happy to know that as of today Miranda is a regular full-time member of our department."

Miranda beamed. Katie didn't know how to react because she had no idea what this news meant. Was Miranda here to keep the Corporate Values Program on a back burner until the time was right to spring it upon the company again?

At this moment, there was a light tap at the door and then a flustered Terry made his way in. He mumbled,

"Sorry I'm late. My regular working hours are nine to six."

"So I've heard," Barry said. "I've just explained to Katie that Miranda is now a regular member of this department."

Terry glanced at Katie. He said, "What about the conference room? Will Miranda want it back?"

In the past few weeks, during Miranda's absence, Terry and Katie had pushed Miranda's belongings into a corner and reclaimed the conference room. Now, Miranda said, "I noticed my office was full of all kinds of stuff that I know I didn't put there." Smiling, she said to Terry, "So you're the culprit, taking over when you thought I wasn't looking."

Terry blushed. "We thought you had left the company. I use the big conference table to assemble materials for my surveys. There aren't any other rooms on this floor with a big enough table."

Barry said, "That's too bad because it will continue to be Miranda's office."

Angered by his smug tone, Katie snapped, "Yes, it is too bad. We really need that space." Three pairs of surprised eyes turned toward her. She said, "Might I ask what Miranda's job in this department will be?"

Barry fixed milky-green eyes on Katie. "Miranda's title is assistant manager. From now on, she'll be your supervisor."

Katie drew a breath. "So Terry and I report to Miranda who, in turn, reports to you?" She couldn't keep the sneer out of her voice. "In other words, you're adding an extra level of management in our department? Isn't that in violation of one of Miranda's corporate values? Having the flattest possible organization structure?"

Miranda looked appealingly at Barry. Unfazed, Barry proclaimed, "Flexibility trumps rules. We do what makes most sense."

Katie met his eyes with puzzlement as well as defiance. Much as she had no love for Barry, she'd always assumed that he was intelligent and efficient.

How could he possibly propose that someone like Miranda take on such a responsibility?

She said, "I don't understand, Barry. How does it make sense? If that's Miranda's job, then what is yours?"

Miranda gasped. Terry's mouth hung open.

Barry looked amused. He said in a kindly tone, "You're worried I won't have enough to do? Well, let me reassure you. Everett relies on me to perform all manner of special assignments for him and he's made it plain he's not going to let me off the hook just because I'm now manager of ESS. So, you see, I really do need someone to oversee the daily nuts-and-bolts running of the department."

Katie said, "But why Miranda?" She turned again to Miranda. "No offense, Miranda, but do you really think you're capable of supervising Terry or me?"

Miranda's doe eyes looked bigger than usual as she stared first at Katie and then at Barry. Barry said firmly, "All right, that's enough. I didn't call the two of you in this morning to debate the pros and cons of my decision to hire Miranda. I just wanted to tell you about it before I announce it to the rest of the department."

He picked up his pen and made a note on the pad in front of him. "Katie reminds me of an important point. I need to find out exactly what kind of work every person in this department does. All I know is it costs the company a bundle in terms of salaries and overheads."

He paused to look around the table at them and added slowly, "In fact, there's a serious question in my mind as to whether the company really gets its money's worth out of ESS."

He scribbled some more. Probably, Katie thought, to allow time for his last devastating remark to sink in. Then he looked up. "I'll have Dorothy schedule individual appointments for Terry and Katie to meet with me to discuss their job duties and we'll take it from there. Okay, we're done here." He gripped the arms of his chair and stood. The others stood also. As they turned to leave, Barry said, "Katie, would you stay behind for a minute, please."

When she saw Miranda's jealous expression, Katie's unease at this summons dissolved into silent glee. But only for a moment.

WHEN KATIE GOT BACK to her office a short time later, she found a fax that someone had left on her chair. It consisted of a draft of the letter that Sherman Granger planned to send to Worthington. The accompanying message asked for her input. A cursory glance at Sherman's document left Katie feeling irritated. Full of boring technical jargon, it had no zip whatever. Wasn't he supposed to be a salesman?

Katie was also irritated at his method of transmitting the letter. The department's fax machine was at the end of a hall near the manager's office, where anyone walking by could see the messages coming in. After her "couple of minutes" with Barry this morning, she felt more than ever that it would be wise to keep her dealings with Sherman under wraps.

While she stood, fax in hand, Terry appeared at the door. Before he could speak, Katie pulled open the bottom drawer of her desk, put the fax inside, and grabbed her purse. "Terry, let's go to the caff for a cup of coffee. I have to get away from this stinking department for a few minutes."

Terry looked at her curiously. "Your little session alone with Barry made an impression, huh?" She shushed him.

In the company cafeteria, they got their coffee and sat at a corner table. Katie looked at Terry. "You know what that ba..." she started. She stopped as someone came to clear an adjoining table.

"That Barry?" suggested Terry.

"That bastard," she spat the word, "had the gall to lecture me on? *Insubordination*! Can you believe it? He told me my behavior in the meeting this morning had been offensive and ill-mannered. He asked how I dared question his decision to hire Miranda."

Terry grinned.

Katie went on. "I reminded the arrogant idiot that, according to dear Miranda's much-vaunted corporate values, 'employee insubordination' is an obsolete term. At complete odds with the ideas of employee empowerment and employee involvement. How can you encourage employee involvement while at the same time accusing people who speak their minds of insubordination?"

"What did he say to that?"

"He as good as told me to stop talking such a bunch of crap."

"I'd like to have been a fly on the wall. But, Katie, do you think it's a good idea to draw up the battle lines his first day on the job?" Katie sipped her coffee, frowning. "I know you were super-disappointed you didn't get Chuck's job, but..."

"Oh, no, I'm over that."

"Really?"

Katie said, "Yes, really. When I got over my initial knee-jerk reaction of wanting to exterminate everyone in my path, I realized the future isn't that bleak."

"Oh?"

"No. You see, Terry, it's widely known in the company that Barry is a man on his way up. Nothing less than a vice-presidency for him. Obviously, Worthington made him manager of our department just so he could gain experience in dealing with mooshy staff departments like ours. He'll be out of here in a year or two, you can bet."

"And Miranda's contract will be up by then," Terry agreed. "But that won't do you much good if Barry fires you in the meantime. You know his reputation."

Katie looked thoughtfully into the distance as she pondered this. She said, "I don't think he could justify firing me, do you? Not to brag, but my management development work here has been written up in national journals."

"And you yourself have won awards from all kinds of professional societies. I know, I know. But, Katie, as we've both said many times, at the end of the day it boils down to not how much you've accomplished but who your friends are."

They looked at each other for a long moment in silence. Katie thought how secure she'd always felt because of having powerful friends in the company. Influential company officers and managers who'd been her clients and who'd expressed their high regard for her and her work. But one of those people, Chuck, had left. And the most powerful person of all, Everett Worthington, seemed now to be under the spell of people like Barry Bryce who had only contempt for her.

If she lost their CEO's support, as Chuck apparently had, wouldn't support from her remaining company contacts vanish too?

She put down her cup. "Oh, God, Terry, you're right. No one is irreplaceable."

BARRY GOT HOME before five that afternoon and was surprised to find his wife there ahead of him. Lila's thin, boyish figure was stretched out on a chaise. She wore shorts and a halter top. With her reading glasses perched on the end of her nose, she was sorting through a stack of file folders and making notes on a pad on her lap. She looked up as he walked out through the sliding doors of the kitchen. "Hi."

"What's this?" he teased. "The senior partner of the city's leading investment management firm goofing off at home and it isn't even five o'clock."

"I'm working," Lila retorted, "What's your excuse?"

Barry removed his jacket and tie and sat on the edge of a garden chair. "Oh, I'd sort of run out of things to do so I thought I'd come home early and surprise you with a barbecue. But, now, alas, no surprise."

Lila took off her glasses and smiled. She sipped from a can of ginger ale beside her. "So how was it? Your first day as manager of the executive support services department?"

"Boring." He leaned forward, forearms resting on thighs, and yawned. "I wandered around the department and introduced myself to everyone. They all looked suitably terrified."

Lila chuckled. "Well, you should act nicer to them."

With mock indignation, he protested, "What're you talking about? I am nice. No one could have been more polite." He remembered Katie. "Well, I did have a run-in with the woman who heads up their management development section. She's been acting manager the past couple of weeks. Given her uppity ideas, I guess."

"Ah," Lila said, "I thought there'd have to be at least one run-in."

"Hey, Lila, this wasn't my fault. The woman is impossible. Today, she was unbelievably rude to Miranda—challenging Miranda's ability to do her job."

Instantly, he regretted having mentioned Miranda. Lila said, "Oh, right. It was your first day as Miranda's boss, wasn't it?"

A couple of weeks ago, Barry and Lila had had a terse discussion about Worthington's request that Barry find a place for Miranda in the company. At that time, Barry had explained to Lila that no one in the company was willing to take on someone as highly paid as Miranda. It, therefore, fell to Barry to find a spot for her in ESS.

Lila asked, "So what is Miranda's job, Barry?"

Inwardly, he braced himself. "Assistant Manager of ESS."

"What!" Lila threw her head back and roared with laughter. "And what, pray tell, will she be doing to warrant that title?"

"Look, at the salary she gets I could hardly make her a junior clerk. And she can't do much damage as assistant manager. She'll have two experienced supervisors reporting to her. She doesn't know anything about what they do so there's no way she can interfere too much."

He slung his jacket over his shoulder and stood up. "What's that you're drinking? Ginger ale? How about a real drink?"

Lila hesitated. "Maybe not. I came home early today because I had a strange episode. For about fifteen minutes, I felt quite unwell. It was weird."

Barry frowned, but before he could press for more details, Lila said, "Barry, wouldn't it be a lot easier, and save the company a lot of money, if you simply suggested to Ev that Miranda be let go? Obviously, you have no need of her services."

He shook his head. "Remember, she has a contract with the company for one year? And, incidentally, that wasn't my idea; it was Ev's. So we either have to utilize her or pay her for the rest of the year anyway."

Barry didn't meet Lila's eye as he spoke. He was sure that she suspected, as he did himself, that RPC's law department could have weaseled them out of that contract if Worthington had insisted.

"Right. I'm off to take a quick shower." He walked back into the house.

As he undressed in their bedroom upstairs, Barry looked down at the patio from the window. Lila had stopped working and was leaning back in the chaise with her eyes closed. She was probably building up all kinds of suspicions about his true motives for hiring Miranda. Quite unjustified suspicions because, in their entire relationship, he had never once been unfaithful to Lila. He felt guilty anyway, because he did, in fact, have a sort of ulterior motive in hiring Miranda. This was to make sure there was at least one person in this hostile department who was on his side during the trying months ahead.

The fact that the person was also mouthwateringly attractive was, of course, irrelevant. He laughed aloud.

As he strode around the bathroom naked, he felt the press of something on his mind. Some unfinished business that was escaping him for the moment. Stepping under the rush of warm water, he remembered. That "strange episode" Lila had mentioned. What was that about?

21

Lorraine Has a Party

ON SATURDAY MORNING, Katie sat at her kitchen table, sipping her first cup of coffee and pondering whether or not to go to Lorraine's tonight for a last-minute summer bash.

Reasons in favor: this past week in the office had been a drag and she deserved some recreation. Also, this would give her an excuse to check out the end-of-summer sales to find some clothes to show off her slimmer figure. Also at one o'clock Ramon, recommended to her as the top stylist at the ChiChi Salon, was doing a complete makeover on her hair— something else to be shown off.

Reasons against: she had brought home a lot of work. She had to revise Sherman's letter to Worthington. Also, she had to prepare for her meeting with Barry to discuss her job duties, a meeting that Dorothy had scheduled for Monday afternoon. But she couldn't spend the whole weekend working on such dreary stuff. Decision made: she would go to the party.

AT NOON, Katie returned home. She hummed cheerfully as she unloaded the car, feeling well pleased with herself. She had bought a summery outfit in a cool, silky material. And stocked up on food to take to the party—ingredients for a big green salad with a cheesy-garlic dressing that was Katie's own specialty. As she made her way to the front door with her purchases, she caught sight of Dan walking down the driveway next door toward his truck. Since the uncomfortable ending of their last conversation, Katie had been avoiding him, but in her present mood she couldn't resist beaming a smile in his direction. He waved. She nodded with her chin at her laden arms, shouting, "Sorry, can't wave back."

He drew abreast of her on the other side of the low fence separating her front yard from Mildred's. "Need some help?"

"Oh, no, thanks." Katie did her best to sound friendly. Although she'd tried to forget about it, she'd been unable to stop feeling guilty at her snippy putdown the last time they'd talked.

He continued to watch as she struggled through her front door. Then he called out, "Wanna go to lunch again?" Katie swung around. He looked strangely appealing as he stood there with his straggly hair and grubby jeans. But lunch was out of the question.

"Not today, I'm afraid. I'm in kind of a hurry. I have to put away my groceries and then rush off to a one o'clock appointment."

"How about a drink after I finish work? I could be ready by six."

Katie so much didn't want to hurt his feelings. "You know, Dan, I'd really like that but tonight I'm going to a party. I'll be leaving here by six. I'm so sorry. Some other time...."

"Sure, no problem." Then, to her dismay, he added, "How about tomorrow? We could maybe...." He caught her eye and stopped. "No, huh?"

"The trouble is I brought a lot of work home with me this weekend and I'll really have to concentrate on it all day tomorrow." In an attempt to lighten the mood, she added, "I've already set my alarm clock for the crack of dawn."

Dan's face fell and, as she watched the light leave his beautiful blue eyes, she felt she had to do something—no matter how much she might regret it later. She said, "You know what? This party I'm going to tonight is a very casual affair. Maybe... um... do you think you'd like to come?"

He looked surprised. And then unsure. And then he said, "No, I don't think so. I wouldn't wanna crash the party." But his tone was so tentative that Katie held her tongue and waited for more. He looked down and shuffled his feet. When he looked up, he said, "It would be awkward for you, wouldn't it?"

"Not at all. It's my friend Lorraine who's giving the party. Remember, you saw her once? The hippie-looking woman with the beat-up car. She's very easy-going."

"The medieval history?"

"That's the one. I'll phone her, of course, but I know the bigger the crowd the happier she is. She won't mind at all if you come." Katie had to suppress a smile as this whopper of an understatement left her lips.

Finally, Dan said, "Okay. What time shall I come for you?"

He'd regained his self-assurance in a flash. But as they discussed logistics for the evening, Katie started to regret her impulsiveness, just as she had known she would. She hoped he had appropriate clothes to wear. From the corner of her eye, she could see his truck, its shabby bulk a blot on the neat little street. Well, she'd been planning to drive anyway.

AT FIVE-THIRTY that afternoon, as she waited for Dan to arrive, Katie checked herself out in the mirror. She was pleased with what she saw. Ramon had done a great job on her hair. Its unruly bushiness had been tamed into soft curls all over the head with wavy tendrils pulled forward to frame her face.

The new clothes looked good too on her so much-more-slender figure. She posed and pirouetted to check out the flouncy pants and matching blouse with their pretty patterns in white, turquoise and gold.

The doorbell rang. When Katie opened the door, her heart soared at the sight of Dan. He was dressed in crisp tan pants and a chocolate knit shirt and looked incredibly alluring. And there was something else. "Dan, you got a haircut. That makes two of us." He didn't say anything but looked at her hair and smiled.

When they walked out of the house, she found a second surprise. There was a late-model, sporty red hatchback parked in her driveway. "Where did that come from? That's not yours, is it?" Katie asked.

Immediately, she felt embarrassed at her display of incredulity and blushed as he teased her. "What, you figure I stole it? Just found it down the street with the keys in it?" But he looked pleased, rather than offended, at her gaffe and stepped ahead to open the car door for her.

As they set off down Alara Way, Dan asked, "So does your medieval friend know I'm coming?"

"Yes, I called her and it's fine." Lorraine had, of course, been ecstatic at hearing Katie had invited Dan to accompany her.

Dan didn't talk much as they drove toward Berkeley. Maybe, Katie thought, he was apprehensive at the thought of meeting her "medieval friends." Katie wondered about that herself. She hoped Lorraine and Peter's academic clique wouldn't be too uppity with her handyman. The men would be jealous of Dan's good looks. The women would be hard pressed to keep their hands off him. That is, except for a couple of militant feminists in the group who would automatically conclude such a *male* male must be a chauvinist pig and, thus, a menace to womankind.

Well, she didn't know about the "chauvinist pig" part, but there was no doubt about the "menace to womankind" part. With a capital M. Katie cast a sideways glance at her date. His new haircut was attractive—short but not too short, the hair layered to fit his nicely shaped head. There was someone else, whom she couldn't quite recall at the moment, who had a haircut like that.

After some patient searching, Dan managed to find a parking spot three long blocks from Lorraine's apartment house. As they hiked down the hill, she remembered who else had that sexy haircut. That bastard Barry Bryce.

AT TEN O'CLOCK that evening, Katie was sitting on Lorraine's living room floor between two bearded members of the U.C. History faculty. Almost nose-to-nose in front of her face, the two men were hotly debating a controversial tenure decision in their department. It seemed to her they'd been at it for hours. Katie yawned. From the sound of things, everyone else at the party was having a good time. Everyone, that is, except for Lorraine who was making angry noises in the kitchen.

Katie drained her glass and lifted herself to her knees. From this higher vantage point, she could see over the two talking heads to where Dan sat a few feet away. He was squeezed into the corner of a couch by a woman Katie knew only slightly, a neighbor of Lorraine's. The woman's body rested against Dan, her spikey-orange hair flopped back on the cushions beside his head. She looked, Katie thought, like a Raggedy-Ann dust-mop.

Dan, his face animated, was relating some story to the people around him. Katie strained to hear. Dan's listeners chortled with him, but Katie worried there might be a trace of condescension underlying their laughter. She resolved to rescue him. She excused herself to the two academicians, who ignored her, and got to her feet.

The room swayed for a moment. Katie paused to steady herself before setting out in Dan's direction. She paused again on observing that Raggedy Ann had encroached still further onto his territory. One of her legs was now trailing across his thigh and the orange mop spilled onto his shoulder. Katie decided to go to the kitchen instead to see what was ailing Lorraine.

Lorraine was standing at the sink, cursing out loud while she attacked a large block of ice with a screwdriver and hammer.

"Lorraine, what on earth are you doing?"

"Peter didn't get us enough ice so I pulled this ancient bag of cubes out of the back of the freezer. It's frozen solid. It must have been there since Christmas."

Holding the screwdriver in place, she swung the hammer down to drive it into the ice. Katie jumped as ice splinters sprayed onto the counter and floor. Lorraine continued, "Of course, Peter is nowhere to be seen. Probably smoking pot on the back porch." She raised the hammer again.

Katie said, "That looks incredibly dangerous. You could hurt yourself. Or the sink."

"If I do, Peter will have to replace it. Serves him right."

Katie retreated to a safe distance as the assault continued. But, in short order, Lorraine put down the tools. She said, "You're right. Why should I risk life and limb? And sink. We both know Peter couldn't fix the sink to save his life. Unlike your Dan." She scooped a couple of loosened pieces of ice out of the sink and placed them in a bucket. "Speaking of Dan, I've been meaning to ask you. Next time you bring him over, do you think he'd be offended if we asked him to take a look at that damp wall in our bedroom? I'm sure the water is dripping down from the roof through the walls. Our slob of a landlord just doesn't want to know."

Katie pulled out a chair and sat down. She felt warm and a bit light-headed. She said, "I'm not sure there'll be a next time."

Lorraine protested, "Why not? The guy's adorable. In fact, I was planning to rub it in how right I was about him. I thought you'd finally seen the light."

Katie leaned her elbows on the table and looked at her hands. "Because... how can I put it? He's gorgeous, but I can't imagine having, say, an intellectual relationship with him."

She regretted saying the word as soon as it left her mouth. Lorraine was sure to pounce on it. Lorraine did. "Intellectual?" she scoffed. "Give me a break. Didn't we go through all this before? It's fun-time, kiddo. Lighten up."

"Well, no, it's not only that. There're other things about him that bother me at times. Things that just don't add up." Katie sighed. She knew that had she been sober she would never have tried to pursue this argument. But, right now, she felt a need to unburden her misgivings and get reassurance.

There was, however, no reassurance forthcoming from her hostess who countered, "Like what?"

Katie thought for a moment. "Well, he told me he used to be a qualified electrician, making good money. Now why would he give that up to become a handyman?"

Lorraine looked exasperated. "Oh, for Heaven's sake! What's so weird about making a career change?"

Katie lowered her voice. "Also, there's his divorce." She stopped, as it occurred to her how pathetic she sounded. Most of the people she knew had been through a divorce. So what exactly was bothering her? She muttered, half to herself, "He's carrying some kind of baggage. I just can't put my finger on it."

Lorraine patted her gently on the shoulder. "You know something, sweetie? The main problem with you right now is you're pixilated. Two sheets to the wind. Or is it three?" Someone came to the kitchen door. Without missing a beat, Lorraine exclaimed, "Lookie, lookie. Here come da baggage."

It was Dan, smiling as he strolled into the room. He said to Katie, "There you are. I was waiting for you to rescue me from the lady with the funny hair." He explained to Lorraine, "A very friendly lady—seemed to think she belonged on my lap."

"Well, that's what you get for being so handsome, handsome." Lorraine affectionately ruffled his hair as she pursed her lips and blew him a slurpy kiss. Katie rolled her eyes at Dan. Privately, she envied Lorraine's hands running through that hair. Lorraine added, "I think this calls for another drink."

Katie said quickly, "Not for me, thanks. I have a full day of work tomorrow and need to be up early with a clear head. In fact..." She glanced at the clock. "...by the time we get home it'll be past eleven. We really should be leaving now. Do you mind, Dan?"

Dan didn't mind, but Lorraine did, and it was almost thirty minutes later by the time Katie had soothed Lorraine and made their farewells to the company at large. At the door, Lorraine gave Dan a hug and said, "Dan, insist Katie bring you back to see us, hear?" Over his shoulder, she gave Katie a look.

The night air was delicious. Cool and velvety. Katie stumbled as she started down the steps to the street and Dan slid his arm around her waist. He kept it around her as they walked back up the hill to the car. She hoped he didn't have any ideas about being invited in when they reached her house. She'd have to remind him again about her need for an early rising tomorrow.

As they drove home, she asked, "So, did you enjoy the party?"

"It was fine."

The tone was polite rather than enthusiastic. But then, Katie reminded herself, Dan was a man of few words—at least, few pretty words. He still hadn't complimented her on her new haircut, even though the women at the party tonight were gushing all over it.

Gushing reminded Katie of the dust-mop. She told Dan, "That woman with the spiky hair, she has quite a reputation, you know."

"Yeah?" he said.

"I can never remember her name. Dottie or Debbie or something. She's been divorced three times."

"It's Carlotta, Lottie for short. She's been divorced twice."

Alarm bells went off in Katie's head. Dan and that woman must have been doing more than snuggling. Talking, getting to know each other. This could be serious. She asked, "Do you find her attractive?"

Dan threw back his head and laughed. "Katie, you're sloshed." He burst into song. "What do we do with a drunken Katie?" Katie never did get to find out what he thought of Raggedy Ann.

When they arrived at her house, Dan pulled into the driveway and switched off the ignition. Katie said, "I have to be up real early tomorrow."

"The crack of dawn. I remember." He opened his car door and she opened hers. He walked around the car to meet her and held her arm to guide her up the steps. A display of affection on his part, she wondered? Or a desire to avoid having to scoop her collapsed, drunken body off the concrete?

When she opened the front door, he said, "Now you get a good night's sleep. If those animals let you." Loud wails reached them from the kitchen where the cats were locked up. "Thanks again for inviting me."

"You're welcome." Katie felt disconcerted. Evidently, she didn't need her pre-rehearsed excuses for not inviting him in because he wasn't planning to stick around to hear them. She had an idea. "How about a cup of coffee? It worries me to think of you driving home without any coffee."

His face was in shadow but she could see the white flash of his teeth as he drawled, "I don't think I'm the one needs the coffee, ma'am. Anyway, I got you here, didn't I?"

He was right, of course. Disappointed, Katie looked up at him as he lounged against the doorframe. She hadn't intended him to come in—but why didn't he want to? Maybe he was disgusted at her for drinking too much.

She said, "Dan, I don't know what happened tonight. I think Peter made those piña coladas extra-strong."

This seemed to move him. He crooned, "O-o-o-h," and leaned his face down until it was almost touching hers. "I was only kiddin', baby. Don't worry about it." Then he added, in a voice barely above a whisper, "Your new haircut looks real nice, y'know. But your hair looked nice before, too. It always looks nice."

The unexpected compliment came as a shock. And there was another shock as he slid his hand up the back of her neck into her hair and she realized that he was going to kiss her. She whispered back, "Oh, Dan," and her mouth reached for his as he pulled her close to him.

All too soon, it was over. Dan pulled back and teased, "Crack of dawn, right?" He kissed her again lightly on the tip of her nose. Then he left.

The feel of his body against hers lingered as she watched him go down the steps and climb into his car. He waved to her once before driving away. The feeling lingered during the half-hour that followed as Katie went through her nighttime time routine of getting herself to bed.

Katie always slept with two pillows: one to rest her head on, one to cuddle up to. She cuddled up now, rubbing her lips against the cool cloth and thinking about the kiss. It had been a wonderful kiss. Not wildly passionate but sexy and romantic just the same. Inside her, a feeling of euphoria clashed with a tension born of arousal. This was due not only to the kiss but also to the wonderful thing he'd said. *Your hair always looks nice.*

As her mind alternately blurred and sharpened with the onset of sleep, Katie wondered if he'd really said those things about her hair or whether her alcohol-hazed mind had imagined it. Whatever. She knew she had to savor her joy to the fullest tonight. Because she also knew that in the cold light of morning things often just didn't look the same.

22

Katie Finds an Angle

IT WAS SUNDAY AFTERNOON and Sherman was at his daughter Ellen's house. Ellen and her husband, George, were frolicking in George's latest pride and joy: their new swimming pool. "Cooling off," they'd said.

Showing off, more likely, Sherman thought to himself. Sherman had obtusely "forgotten" to bring his swimsuit so he sat alone at the patio table, his feet planted firmly on dry ground, even as the thermometer under the eaves climbed to the high 90s. How ridiculous, he fumed, to have all that air-conditioning indoors going to waste while he sweltered out here.

After a while, his son-in-law climbed out and sat on the side of the pool, kicking his thin hairy legs in the water. He said, "Hey, Sherm, I have some news that might interest you." Sherman kept a blank expression on his face.

But, when his daughter swam over toward them, the expression turned to one of affection. To Sherman, Ellen looked so much like her mother at that age with her cherubic face and curly blonde hair. Standing up to her waist in water, Ellen leaned her arms on George's knees and asked her father, "Don't you want to hear George's news, Dad?"

In truth, he didn't. Anything George had to say was usually something that illustrated how skillful, cunning, or lucky George was. Sherman said, "So what is it?"

George smoothed his dripping hair back from his face. He said, "Our company's opening up a new branch office soon in Beresford and I just heard they're looking for a sales supervisor. It's an office job, someone to schedule appointments for the salesmen, stuff like that.

Sounds like a good job for you, Sherm." Sherman gazed into the distance.

George worked for a company that designed software systems and that had been phenomenally successful in recent years. As a result, the company, headquartered in San Francisco, now had branch offices mushrooming all over the state. George added, "You're a bit older than the applicants they would normally consider, but I can put in a good word for you."

Sherman said, "Thanks but I already have a job."

George looked surprised. "If you're talking about your position with Sequoia Enterprises, I understand things are a bit rocky there right now." He looked at Ellen as though appealing to her to back him up. Sherman caught the look and felt a stab of anger. Ellen must have blabbed to George what Sherman had told her in strict confidence—that business was drying up at Sequoia.

Ellen said quickly, "Dad, this job George is talking about is a real good deal. Their company has great benefits. Medical, dental, pension plan. And the salary..."

Sherman said, "The job with Sequoia is just a stopgap. I have other irons in the fire."

George stared at Sherman with disdain. "What irons?" he asked. "You're surely not talking about that cogeneration thing?" As Sherman opened his mouth to respond, George said quickly, "Okay, I'm sure it's a great invention and all but, Sherm, your business model is no good. There's no way a company like RPC would give you the time of day."

Ellen broke in, "Yes, Dad, George should know. Remember, he's the director of product development for his firm."

Sherman drew his shoulders back and thrust out his chin. "I'm well aware of George's title. But I'll have you both know that I have real strong support at RPC. Even as we speak, a high-level executive in their head office is reviewing the draft of a letter I'm sending to their CEO.

She's going to tweak it for me to make sure it gets his full attention. I expect to hear back from her this week."

George's mouth dropped open. He exchanged a glance with Ellen, who said, "High-level executive? I didn't realize...?"

"Yes, she has a lot of influence in the company." Sherman didn't usually stretch the truth but there were times, like now, when such action was necessary to preserve a man's dignity.

George shrugged. "Well, let me know if you change your mind." He slid back into the water. As he swam off on his back, he called out, "Salary is fifty-three thousand. That's to start. With a review after six months."

Fifty-three thousand?

Sherman's throat constricted. Never in his life had he earned that kind of money. Fifty-three thousand. Plus benefits. Poor Judy. She had died without ever having enjoyed such advantages. He felt his resolve draining away. What reason could he possibly have for turning down such an offer? He said, "I guess I could think about it."

George's smugness reappeared in a flash. "Better not think too long," he said. "I won't be able to hold it open for you forever."

Sherman grabbed his empty beer bottle, shook it over his mouth as though determined to coax out the last drop, and then slammed it back down on the table. He had just thought of a million reasons not to accept this offer. They were all called George.

WHILE SHERMAN was weighing the job prospect being dangled in front of him, the "high-level executive" from RPC was stretched out on a chaise in her back yard. Until a couple of minutes ago, Katie had indeed been tweaking Sherman's draft. Now she leaned back and looked up at the sky, which was a cloudless deep blue. The temperature was a balmy 75°. A light breeze rustled through the poplars next door and Katie closed her eyes, relishing the cool waft as it reached her. It was criminal, she told herself, to have to work on a gorgeous day like this.

This morning, she had compiled a portfolio of her projects to present to Barry. With care, she'd selected the pieces of work that best exemplified the creativity and thoroughness of her investigations. She didn't include a summary of her Manifesto. She wasn't interested in sharing any ideas about the department that might benefit Barry.

Her lunch break today had been a short one because she found that any time she wasn't absorbed in work, her mind had a distressing tendency to ruminate about yesterday evening. Things did indeed look different in the cold light of day.

Today, she wasn't hugging herself over Dan's kisses and compliments. Today, she couldn't stop reproaching herself for having had too much to drink last night. And for throwing herself at him in such an undignified way. Like inviting him in for coffee. What had she been thinking?

Since lunchtime, she'd focused on Sherman's letter—and found herself weighed down by a feeling of guilt. When she'd first suggested to Sherman he write this letter, it truly had seemed like a good idea. But, now, as she read it through the eyes of whoever on the executive floor was likely to review it, she could see this strategy wasn't going to work.

True, Sherman's letter had spelled out how his invention would benefit RPC's customers, but it didn't make it clear why the company should adopt it—after all, it was hardly a moneymaking proposition for them. What the letter needed was some angle, some sales pitch, that would leap out of the page and make someone in top management exclaim, "Hey, we need this."

As it was, the fate of this letter was sealed. Worthington himself would probably never see it. Shortly, Sherman would get a letter penned by one of the CEO's aides, thanking him for "considering Redwood Power Corporation" and assuring him he'd be contacted if the company ever wanted to pursue the matter. Which they never would.

Katie sat up and rubbed her forehead. It was time for a cup of tea.

In the kitchen, her eyes fell on her briefcase which she'd left on the counter. Lying on top of it was the Statement of Corporate Values. Just the other day, at a staff meeting, Miranda had—eyes shining—told them she'd recently talked to Everett Worthington about the defunct program. "He agreed with me," she'd claimed, "just because the pilot is over doesn't mean the values aren't still core to how the company conducts its business."

At the time, Barry's eyes had glazed over, along with hers and Terry's, but now... now something suddenly occurred to her. She sat upright and pulled the Statement of Values to her, her excitement growing as she ran her eyes over the familiar hackneyed statements. *That's it, Katie*, she told herself. She had found the angle she was seeking.

KATIE GOT TWO phone calls that evening. The first, shortly after seven, was from Sherman. "Sorry to disturb you on a Sunday," he said. "I just wondered if you'd had a chance to look at my letter."

"Sherman, I'm glad you called. First, I should tell you I thought you wrote a really good explanation of your invention, but I felt your letter lacked a strong argument for why the company should bother to do business with you." He gave a discouraged mumble and she added, "But the good news is I think I know how to fix it. Have you heard of our Corporate Values Program?"

"Sure have. Mike told me the company finally abandoned it."

"He's right. Our pilot program at Beresford has ended. But, at the same time, it seems our CEO still thinks the values themselves are core to how RPC conducts its business. This can work to your advantage,

Sherman. Because guess what some of the values are? Just let me read you a couple."

She reached for the statement and read aloud. "'We value our customers and are committed to supplying their needs at the lowest possible prices.' And how about this? 'We value technological advancement and constant innovation in the development of new products and services.'"

Sherman hesitated. "Yeah?"

"It seems to me your cogeneration unit is custom-designed to help the company live up to those two values, so your letter needs to stress that connection."

"Hmm. If you say so. All I ever knew about that values business was what Mike told me. 'A giant pain in the butt,' he said."

Katie laughed at this reminder of Mike's irritation. But now a red flag waved in her mind. There was something she needed to tell Sherman.

Sherman said, "So I need to rewrite the letter?"

"That's right. In fact, I've redrafted it for you, making direct links between your cogen unit and our corporate values."

Sherman clucked. "Gee, the games you people play. But, Katie, I sure do thank you. I'd never have thought of this stuff myself. Do you think you could fax your draft to me tomorrow?"

"As soon as I get into the office, I promise."

"That's great," he said. "I'll get the letter finalized and mailed this week."

As soon as she hung up, Katie realized she'd forgotten about the red flag. She'd wanted to warn Sherman not to tell Mike Weston she was helping with this letter. Because good-ole-boy Mike seemed like just the kind of person who would spread the word. She'd make a note to mention it next time she talked to Sherman.

KATIE WAS EATING a peach when the second call came half an hour later. She answered the phone with a muffled, "Hullo."

A male voice said, "Gotta a mouthful. I can tell."

Katie jumped and swallowed. "Dan. How are you?" She was surprised, delighted, and wary, all at once.

He said, "Just checkin' to see if you got all your work done."

"Yes, I did. I had a most productive day. How about you? Did you have a good day?"

"Sure did. Drove up to Huddart Park, off of Skyline, and went hikin' in the redwoods. Sure was beautiful up there."

"Spectacular views, I bet." Katie was genuinely envious. "Oh, Dan, it sounds wonderful. None of my friends much enjoy hiking and I love it."

"Yeah? I woud'a asked you to come along but you said you'd be busy. Maybe some other time."

Katie, emboldened by his call, found she was throwing herself at him all over again. "Why don't we go next weekend?"

Dan hesitated. "I don't know. I work Saturdays. And next Sunday I'm going to go visit my son." After a moment, he added, "I know you said you'd come with me sometime but I wasn't sure if you meant it."

There really was no way out of this one. "Sure," she said, "I'll come with you."

23

Complaints and Counter-Complaints

At three o'clock on Monday afternoon, Katie presented herself in Barry's office. He motioned for her to sit down. There was an open folder in front of him and she could see a document with the single-space layout of a job description. Hers, no doubt. She clutched the portfolio she'd prepared over the weekend.

She had a lot to accomplish during this one-hour meeting. For a start, of course, she had to impress upon Barry the depth and importance of the work she did in ESS. Also, she'd had a disturbing interaction with Miranda this morning that Barry ought to know about.

Barry said, "So job duties." He picked up her job description and read aloud. "Supervisor, Management Development Programs. Special Projects Consultant." He looked up at her with his strange chameleon eyes. "Special Projects Consultant?"

"I thought I might have to clarify that. As you know, Chuck was called on to assist top management with many sensitive issues. Things like poor performance of high-level people, conflicts between departments, decisions to eliminate departments, and so on. I worked with him on many of these projects." She thrust her portfolio across the desk toward him. "This is a sampling of my project reports to give you a sense of the work I did."

Barry opened the folder, flicked quickly through the pages, and closed it again. He said, "Give me an example of a special project."

Katie took a breath. Conscious of how intently he was listening, she chose her words with care.

"Let's see. One recent example involved the office equipment and supplies department. People were constantly complaining about how slow they were to respond to requests and how they so often filled orders incorrectly. Everett asked Chuck to look into the situation and Chuck handed the project over to me."

Katie noticed an oddly eager expression come onto Barry's face. He said, "Yes. And then?"

"I interviewed people throughout the department, examined their policies and procedures. The department had good written procedures, but discipline was lax and management was not enforcing them."

He nodded. She went on, "One of my recommendations was to hire an executive coach to work with the manager in improving his leadership ability."

Katie had been pleased with herself for thinking of engaging an executive coach. It was something the company had never tried before. Chuck had called it a "creative stroke" on her part.

Barry said, "Wasn't the main problem having the wrong person in charge? If a manager can't identify and correct his department's problems, he should be replaced."

Barry's words so confirmed to Katie what she'd heard about Barry—that his preferred solution to any problem was of the "give-'em-the-ax" variety. She said slowly, "Chuck's philosophy, with which I agree, was that it's seldom necessary to fire people. Firing people is expensive. It takes time and money to hire new people and bring them up to speed. Most people can be rehabilitated if their errors are pointed out to them."

The corners of his mouth turned up. "It also takes time and money trying to rehabilitate incompetent people. Usually, it's not worth it. Take your example. Did the manager get the coaching you recommended? Did service in office equipment improve as a result?"

"Yes, I've heard service in their department has greatly improved of late."

"Because of your recommendations?"

Katie hesitated. She felt her face grow warm as he continued to stare at her. One weakness of so many of their studies—hers and Chuck's—was that typically there'd been little follow-up. As long as the client had been happy with the final report, they'd considered their job done.

Barry said, "You didn't bother to check, did you? Well, let me fill you in. Nothing changed as a result of your study. No one got coaching or training or anything like that." Katie fidgeted uneasily as he went on. "It turned out there was a spot of hanky-panky going on there. The manager was taking kickbacks from suppliers. Everyone in the department knew about it, even if they weren't directly involved. It was pretty obvious the manager was being blackmailed by his employees into allowing them to get away with poor performance."

Katie's mouth dropped open. "I had no idea."

"No? I'm pretty sure Chuck did. But then he was a 'don't let's rock the boat' kind of guy, wasn't he? That's probably why he assigned that particular project to you. He figured you'd never succeed in digging that deep."

Katie inhaled sharply at this unpleasant dig at Chuck. And at her. Barry said, "Anyway, it's all taken care of now. Everyone in the department is on notice to shape up by year's end, or else they'll face disciplinary action. The manager is taking early retirement." He gave a tight-lipped smile. "That's why performance has improved in the office equipment and supplies department."

Katie looked down at her carefully prepared portfolio lying on the desk in front of Barry. How many of her other projects would he be able to demolish? She could feel Barry watching her and finally looked up, reluctantly, to meet his eyes. He said in a gentler tone, "I know. It's not really your fault. You just did things the ESS way—yet another study. When Worthington realized you hadn't uncovered the real source of the trouble, he asked me to get involved. He knew I wouldn't be afraid to come up with hard-hitting recommendations that would fix the situation."

As he spoke, some things were becoming clear to Katie. Chuck must have considered Barry to be a competitor from the very first because Worthington used both of them to do the same kind of investigations. Barry's methods and results were, however, very different from Chuck's. And, in retrospect, it seemed Worthington was losing faith in Chuck's velvet glove approach and leaning instead toward the big stick favored by Barry. For the first time, it seemed to Katie that Terry had been right in suggesting that Chuck had indeed been "pushed," rather than "jumping."

Barry said, "So, you see, I am basically carrying on the work Chuck did but with a different approach." His hypnotic green eyes met hers again as he added, "However, I'm not sure we need any *more* people to do this kind of work. Other than me, I mean."

Katie swallowed. He was saying that the part of her job she'd most enjoyed—and that most qualified her to be promoted—was to be eliminated. He closed her portfolio and pushed it aside. "Okay. I'll look over this and get back to you if I have any questions."

Quickly, Katie said, "Barry, something else came up today." She pulled out the document she'd been holding on her lap and waved it at him. "This is the schedule of management development classes for the fall. Last week, Miranda asked to see this so I gave her a copy." In a muttered aside, she added, "Not that I thought it was any of her business."

Barry frowned. Katie went on, "And then this morning, I found it back on my desk." She put the document down in front of him. "As you can see, she has marked up the entire schedule with changes on every page. Does she really think I'm going to change the schedule at this late date?"

Barry took the document and riffled through it. Katie was annoyed that his immediate reaction appeared to be one of mild amusement. He said, "Yes, we should get together with Miranda to discuss this. But not now." He glanced at the clock.

"Discuss?" Katie's voice rose. "What's to discuss? I've run our management development section for over five years to everyone's satisfaction. Who does Miranda think she is, interfering like this?"

Wryly, he suggested, "Your supervisor?" And then, "Okay, okay," as Katie opened her mouth to respond. "I'll take care of it." Then, to her surprise, he changed the subject. "I'm interested in learning more about the employee satisfaction survey. I understand you and Terry conduct this every year. How do you split up the work between you?"

The survey was the least impressive of her duties. Katie forced herself to refocus. "Terry develops the survey questionnaire and analyzes the data. I do a lot of the fieldwork for him."

"Fieldwork?"

"That consists of making visits to each division manager to explain how to administer the survey. Then, after the data have been analyzed, I go back into the field to help the local managers develop action plans to address problem areas."

Barry nodded, looking thoughtful. He said, "Next time you're due to make a field visit, ask Dorothy to check my calendar. I'd like to go with you."

With this bombshell, he rocked back in his chair and said, "I think we're through here. Thank you."

Katie stood and was on her way to the door when he dropped a second bombshell. "By the way, do you know a man called Sherman Granger?"

Katie froze. Her first terrible thought was that when she faxed the material to Sherman this morning she must have left some incriminating papers by the fax machine. She turned back toward him. He was looking at a note he'd pulled out of a desk drawer, "Apparently, he knows Mike Weston, the manager of Beresford Division. Miranda thought you might have met him."

Katie, in a voice so calm she was sure it would make him suspicious, said, "That's right. Mike introduced me to Sherman when I was out at Beresford telling them about the pilot study."

Barry crumpled up the note and threw it in the wastebasket. He didn't look suspicious. He said, "This man has invented some energy-saving device he's trying to sell the company. Keep me informed, would you, if he approaches you at any time. I can't imagine he would, but it seems he's been calling on other people in the company to help him, so you never know."

Katie said, "Sure." She paused for a moment before asking, "Any reason we shouldn't help him?"

"People like that are nothing but a time-wasting nuisance. And there are probably legal implications. Don't get involved. Refer him to me if he calls."

"Right."

Katie hurried back to her office mentally making note of what she had to do. She had to be sure to call Sherman tonight and warn him not to tell Mike Weston about her collaboration. She had to come to terms with the suddenly diminished importance of her job duties.

But the words "field visit" crowded out pretty well everything else. Barry's stated desire to accompany her suggested he wanted to monitor her performance. Most worrying, Katie wasn't sure she had the physical, mental or emotional stamina to spend an entire day out of the office with Barry Bryce.

A FEW MINUTES before five, there was a tap at Barry's door and then Miranda's cheerful face peeked around it. "Hey, Boss, time to wrap it up."

"Just the woman I wanted to see. There's something I need to discuss with you."

"Same here. In fact, how about we amble down to the waterfront and have a drink at Emilio's? Then we can both discuss away." She beamed. "Good way to end a Monday, huh?"

Barry considered this for a moment. Lila and her partners were having one of their periodic heavy-duty planning sessions this evening so she'd be late coming home. But, he decided, better not. Barry liked Miranda, but he was wary of her too. She was just the sort of woman who causes men to come undone. And Barry was darned if anyone was going to undo him.

He said, "No, this will only take a minute. Have a seat."

She sat down opposite him at his desk, leaned back and crossed her legs. Barry said, "I had a meeting with Katie this afternoon to discuss her job duties."

Eagerly, Miranda sat forward. "Oh, yes, I meant to tell you. I proposed a whole bunch of changes to her fall lineup of Management Development programs. Much of her stuff is so old-hat."

He said, "That's most praiseworthy of you, Miranda. However, you do realize it's completely up to Katie whether she considers your suggestions. She's the MD guru in this company and what she decides goes."

Miranda pouted. "You seem to be overlooking the fact that I'm now her supervisor. Isn't it my job to suggest ways for her to do her job better?"

"No, it isn't," Barry said. "It's your job to keep out of her way and let her do her thing." His voice hardened as Miranda started to protest. "Look, don't push this supervisor thing too far. Remember, I created the assistant manager position for you because I was trying to find something that would justify your salary, not because I intended you to interfere with ongoing work that's going smoothly."

Miranda looked upset. "Next, you'll be telling me I can't do her performance review."

Barry had forgotten that the annual performance reviews would be coming up soon. He said, "I guess that makes sense, seeing you're her supervisor. But I have to approve it."

Miranda nodded. She asked, "And how about the queer guy, Terry? Am I allowed to supervise him?"

Barry's mouth dropped. He repeated in a hushed voice, "'Queer guy?' Is that really what you said?"

Miranda corrected herself. "Gay, or whatever."

"Miranda. No, listen to me..." His voice sharpened as she started to smile. "This is important. This company may not care as much as it should about mundane things like efficient operations and customer service. But, believe me, it cares a whole bunch when it comes to anyone, especially supervisors, saying anything that has the slightest tinge of racial, sexual, religious, or homophobic bias. Don't ever use an expression like that again about anyone at RPC."

The rebuke removed the smile from her face and she flushed a deep pink. She pushed back her chair and stood. Barry said, "Wasn't there something you wanted to ask me about?"

She snapped. "There was, but what's the point? You'll just say no."

"Try me."

Miranda sat down again. She said, her eyes roving around the room, "Katie and I were talking this morning and she came up with a great idea. She... we... thought that what this department needs right now is a retreat. A day spent off-site."

Barry gave a loud groan.

"Now, Barry, don't be that way. You're a new manager with a completely different style and different expectations from what these people are used to. A retreat will give you the opportunity to let them all know what you stand for and what you expect from them." She looked up and their eyes met. He smiled.

She continued, "It doesn't have to cost a lot of money. We could meet in a local hotel...."

"Or," Barry interrupted. "We could meet in your office. It's big enough, as we know." His smile broadened. He knew how it bugged Miranda when people complained about the size of her office.

She again rose and turned to leave, muttering something about "waste of breath." But, in fact, much as he disliked departmental retreats, Barry knew that Worthington and some company officers positively revered them. This particular battle just wasn't worth fighting.

He said, "Why don't you go ahead? Just be sure to show me the estimates before you spend any money."

Miranda stopped and looked back at him with a small smile of both surprise and relief. She pouted again to show she hadn't forgiven him. Then she flounced out of the office.

Barry knew why Miranda was proposing a retreat. And why she busied herself with Katie's program schedule. It was because she had hardly anything to do these days. In fact, he wondered how on earth he could keep her occupied until the end of her contracted term of employment.

His limbs felt cramped and he stretched. It was time to go home, get something to eat, and wait for Lila to come home. He wondered what sort of mood she'd be in. These intensive meetings with her partners often left her on an adrenaline peak and she couldn't stop talking when she got home.

When bedtime came, sometimes she just wanted to sleep. But when she was in the mood for physical comfort, she would cuddle up and her fingers would start caressing him. Lila could do things with her fingertips that were obscenely exquisite. He hoped she would be in the mood tonight.

24

Storm Clouds Gather

ON FRIDAY, KATIE got an e-mail from Miranda. "Katie. Great news. The departmental retreat is a go. Stop by ASAP and we can get this baby rolling."

Katie e-mailed back. "Sorry, Miranda, no time right now. Up to my ears on the employee survey."

Katie felt smug as she pushed the SEND button. She'd been arguing with Miranda that now was not the right time for a retreat—not with the employee survey looming. And she had a feeling that Barry would back her up on this.

Shortly before noon, Terry stopped by. "I'm off to get a sandwich from the caff. Wanna join me?"

Katie agreed. She'd seen Terry leaving Miranda's office a couple of times this week with a long face, and suspected he needed a shoulder to cry on.

In the cafeteria, they bought their food and found a table on the terrace. Katie asked, "How's it going?"

Terry shook his head and munched on his sandwich for a while before answering. "That bloody woman! What she knows about data analysis you could stick on the head of a pin, and here she is..." He shook his head again.

Katie said sympathetically. "I know, showing you how to write computer programs. She just doesn't have enough work to do."

As she spoke, Katie shivered. It was a typical summer day in San Francisco. The gray morning overcast had receded, leaving in its wake sunny skies and cold winds.

Terry said, sounding grumpy, "She tells me she has to learn all about my job because she'll be doing my performance evaluation this year. Ain't that one for the books?"

"That's ridiculous. There's no way she's qualified to evaluate you. If she gives you a bad rating, go to BB and threaten to sue."

"Is that what you'd do?"

"I don't think she'd have the nerve to suggest evaluating me. Besides, I'm pretty sure Barry's the one who's keeping on top of my performance. On Monday, he told me he wants to accompany me on one of my field visits for the employee survey. Presumably so that he can evaluate me."

Terry looked thoughtful. He said, "Going on a field trip with Barry could be a big opportunity for you, couldn't it?"

"It could?"

"Think about it. You'll have him all to yourself all day. Lots of chances to slip in a few comments about your bright ideas to revamp the department."

"Could be." Katie spoke absent-mindedly. She'd been watching Terry as he spoke and had noticed for the first time the hollow cheeks and bags under his eyes. "Terry, is anything wrong? Are you that worried about your performance review?"

"I suppose not." He sighed. "It's just...well, it's Stefano. He hasn't been well for a while and I finally persuaded him to go for tests."

"And?"

He said, almost in a whisper. "It's as bad as it can be."

"Oh, Terry. AIDS?"

He nodded and she put out her hand to stroke his arm. The AIDS epidemic had hit RPC hard. Katie had not even realized so many of her fellow workers were gay until one familiar person after another had fallen ill. So far, there appeared to be no viable course of treatment for this horrible epidemic. She had no idea how to comfort Terry.

Suddenly, Terry leaned back, shaking off her arm. "Speaking of Stefano, the two of us went to a summer symphony performance last night. Here's a piece of gossip for you. Guess who we saw?"

"Who?"

"Our chief executive officer, Mr. Everett W, accompanied by the worthy Mrs. Everett W. And guess who was with them? None other than Mr. and Mrs. BB."

"Really?" Katie sat upright. "You saw Barry's wife? What does she look like?"

He seemed surprised at the question. "I didn't pay much attention. Let me think. Blondish, slender, sort of wispy looking. She's no Miranda, that's for sure." He added, "She looks quite a bit older than Barry."

Katie exclaimed, "That's strange. Why would someone like him—I mean, he's quite good-looking in his own sinister way—why would he be attracted to a woman who's older and not even that attractive?" Her voice trailed off as her own words replayed in her mind.

Terry said, "I wouldn't know." He snickered. "For money, perhaps?"

He talked on about May-December couples he'd known but Katie's thoughts had drifted to Dan. A beautiful young man who appeared to be in active pursuit of a far-from-beautiful older woman. Herself. Why was he pursuing her?

AT THREE O'CLOCK that afternoon, Katie, a stack of employee survey printouts in her arms, walked past Miranda's open door. She was headed for Terry's cubicle but stopped when a familiar voice hailed her. "Katie, got a minute?" Miranda sounded friendly.

Katie said, "Sure," and walked into the big office. Miranda waved at her to sit down but Katie remained standing. She wanted to make it clear she was in a hurry to move on.

Miranda was fussing with a thread unraveling from a button on her jacket. "Don't you just hate it when this happens?" she muttered. "This is an expensive suit too.

You wouldn't happen to have a needle and thread, would you?"

"Sorry, no."

Miranda tsked and continued to fiddle. Katie said, "Miranda, I really am kind of busy. Terry and I need to check over these printouts before five o'clock. Field visits start next week."

Miranda, still fiddling with her errant button, said in a dreamy voice, "You know, Katie, I've been remiss in not keeping on top of the work you're doing. I think we both keep forgetting that I'm your supervisor now."

She looked up to meet Katie's eye and gave a girlish giggle. "Fortunately, Barry keeps reminding me that I need to be fully aware of what you're doing. Or else how can I do your performance review?" She pulled the button loose at last and flashed Katie a radiant smile. "And that's important, isn't it? Considering your raise for next year depends on the rating I give you?"

Katie was startled, both by the words and by the almost menacing tone with which they were spoken.

Miranda went on, "I'll be checking your daily calendar from now on so I know where you are and what you're doing at all times. So let's set a time to meet every week. How about every Friday morning at ten?"

Katie forced herself to stay calm while a growing lump of anxiety formed in her stomach. "I can't commit to anything, Miranda. I'll be out in the field a lot from now on."

"Yes," Miranda murmured. "And there's the department retreat, isn't there? You're going to be busy."

With this, she picked up her button and stood up, brushing past Katie on her way out the door. "Now I must find someone with a needle and thread."

SHORTLY AFTER KATIE returned to her office at five, Sherman Granger phoned. "Hi, Katie. Just calling to let you know I finally got that letter mailed to Mr. Worthington. Thanks again for all your help."

"You're very welcome. Hold on a second." Katie moved around her desk and closed her office door. She said, "Sherman, I wanted to make sure you got that message I left for you." Sherman was silent. "You know, about not telling Mike Weston that I was helping you? I left a message on your recorder on Monday evening."

"Oh, yes." He cleared his throat. "You know, Katie, I don't think you need to worry about Mike. He's a blowhard at times but he's usually pretty discreet."

Katie's heart sank. His words meant just one thing to her. He'd already told Mike. His next words confirmed her fears. "Fact is, I may have... well, I already have said something to him. It was one day when he was complaining about the people at your head office; how they spend all their time trying to think of how to mess up division operations. Anyway, I felt I should put in a plug for you, tell him how helpful you've been."

Katie groaned. "Oh, Sherman."

"If you want, I can call and ask him to keep quiet but, to be honest, that might make things worse. The way he is, he's probably forgotten I said anything in the first place. If I bring it up, it'll just remind him."

Katie was surprised at the sudden rush of anger she felt, more toward herself than at Sherman. She should have sworn him to secrecy before ever agreeing to help him with his letter. It didn't improve her mood when Sherman asked, "Does it really matter that much?"

What he didn't realize, of course, was that she was in jeopardy because she had deliberately disobeyed both her former manager and her current one. Guilty of insubordination. Sherman wasn't responsible for this but damn him anyway. Damn all men.

She snapped, "Actually, it does. But I guess it's no use fretting over spilled milk."

"Gee, Katie, I'm real sorry. I had no idea it was that important."

"Yes, well, I have to go. Good luck with the letter." She put the phone down before he could say more.

She rode her wave of anger for all of ten minutes, after which she was filled with remorse for acting like a shrew. Sherman was always so gentle and gentlemanly. He'd thought he was helping her by saying nice things about her. And now in her guilt-induced eagerness to make it up to him, she'd likely end up doing even more career-limiting things on his behalf.

25.

A Family Visit

DAN ANNOUNCED, "It's gonna be hot and windy in the Valley." It was nine o'clock on Sunday morning and they were driving along the freeway on their way to Merced.

Katie asked, "So what are the plans for today?"

"We'll pick up Danny, get some lunch. Then we'll go to the park or someplace for a coupla hours. I usually get him home by three or so. That's a plenty long enough day for both of us."

Neither of them spoke much over the next few miles. When they reached the Altamont Pass, Katie was fascinated, as always, by the strange landscape—rolling bald hills covered with multitudes of windmills, their blades spinning furiously in the hot winds.

"This place is so eerie, "she exclaimed. "Don't those things look like alien creatures that might march down at any minute and swallow us up?"

Dan's flat, "Mmm," stemmed any further fanciful outpouring on Katie's part. She glanced at him. He seemed to be in some faraway place beyond the reach of small talk. She was caught off guard by his next question. "This inventor friend of yours. What's his story?"

Katie wasn't comfortable being reminded of Sherman. Poor Sherman was probably still wondering why she'd been so irritable with him. And, given the confrontational tone of her last conversation with Dan on this subject, she was surprised he'd want to talk about it.

"Sherman Granger? Now where should I start? Well, I was introduced to Sherman the first time I visited RPC's Beresford office."

Dan seemed excited. "No kiddin', Beresford? We'll be passing close to there on the highway today."

"Yes, I know. Sherman has an office in town but he lives in some small place outside town. Anyway, the day I met him I'd just had a really tiresome meeting with the division manager at Beresford."

Katie almost forgot about her listener as she became immersed in her reminiscences about Mike Weston and his boorish management team and what a gentleman Sherman had seemed in contrast to Mike and his goons.

Dan listened intently, but when Katie said, "Well, that's about it really," he glanced at her in surprise.

"But what about the invention? You said it's a small cogenerator unit. Is it hooked up to an existing power source? How can he make such a small unit cost-effective?"

Katie chuckled at his accusatory tone. "Dan, there's no way I can answer questions like that. I haven't a clue about the technical details. I've never even seen one of these units."

Dan gasped. "You gotta be kidding. If you don't know how the thing works, how can you help him sell it to your company?"

Katie sighed and twisted her body away from him to look out the side window. It was a fair question but it annoyed her just the same. Once again, the subject of Sherman was putting her at odds with Dan.

After a moment, he said in a more conciliatory voice, "Sorry. I guess women aren't much interested in stuff like that. But, like I told you before, one day I'd like to have my own shop making machines and things. I got a lot of mechanical experience that'd come in handy."

"I thought you were an electrician."

"Yeah, that too. Anyway, that's what I'm aiming for. A proper business. Not all this odd job stuff."

"Yes, I remember you said that before." Katie spoke without enthusiasm.

He said, "I bet you're thinkin' I could never find the money to get going. But, see, I wouldn't need much money. My brother-in-law—my ex-brother-in-law, that is—runs a big machine shop near Merced. It has all kinds of equipment: mills, lathes, saws, grinders. Everything you can think of. He told me if I ever wanted to get started on my own business, he'd let me use his place, rent-free, nights and weekends when he isn't using it."

"That's nice."

"Yeah, he's a real nice guy. Bin real good to me. All's I need to do is find something to make. Some great product people would want to buy." Then Dan surprised her a second time by saying, "You know all about business. Do you have any advice for guys like me?"

She was moved by the request. She said gently, "I really don't know much about starting a business from scratch. At RPC, I work with top management to help them with organizing their operations. At least, that's what I used to do. I'm not sure what my new boss has in mind for me."

"Things a bit rocky right now, huh?" He added, earnestly, "You know, Katie, some day, if I can get a proper business going like I was talking about, you could maybe come work for me."

"Mmm, thanks for the offer. Unfortunately, I can't imagine being much good at operating a lathe..." Then, she couldn't hold in the laughter any longer.

To her relief, he chuckled too. "Pretty wild idea, huh?" He added in his down-home ingenuous way, "But nice to think about. I like being around you."

When she recovered her breath, Katie managed a weak, "I like being around you too."

When they reached the outskirts of Merced, Dan turned off the freeway onto a city street, and, a few minutes later, into a suburban housing tract. Katie surveyed the passing homes. The developers had tried, but not succeeded, to lessen the stamp of uniformity by varying the colors and styles of the houses. God, she thought, how she would hate to live here.

After some weaving and turning, Dan pulled into a cul-de-sac and stopped in front of a pink split-level house. There were two cars parked in the driveway. A small boy who had been sitting on the ground near the street climbed to his feet as they approached and ran toward the passenger side of the car. Dan wound down the window and called out, "Danny, get in back today."

The boy stopped by Katie's window and stared in at her. He was thin, blond, and dressed in a blue and white checkered shirt and blue jeans. His resentful expression made it plain he hoped he hadn't heard correctly. Dan repeated, "The back, I told you."

With reluctance, Danny opened the rear door and climbed in. Katie felt like an interloper. Obviously, she was occupying his customary seat. She twisted around and said in her friendliest voice, "Hi, Danny."

He looked like his father, as she'd always imagined, with the same bright blue eyes. He returned Katie's greeting with an indifferent, "Hi." As he struggled to buckle himself into the seat belt, he complained, "I'm not used to the belts in the back here."

Dan winked at Katie as he pulled away from the curb. "That's life, kid. One danged challenge after another."

Katie smiled but she couldn't help feeling sorry for the displaced person in the back.

DANNY'S RESENTMENT toward Katie was short-lived. In fact, during the next few hours she mentally declared him to be a lovable, well-mannered child. They took him for lunch—hamburgers and shakes, to Katie's guilty delight—and then to the zoo.

Afterward, they stopped for gas. While Dan pumped gas, Danny leaned over the seat and chatted with Katie. He informed her, "Auntie Jen and Uncle Cliff are visiting us today. After I get home, we're all going bowling."

"Do you like bowling?"

"Yeah. I'm aiming to get real good at it. Just like my dad; he's a champion bowler."

"Is he really?" Katie grinned. "I didn't know that." She ducked her head to look at Dan as he stood with his back to them, watching the gauge at the pump.

"Oh, yeah," her informant enthused. "He got a silver cup for being top bowler in the whole league."

"For heaven's sake." So Dan had hidden talents. Bowling indeed!

When they arrived back at Danny's home, Danny leaped out of the car without even a goodbye to Katie. But he called to Dan, "You wanna come say hi to everyone?"

"Sure, why not?" Dan raised his eyebrows at Katie who shook her head. Meeting Josie and the new husband would have been bad enough, but having to meet Auntie Jen and Uncle Whatever as well was more than she was prepared to deal with right now. Father and son tromped up the driveway toward the house. The front door opened before they got there and a young woman stepped out. She put out her arms to little Danny. Katie felt a pang of envy watching the affectionate hug that followed.

Dan's ex-wife was several months pregnant. She seemed very young, no more than her mid-twenties. She smiled at Dan who leaned forward over his son's head to kiss her cheek. They chatted in an animated, friendly fashion for a few minutes.

When Dan came back down the driveway, he looked cheerful. He climbed into the car. "Josie wondered if you'd like to come in, but I didn't think you'd be interested. You know, with the company and all."

Katie nodded. He'd got that right.

As they drove back to the highway, Katie kicked off her sandals and relaxed back into the seat. She said, "So Josie's expecting? How will Danny take to that?"

"Same way he took to the others, I guess. They have two other kids." He fiddled with the radio as he spoke.

"Really?" Katie said, "By the way, I enjoyed meeting your son. Oh, and I learned something about you I didn't know before." She smiled mischievously.

He said sharply, "What?"

"That you're apparently the world's championship bowler."

"*Bowler?*"

" Well, that's what your son thinks anyway."

"Oh." Dan's expression cleared. "He wasn't talking about me. He was talking about Bill, his stepfather."

"That's funny. Why did I think he meant you? Oh, I remember, he said, 'My Dad is a championship bowler.'"

"Yeah, well, he thinks Bill is his Dad. Which he is really. Bill adopted him when they got married. Danny hasn't seen much of me since he was a baby."

"I thought you said you visited him every month."

"Yeah, well, I haven't always done that." Abruptly, he changed the subject. "It's not four o'clock yet. How about we take the back roads home? Like I was telling you, it's much prettier."

"Sounds great."

Some ten minutes later, they found the back road Dan had been seeking. The scenery was certainly more varied than on the main highway. They passed a rag-tag mix of properties: a farm machinery repair shop, a dog-boarding facility, parched-looking feed lots with cattle standing around.

After a while, Katie asked, "If Danny doesn't know you're his father, who does he think you are?"

"Ha. Good question. A family friend, I guess." After a pause, he added, "We'll get around to telling him when he's older. But while he's little, it seems best to keep him in the dark. This way, he thinks he's a regular kid with a regular mother and father, just like his sisters."

Noble intentions indeed, Katie thought, but were she in his shoes she'd have been devastated for her only child not to know she was his parent. She wondered if she knew him well enough to ask what was uppermost in her mind. "Dan, why did you and Josie divorce?"

"Because she met someone else."

"You mean *she* wanted the divorce?"

A mirthless chuckle from Dan. "Why does that sound funny? You think it's always the guy who wants out of a marriage?"

"Of course not." Without thinking, she added, "But I couldn't imagine any woman giving up a guy like you."

Dan gave her a thoughtful look. Maybe, Katie thought, he took that for sarcasm or maybe he was shocked at such a forthright statement. He asked, "What's so special about a guy like me?"

Katie felt her face getting warm. "Well, you are incredibly good-looking, you know. Or hasn't anyone ever told you that?"

Dan said seriously, "But that's not enough to make a good marriage, is it?" He was right, of course. Being young and handsome and sexy was good enough for someone to play around with. But marriage was something else.

Dan said, "For one thing, I wasn't too good a provider. Bill has his own business. He's really made a go of things. Josie and Danny live a pretty good life."

Engrossed in their conversation, Katie almost missed the signpost that flashed past them. *Pine Flats 2 mi.* The arrow pointed to the right. The name was naggingly familiar. Then she remembered where she'd seen it.

"Are we near Beresford here?" She asked Dan.

"Pretty close. It's about five miles off to the right on the main highway."

"How about that? Pine Flats is where Sherman Granger lives. You know, the inventor I was telling...*Whoa!*" She grabbed the armrest as Dan veered off onto the shoulder and squealed to a stop.

He turned to her. "Let's stop in and say hi. We have time."

"Good heavens, no. I wouldn't dream of calling on someone uninvited. I don't even remember his address. Besides..." She grimaced, "...when we last spoke on Friday, I cut him off rather rudely."

Dan was undeterred. "Even more reason to stop and be sociable. We can call ahead if it makes you feel better. I went through Pine Flats one time. There's a crossroads with a store. They must have a phone."

Having seemingly persuaded himself he had settled all objections to his proposal, Dan checked to see the road was clear and made a U-turn to return to the signpost.

Agitated, Katie squirmed, muttering, "I just don't believe this."

Dan continued moving forward. He said, "Look, I'm real curious to meet this guy. I'd really like to find out more about his invention."

"That's not the point. It's not a case of what you want. It's a Sunday afternoon. Most people would just as soon not have their private family time interrupted by uninvited guests."

Dan said airily, "You're talking 'bout city folks. Country folks call on each other all the time. I know. I was raised in the country."

Katie sighed. It seemed that, short of wrenching the wheel from his hands, she couldn't stop him from taking them to Pine Flats.

A few minutes later, they drove into Pine Flats. *Population 250*, as the signpost informed them. There was a small grocery store near the crossroads with a pay phone inside. Katie found Sherman's number in the directory and dialed. After four rings, the answering machine clicked on. *"This is Sherman Granger. I'm sorry I missed your call."* Relieved, Katie hung up without leaving a message. She walked over to where Dan stood chatting to the woman behind the counter. "He's not in," she said. But, while she'd been dialing, the woman, who apparently knew Sherman, had told Dan how to get to the Grangers'.

"Barely a mile down that street there," she said, pointing.

Dan said, "Great. We'll just drive by."

In spite of her annoyance at Dan's pushiness, Katie was curious, wondering what sort of a home Sherman had. As they drove, she joined Dan in checking the numbers on the rural mailboxes.

Then, Dan said, "This is it." He stopped in front of a small clapboard house, lodged between two parcels of weed-strewn vacant land. The wood siding on the house was so badly in need of painting it was hard to determine what its original color had been. An unpaved driveway ran alongside a close-cropped brown lawn in front of the house to a ramshackle garage.

For a time, they peered at the house through the car windows. Dan said, sounding sad, "Inventing don't pay that much, I guess."

"Oh, look, Dan." A car coming down the road toward them signaled and turned into the entrance of Sherman's driveway. The driver stopped and got out of the car. It was Sherman.

Katie's first thought was to scrunch down onto the floor and ask Dan to drive away as fast as he could. But Sherman's car was partially blocking their way and now Sherman walked over to them, staring and frowning as he tried to see who they were. Dan leaned out his open window and called out a cheerful, "How ya doin'?"

Sherman reached their car and looked in through the window. "Katie?" he said. "What on earth are you doing here?"

26

Barry and Lila Reminisce

THAT SAME SUNDAY afternoon, Barry Bryce was taking part in a twice-annual domestic ritual in his San Francisco home: watching his wife try on new clothes.

When it came to advising clients on investment strategy, Lila was enthusiastic and sure-footed. But when it came to selecting a wardrobe for herself, she tended to be apathetic and wavering. Barry enjoyed looking at women's clothes, and he seldom shrank from making a decision about clothes or anything else.

Thus, twice a year, when the spring and fall fashions came out, Lila would bring home an armful of outfits on approval from various women's clothing stores in the city. She would then model them for Barry, as she was doing now, and he would help her decide what to keep and what to reject.

Sitting in the wingback chair by the window, Barry watched Lila pulling on the skirt and jacket of a soft woolen suit. He stretched his legs. "Another suit? Don't you have enough already?"

"This is the last one. It comes in gray and olive. Which do you think I should get?" She pointed down at the gray skirt she was modeling and held up an identical skirt in olive-green.

Barry wrinkled his brow as he concentrated. Like most of the other things Lila had tried on today, these suits were tasteful and quiet. And boring. But somehow appropriate for someone in Lila's position. "Get the olive," he said and stood up. "Look, we seem to have been at this for hours. It's too nice a day to be stuck indoors. Let's go for a walk."

Lila continued to look into the mirror, comparing the olive suit with the gray. It struck Barry his tone of voice may have sounded more abrupt than he'd intended. To reassure her, he walked up behind her and lightly rubbed his head against her hair. Catching his eye in the mirror, Lila's lips curved upwards in a smile and her eyes sparkled.

"You know what I was thinking of, Barry? The day we snuck out of that dreary seminar and went wandering around Macy's. The fashion show, remember?"

"The day we met?" He was surprised at her nostalgic outburst.

"Yes, and some model was wearing a flashy metallic dress and you told me I'd look great in that and I disagreed."

"And you told me how you hated buying clothes."

"And then..." Lila looked up at him over her shoulder, the laughter still in her face, "...you said, 'Why don't you let me dress you from now on? From the skin out.'" She chuckled. "This from someone I'd met for the first time only a few hours before. I was shocked."

Barry kissed her on the cheek. "The hell you say. You were thrilled to the core." She didn't deny it.

BARRY COULDN'T REMEMBER what that long-ago seminar was about or why he'd gone to it in the first place. But he remembered that fifteen minutes after the lecture started, a petite blonde latecomer struggled over his feet and slid into the seat next to him. She'd whispered an apology for disturbing him. He'd looked at her, she'd smiled at him, and he was smitten.

The seminar had indeed been dreary. The speakers droned in monotones, and the room was hot. Barry had helped to speed the endless morning along by whispering wisecracks to the lady by his side. She had, in turn, snickered her appreciation. When the noon break arrived, he had lost no time getting the two of them out of the hotel ballroom "for some cool fresh air." They merged into the lunchtime crowds in Union Square and later, when the February day made them shiver, slipped into Macy's "for some stale warm air." They'd played hooky at a fashion show for the rest of the afternoon.

In the ensuing weeks, Barry had discovered that underlying Lila's friendly smile and ladylike demeanor was a passionate nature, a keen intellect, and a drive to succeed that matched his own. She was, in other words, the perfect partner for him.

Now he slid his arms around Lila's waist and with one hand smoothed the soft gray skirt over her stomach.

Lila said, "Barry, do you think I'm too thin?"

He looked at her reflection and wondered how to respond. He did, in fact, think she was too thin, but that wasn't the worst of it. It was her paleness that seemed to age her. The almost translucent lightness of her complexion that had once made her look delicate and appealing now made her look anemic. He said, "Tell me again, why are you so determined to stay out of the sun these days?"

Lila sighed. "Because of those anti-wrinkle treatments I'm taking at the dermatologist's. It makes me more sensitive to skin cancer."

"Oh, right."

She pouted. "And don't tell me—yet again—you'd rather see a wrinkled brown face than a smooth white one."

"Okay, I won't."

His laugh was insincere because there was something that had been bothering Barry lately about Lila. It had come over him with a vengeance the other night at the symphony.

He and Lila had gone with the Worthingtons to a Midsummer Mozart concert. At the intermission, Barry had sensed someone watching him and had turned to see Terry Lynch from the office on the other side of the lobby. Terry had swung away quickly to avoid meeting his eye but Barry thought he could feel him looking over again later. Most likely, at Lila.

Lila had always looked young for her age but now that she was approaching fifty, this was no longer the case. Although Barry felt guilty about it, he was a bit self-conscious these days about having a wife who looked so much older than he. Sometimes, he was even fearful that one day he might be tempted to forsake her.

They left the house a short time later, Lila swathed in sun cream, sunglasses and a broad-brimmed hat. She said, "No huffing and puffing up hills for me. How about we just stroll over to the park?" She was referring to the eucalyptus grove three level blocks from their home. It was a pleasant, physically unchallenging walk.

Barry glanced at Lila as they walked. Things had been difficult for her at her firm this year. Some anticipated business had not materialized and Lila had been at odds with the senior partner who wanted to bring his nephew into the firm "to breathe new life into us," a move Lila opposed. On a couple of occasions, she'd left work early because, she said, the stress had made her ill. It was no wonder she was looking haggard.

He said, "You know what we both need? A vacation. We haven't had one in—what is it?—three years. Let's just do it."

"Barry, you've just started a new job and already you want a vacation."

"That's right," Barry retorted. "It's because of this blasted job that I need a vacation." He reminded himself he had to stop complaining to Lila about the job he was supposed to be thankful for getting. He went on quickly, "No, seriously, over the next few weeks there'll be some dreary business with next year's budget and this year's performance reviews, but, come November, I can take a break."

He lifted Lila's hand to help her over a tree root pushing up the paving. "Why don't we go to Italy," he said. "Lake Como?"

They had honeymooned at Lake Como. The very words evoked hazy summer skies with puffy white clouds, picturesque villas, lazy breakfasts at the water's edge.

Lila said, "Are you kidding? In November? We'd be

rained out."

"You're probably right. How about Hawaii? Or Mexico?"

Lila said firmly, "No, Barry, I can't take any time off for a while. There's this brouhaha going on about the new partner. I have to stick around till that gets resolved."

"Look, Lila, surely there's no way the firm could take on a new partner without your approval. Isn't that in your partnership agreement?"

Lila shook her head. "You have no idea what it's like to be a lone woman trying to stand her ground with a couple of male colleagues."

They had reached the eucalyptus grove and Lila lifted her head as though to drink in the sight of the trees. "I just love these beautiful trees." She sniffed the air as she spoke. "We must take a trip to Australia when we have the time."

Barry scowled. "Which means never, I suppose."

Lila broke into reminiscences about a travel program she'd lately seen on TV about Australia. Barry looked down at his feet and grumbled to himself that sometimes Lila was just asking to be forsaken.

27.

Sherman and Dan Hit It Off

IT WAS EVIDENT that Sherman was far from annoyed to see Katie outside his house. After his initial exclamation of surprise, his homely face lit up with pleasure. Katie explained, "Sherman, we were just driving by. Er, this is a friend of mine, Dan Erickson. And, Dan, this is..."

But while she'd been talking, Dan had leapt out of the car. He now extended his hand across the hood. "Hey, Sherman, Katie's told me so much about this generator you've invented. Sure would like to find out more about it."

Sherman's smile grew even more welcoming. "That's great. It so happens I have a demo unit installed in my house. Would you like to come see?"

Dan needed no further urging. He hurried around the car to join Sherman and the two men walked down the driveway and around to the back of the garage. After a moment, Katie reluctantly left the air-conditioned coolness of the car and followed them.

The men stopped in front of a gray metal box, about the size of a house furnace, which was stationed in a sort of closet abutting the garage. This was, presumably, the famed portable cogenerator unit. Sherman pulled open the metal front of the box and started on a description of the contraption.

There was no shade. Almost immediately, Katie felt her sweat-soaked blouse and cotton skirt sticking to her. But the two men seemed too engrossed—Sherman in talking and Dan in listening—to be concerned about the temperature. Soon, Katie could take it no longer. "I'm sorry, Sherman, but I'm about to collapse. I'm just not used to this heat."

Two pairs of eyes turned to her. Sherman apologized. "I'm afraid I get carried away once I get onto this subject. Let's go in the house and have something cold to drink." Dan made a mutter of disappointment and Sherman assured him, "I have all the specs and blueprints inside. We can take a look at those while we cool off."

The interior of the house was a somber contrast to the glaring brightness outside. Window blinds and curtains were closed against the heat and Katie struggled to adjust her eyes to the gloom. From the kitchen fridge, Sherman got them each a can of Budweiser—and, after a moment's reflection, a glass for Katie. "So where are the drawings?" Dan asked.

Sherman went to a closet and pulled out several accordion folders of papers and an easel-sized cardboard case containing blueprints and carried them all to the dining table.

Katie headed for the couch in the living room and sank into it. It was soft but decrepit in appearance, like— she observed—the rest of the house.

For the next hour or so, Sherman spread out one set of materials after another on the dining table, giving detailed explanations to Dan. Dan frowned in concentration as he listened, occasionally tossing out a terse question or comment. Katie listened to him with some amusement. Dan was acting, she thought, for all the world like an auditor examining a tax return.

During one of Dan's silent spells of concentration, Sherman turned to Katie. He asked, "Have you heard anything yet about my letter?" She shook her head. Sherman explained to Dan, "I wrote to RPC's CEO. Gave him a sales pitch on my unit. Katie here sure was helpful in putting that letter together."

Katie took a breath. Sherman, she thought, just couldn't get it into his head how much she didn't want anyone to know about her involvement. Dan dragged his eyes away from the blueprint in front of him. "You're telling me RPC is considering buying these things offa you?"

Sherman said, "I'd like that but I don't have the wherewithal to set up a manufacturing operation. What I'm really hoping is that they'll be willing to bankroll me."

Dan glanced at Katie and back at Sherman. He asked, "Why'd they want to do that? More like, they'll steal your patent and make the things themselves. That is, if they even want 'em."

Alarmed, Katie sat forward, trying to catch Dan's eye. She knew his words were playing right into one of Sherman's deepest fears. Dan went on, not looking at her, "I mean, why would that company be interested in somethin' that reduces the amount of electricity they sell? Seems to me like they'd do their best to make sure you never got going."

Sherman's face turned red. His shoulders slumped. Katie longed to interrupt but couldn't think what to say. Only Dan seemed at ease. He took a mouthful of beer and in a cheerful, avuncular voice told Sherman, "Now, Sherm, if I was in your place, this is what I'd do." And he proceeded to speak.

In spite of herself, while Dan talked, Katie felt as mesmerized as Sherman appeared to be.

"First off," Dan said, "you got a great contraption here. I can't pretend to follow all the ins and outs just yet but one thing I gotta tell you is..." His hands chopped the air in emphasis. "...don't let go control of it. 'Specially not to one of them big companies with all them fancy lawyers and such. If they want it, they'll steal it or tie it up in legal stuff so's you can never use it."

Sherman leaned forward, his hands on his knees. "So what do I do?"

Katie found her eyes swinging from Sherman to Dan. Dan said, "Make the things yourself. Find other markets for them. Don't sell yourself short dickering around with a regional outfit like RPC. Think the whole country. Think the whole world. You gotta think big, Sherm."

Katie couldn't help but feel a kind of stunned admiration. Dan's pitch was so smooth. The words rolled out of him as though he'd been reading from a script. Of course, everything he'd said was just impractical meandering from a dreamer who'd never had to face a real-life situation of the kind he was fantasizing.

Sherman was silent for a time. Then, he said, "Dan, I know you're right. But you know what they say. You gotta have money to make money and I don't have a dime." His eyes wandered around the room. "Even this house I don't own. Some years back, I mortgaged it to the hilt to finance one of my business ventures. I lost every penny. Now I rent it back from the property company. Even my sales job with Sierra Enterprises isn't bringing in much these days."

He hesitated and then continued in the same flat voice. "There is one good thing that came up the other day. My son-in-law, George, reckons he can get me a job in his company's Beresford branch. It pays good money. Even has medical benefits. If I take him up on this offer, I should be able to save a tidy sum in a couple of years. Then, who knows?"

Katie exclaimed, "Why, that's wonderful, Sherman."

But Sherman was watching for Dan's reaction. Dan shook his head. "That's no good. Who knows what'll happen in a coupla years? You gotta strike while the iron is hot."

At this moment, the phone rang. "Hi, honey," Sherman said into the phone.

From where she sat, Katie could hear the voice on the other end of the line. "Dad, what are you doing?"

There followed some mumbled conversation from Sherman. After he hung up, he explained. "My daughter. I was supposed to be at their house for dinner at five o'clock."

Katie glanced at the clock. It was almost six. She scrambled to her feet. "I'm so sorry. We've taken up far too much of your time."

"No, that's okay." Sherman said. He turned to Dan as they all stood. "Dan, it's been a real pleasure. Let me find you a business card." As the two men exchanged cards and made promises to keep in touch, Katie thought back to the misgivings she'd had earlier that afternoon about calling on Sherman. Those particular misgivings had turned out to be unfounded, but they had been replaced by other, more worrisome ones.

DAN LOOKED PLEASED with himself as they drove away from Sherman's house. He said, "Well, me and Sherm sure got along okay."

"Mmm."

"Me and him'd make great partners. I didn't have a chance to get into details about my brother-in-law's offer." He glanced at Katie, blue eyes sparkling. "About using his machine shop, remember? But I'll be talking again with Sherm real soon."

Katie wrestled with her emotions. She was dismayed at the way Dan was getting Sherman worked up. He was acting as though he were in a position to offer material help to Sherman, which she knew not to be the case. Also, even more worrying, Sherman might think that Katie was personally vouching for Dan.

She said quietly, "You know, Dan, it's important not to get Sherman's hopes up too much. He's a bit of a dreamer. This job with his son-in-law sounds like a really good deal for him. It's not fair to try to talk him out of it."

Dan reacted with one of the flare-ups Katie was beginning to realize was a part of his nature. He said, "What do you know about people having dreams? You and your college degree! You think Sherman *wants* this job with his son-in-law? Didn't you see his face when he was talking about it?"

"Well, yes, he did seem ambivalent. But, even so, he must find a way to get money. He can't do anything without it."

Dan gave a cluck of disgust. "You're always talking money. Money isn't everything. Having a good product is even more important. Sherman has a great product. And I know enough about machinery to help him build it."

Katie felt more worried than ever.

As they continued their drive home, Dan looked sullen. He didn't even suggest they stop off somewhere to eat. Katie told herself to be sensible about this downturn in their relationship. She reminded herself that he was just a short-term fling. There were so many things about him she couldn't stand. His arrogant know-it-all fits, his bad grammar, his.... *Oh, what did it matter anyway?*

Her eyes fell on his hands on the wheel. Square, tanned, with tiny gold hairs on the backs of the fingers. Suddenly, she longed to touch him. Any part of him. Hands, arm, face. She knew full well that her sole reason for coming today was the thought of the day's end.

She had played it over in her mind more than once—the time when the two of them would pull into her driveway after a long day spent together. She would invite him in for coffee. He would smile in that tender, half-amused way of his as he accepted the invitation. As for what might come next—her mind was an erotic jumble of indistinct thoughts about the feel of him against her, his soft mouth. She rested a hand on her stomach. It felt hollow in there. Because now nothing was going to happen. All because of Sherman.

It was almost eight when they arrived at Katie's house. Dan switched off the ignition and looked at her. There was an awkward pause before she said, "Well, Dan, thanks for taking me with you today. It... it was quite a day. I enjoyed myself."

Dan gave a snort of disbelief and she added, "Well, most of it anyway. Until we got into this sort of squabble over Sherman."

He looked away from her and lightly tapped his hands on the wheel. She said, "I didn't mean to sound so negative about everything. I know Sherman has a great invention and I understand how much you want to help. It's just that...." Her voice trailed off.

Dan said, "You really care about Sherman, don't you?"

Katie stared at him in surprise. He said, "I don't mean you have the hots for him. I mean, you really care about what happens to him."

"Yes, I do. He's such a sweet guy." She added, "Part of it is he reminds me of my father. Dad wasn't an inventor but he was full of bright ideas that none of us took seriously. I felt so guilty after he died that we'd never appreciated him enough."

Immediately, she felt embarrassed at her confession. She picked up her purse and draped her sweater over her arm. As she opened the car door, she waved the sweater at Dan. "Can you imagine—I took this with me today!" Her laugh stuck in her throat.

He got out of the car too and followed her up the steps to the front door. She turned to him after unlocking the door. He was standing very close, their faces almost touching.

He said, "Katie, you still have the hots for me, don't you?"

Her heart leapt. Maybe it wasn't the end after all. It seemed their tussle over Sherman had created a dilemma for Dan also. Maybe he too had been looking forward to some kind of payoff tonight. And, in typical male fashion, he was determined not to let a silly disagreement over principles keep him from getting what he wanted.

Katie resolved to play it cool. Looking him steadily in the eye and with a more or less straight face, asked, "What makes you think I ever had the hots for you?"

But he started laughing after the first four words and the laughter spilled out of her too before she'd finished the question. He stepped in through the door right after her and his arms closed around her. As his mouth pressed down on hers, she reached out behind his back to push the door closed.

28

Bad News for Sherman

A MONTH LATER—a hot Monday in the middle of August—it was a day of gloom for Sherman. The misery began the moment he arrived at his office and found a letter in the mail with the *Redwood Power Corporation* logo. His heart leapt with twin feelings of hope and impending doom. He delayed opening the letter, taking as long as possible to remove his jacket and settle himself at his desk.

> *Dear Mr. Granger:*
> *Thank you for your letter of July 14 describing the portable cogenerator unit you have recently patented. After careful consideration, we have decided our company has no interest in accepting your business offer.*
> *We appreciate your thinking of Redwood Power Corporation and wish you luck in pursuing your endeavors.*
> *Yours truly,*
> *Everett Worthington, Chief Executive Officer*

Sherman felt as though he'd been punched in the stomach. Then, right on the heels of disappointment, there was anger. *Careful consideration*, baloney! This brush-off had most likely been written by some lackey who hadn't even bothered to read Sherman's letter.

Sherman's next thought was to wonder whether Katie knew about this. Although he was reluctant to acknowledge it, he was aware that a part of his anger was directed at her. How could she have so badly misjudged the reaction of people in her own company?

Hands shaking, he walked over to the coffee-maker in the corner of the room. It was unfair to blame Katie. Both he and she had allowed their judgment to be clouded. Only Dan had seen the truth—that the odds of RPC's being interested were zero.

After getting the coffee started, Sherman sat down at his desk with his card file. Today would be another day on the phone trying to drum up sales for Sierra's products. Sales the past month were the most dismal in what had been an all-round poor year. Suddenly, he was gripped with a depression so paralyzing he was unable to move. He desperately longed for someone to boost his confidence.

He thought of Dan.

Since their meeting last month, Dan had phoned him a couple of times. "To keep in touch," he'd said but also, Sherman suspected, to prod Sherman into getting moving on the cogen unit.

Sherman recognized that Dan's optimism came from the naiveté of the innocent more than from a realistic understanding of the situation. Nevertheless, the younger man's energy and enthusiasm were infectious. A conversation with Dan left Sherman feeling twenty years younger.

But Sherman knew he couldn't reach Dan in the middle of a workday so instead he called his friend, Mike Weston. As usual, Mike was too busy "fighting fires" to talk for long but he offered to take Sherman to lunch to cheer him up. They agreed to meet at noon at the Golden Nugget.

Before tackling the depressing card file, Sherman decided to make one more call. He looked up Katie's number.

SHORTLY AFTER she had arrived at work that morning, Katie had also received an unexpected message. Barry's secretary had phoned. "Katie, great news!"

"What's that?"

"Well, Barry was scheduled to be in a budget meeting all day Thursday but it's been postponed. And, according to my notes, you are due to make a field visit on Thursday to present employee survey results. Remember, Barry wanted to come with you on one of those visits? So now he's free to go with you on Thursday."

Katie's heart sank.

Then, she consulted her own schedule and saw a way out. "Dorothy, you know what? The place I was scheduled to visit on Thursday is Beresford Division. That's one place I don't ever want to see again. Remember, my meeting with those people last February was a real fiasco? So I've asked Terry to take my place."

Dorothy was the most deferential of secretaries so Katie was surprised at her firm response. "No, Katie, you'll have to go yourself. It's been so hard scheduling Barry for one of these trips. Anyway, I've already told him. If you back down, he'll think you're just trying to avoid having him accompany you."

Katie strangled a laugh, but Dorothy continued in a no-nonsense voice. "I'll call the travel office and ask them to make plane reservations for both of you."

Katie was still trying to come to terms with this development when Sherman phoned. She was sad, though not surprised, at hearing his news. She said, "I'm so sorry, Sherman."

Sherman said bitterly, "I guess Dan was right all along when he said there was no way a company like yours could possibly be interested."

Katie tried not to sound defensive, "Well, it was worth a shot. The letter, I mean. It's not as though Dan had anything better to suggest."

"I guess not." He added, "Please don't think I'm blaming you, Katie. You did your best and I'm grateful."

His words stung her like a slap in the face because his tone seemed to imply the opposite of what he was saying. Funny, she thought, any time Sherman came into the picture, he introduced a sour note into her relationship with Dan. Which, since the night Dan first slept over, had been proceeding extremely well.

THE SECOND PIECE of misery in Sherman's day arrived that afternoon, also via the U.S. Postal Service.

Sherman had just returned from lunch with Mike, a meal that had alleviated his hunger, if not his dejection. Although Mike had expressed gratifying indignation at RPC's shortsightedness, he had annoyed Sherman by attacking Katie. "It's terrible the way that woman let you down—raising your hopes, making you think she could help you."

Sherman defended Katie fiercely. Perhaps especially fiercely because he was trying to drown his own doubts about her contribution. "Mike, you're quite wrong. She worked hard to find people to help me. And there was all the time she spent on that letter to the CEO. Remember I told you—she basically wrote the thing."

"Hmm." Mike said.

Mentally, Sherman kicked himself, remembering that Katie didn't want Mike to know about her help. He walked back to his office feeling he would have been better off to have eaten a solo sandwich at his desk that day.

And then he saw the afternoon mail, lying on the floor, with a letter from Sierra Enterprises on top of the pile. Now what was this? He wasn't expecting any written communication from Sierra. He opened the letter with a heavy heart thinking it might be a reprimand because of his poor sales performance.

It wasn't a reprimand. It was much worse than that.

Without preamble, the letter stated the company had decided to combine Sherman's sales region with the adjoining Sacramento region. "We have decided," the letter went on, "that the combined territories would best be handled out of Sacramento. Therefore, we regret to inform you we will have no further need for your services as of the end of the month."

The letter concluded, "At your earliest convenience, we would appreciate your calling at head office in San Francisco to settle up accounts."

Sherman slumped back in his chair. That final request was an added kick in the head. Because "to settle up accounts," as Sherman well understood, meant the company would be asking for repayment of advances he'd received that had not been covered by commissions earned. These would amount to a fair sum to be repaid with money he didn't have.

Sherman reread the letter. As he did so, an image of his son-in-law's smug face hovered in front of him. Now, Sherman thought despairingly, he really had no option whatever but to accept George's help. He felt sick.

Later that afternoon, Mike Weston phoned with a "by the way" piece of information. Katie and her boss, Barry Bryce, were planning to visit Beresford division on the coming Thursday. Mike joked, "Do you think I should bawl her out in front of her boss for making such a hash of things for you?" He laughed shamelessly at Sherman's whoop of protest and cried, "Kidding, kidding!"

Sherman hadn't intended to tell Mike yet about the letter from Sierra. Being fired for poor performance was such a shameful fate. But his longing to unburden his woes overcame him. "Guess what, Mike? I just got this letter from Sierra. They're terminating my services as of the end of the month."

Mike was silent for a few seconds. Then, he said, "My God, you poor guy, clobbered twice in one day. Aw, they're going to regret it, giving the ax to a really good guy like you. Wanna go for a drink after work?"

"No, I'll be okay. You know what they say, 'It's always darkest before dawn.'"

"Right. And there's that other old saying, 'when you hit bottom, there's nowhere to go but up.'" He gave a humorless guffaw, as did Sherman. In the past, the two of them had joked about the cold comfort in this particular platitude.

SHORTLY AFTER six o'clock that evening, Sherman was sitting in front of the TV with a can of Budweiser when the phone rang. It was Ellen. She sounded breathless. "Hi, Dad. Have you had dinner yet? George just brought home a big tub of Kentucky Fried. Why don't you come over and help us eat it?"

Sherman hesitated. He was surprised at the last-minute invitation, unusual for Ellen. He'd planned to spend the evening wallowing in gloom, but he felt hungry and all he had in the fridge was a half can of tuna and some bread. So he said, "Okay, honey. That'd be nice."

A short time later, as he drove over to Ellen and George's neat modern house in the Oaks Estates, he mentally kicked himself for accepting. Now there was no way he could postpone telling them his news. Was fried chicken really worth it?

As soon as George opened the door to him, Sherman suspected there was something up. George said politely, "Come on in, Sherm." Ellen set out the food and they all sat down to eat. Throughout the meal, his two hosts were uncharacteristically quiet. Ellen's constant chatter and George's customary smirking stories about the misfortunes of others were absent.

But, as Sherman slowly ate his chicken and mashed potatoes, he barely noticed the change in their demeanor. He was too busy mentally framing the humiliating news he would have to tell them.

Finally, Ellen cleared the table and set out dessert. "Ice cream. Cherries Jubilee." She smiled brightly at Sherman. "Your fave, Dad."

George said, "I'll get coffee."

After they finished dessert, Sherman cleared his throat. "You know, I had some bad news today." He stared fiercely down at his coffee. "In fact, two pieces of bad news. One from RPC and one from..." he swallowed. "...Sierra Enterprises."

There was silence and he willed himself to look up and meet Ellen's eyes. She reached out a hand and patted his arm. "We know, Dad. I found out by accident. I bumped into Mike Weston in the bank after work and we got to chatting."

So blabbermouth Mike had spilled the beans and that was the reason for Ellen's last-minute dinner invitation. She went on, "Don't get mad at Mike for telling us. Obviously, you were going to tell us anyhow."

Then George, speaking in a matter-of-fact voice, said, "All this must be very disappointing for you, Sherm. But you don't have to worry about the money side of things. That office manager position is still open and if you don't want that I'm sure we can fix you up with something else."

Sherman lowered his head into his hands and whispered, "Thank you." This was the moment of utter humiliation he'd so dreaded. But all he could feel right now was a sense of profound gratitude that brought tears to his eyes. Why, sometimes, even people like George could act human.

29

Lunch at the Eagle's Nest

BARRY SLAMMED DOWN the phone. "Dorothy," he called out. "Would you find Miranda and ask her to come see me? ASAP, please."

A few minutes later Miranda was at his door, a folder in her hands, her face bright. "You wanted to see me, Barry?"

"Come in. Close the door, would you?"

He watched her as she sashayed across the room toward him. She walked like a model on the runway, body thrust forward, hips shifting suggestively from side to side. She sat down and said happily, "I hope I can guess what this is about."

Barry cleared a space on the desk in front of him. "I doubt it."

"Not the department retreat?" She placed her folder on the desk. "Barry, the retreat is coming up next week. At least, it is if you ever get around to approving the hotel contract." She drew the contract out of the folder and waved it at him.

He grimaced. That retreat was far enough down on his list of priorities to be off the screen entirely. "I know. That's next on my list." He went on talking before she could remind him of how many times he'd said that. "No, I wanted to talk to you today about a call I just received from Joe Beretsky."

Joe Beretsky was Senior Vice President of Public Relations and a personal friend of Worthington's. There'd been complaints about slow service in PR, and Beretsky had asked for a staffing study in an attempt to justify adding to his headcount. With some misgivings, Barry had assigned the project to Miranda.

Miranda's face lit up. "Good old Joe! I did a study for them, remember?"

"I know. Apparently, good old Joe was not too happy about the results."

Miranda's smiling eyes searched his face. "You're kidding, aren't you?"

Barry smoothed out the yellow-lined sheet on which he'd written his notes from Beretsky's call. He said, "It seems that Joe and his managers have been discussing your report and have a hard time understanding how your findings were actually supported by the data."

"What's he talking about?" Miranda's indignation sounded genuine. "Barry, this was a good study. I did it just as we'd discussed ahead of time. The goal of the study was to find out how satisfied clients were with the services of the PR representatives. So I interviewed all those people: their clients, the PR managers, the reps."

"And you concluded?"

Miranda wrinkled her brow. "Let's see. The main finding was that all their clients were very happy with the service they were getting from PR."

Barry asked, "And nobody complained that the clients got very slow service. That there weren't enough reps to handle all the calls?"

"Oh." Miranda looked relieved. "Now I know what's going on. I bet Joe was mad because he had wanted me to say they were short-staffed so he could make a case for increasing his headcount. But, Barry, everyone is always trying to justify the need for more people. So I told him his people need better training."

"Training?"

She returned his surprised look with a steady gaze. "You know," she explained, "to teach them to do their work faster."

Barry shook his head. "Miranda, you know anything you report as a result of a study has to be backed up in some way. You can't just wing it. Did you present any figures showing how many people said what about what?

Any info on comparative staffing levels in other departments?"

She said quickly, "No. But it's all in my notes."

Barry sighed. Beretsky had asserted fiercely that their training program was the best in the company. Furthermore, he'd insisted that most of the people Miranda had interviewed had impressed upon her that shortage of staff was the main factor causing their slow customer service. Barry knew this didn't mean Miranda was wrong, but it did mean she'd have to produce evidence to back up her conclusions. Especially when dealing with a feisty Senior V.P. hot on the trail of additional headcount.

Barry said, "We've got to take him seriously, Miranda. He's a close friend of Everett's. So let's do this. Give me your interview notes and let me look them over." Miranda abruptly sat upright. Barry continued, "We have to present them so they back up what you're saying. Maybe you can get Katie to help."

He almost laughed aloud at Miranda's expression. She looked downright scared. He guessed that her interview notes, to the extent they even existed, were sparse and unintelligible.

Not for the first time, Barry reminded himself it wasn't Miranda's fault that she was on the payroll for the remainder of her one-year consulting contract. Worthington just didn't understand that her uselessness was not the major problem. It was the damage she did when she tried to be useful.

Her eyes met his across the table. Her expression was pleading. Pleading for him to be nice to her? The heck with it. Why not? He'd figure out how to deal with Beretsky later.

He asked, "Are you free for lunch today? Because, if so, I have an idea. There's this great place in Sausalito called The Eagle's Nest. Heard of it?" Miranda nodded eagerly. "How about I ask Dorothy to reserve a table? Then we can eat lunch, look at the view, and..." He nodded at her folder, "...go over your ideas for the department retreat."

"Oh, Barry, that would be wonderful."

Her joyous cry sent his spirits soaring too. It reminded him that for all his griping to the contrary it could be a lot of fun managing women. Well, women like Miranda anyway.

SHORTLY AFTER NOON, they arrived at The Eagle's Nest. Barry drove the car up to the portico entrance where two parking valets stepped up to open their car doors. Then he ushered her through the double doors into the cool of the cavernous entrance hall. With a touch on her elbow, he guided her past the dimly lit indoor dining room and up the stairs to the outdoor terrace. The maître d' led them to their reserved table, tucked into a secluded back corner of the terrace.

Before sitting down, Miranda raised herself on her toes to get a glimpse of the panorama that could be viewed from this hilltop. "What a shame we couldn't get a table in the front there," she exclaimed. "It's such a gorgeous view."

Barry said, "Never mind. From here, we can look down into the parking lot and see who's coming and going." He smiled flirtatiously at her as he sat down. "Besides, from where I sit, the view is pretty nice anyway." Miranda's eyes crinkled with pleasure.

The compliment was a genuine one because it seemed to Barry that Miranda did look particularly fetching today. Her creamy complexion and auburn hair were beautifully complimented by the short-sleeved summer suit she wore: nubby burnt orange and navy checks with white trim at the throat. A color combination that would look dreadful on Lila, Barry mused.

Miranda said, "What are you looking so happy about?"

Recklessly, he replied, "You. And me. Being the lucky guy who's having lunch with the prettiest woman for miles around."

Miranda fluttered her eyelashes and affected a Southern drawl. "Wah, Mr. Brahce. Ah do declare!"

He said, "Of course, if you tell anyone I said that, I'll deny every word."

They both laughed but Barry felt a momentary disquiet at the prospect of his words coming to the attention of certain people. Like Worthington, who might pass them on to Lila.

The waiter hovered beside them. "Something to drink?"

"Iced tea?" Barry suggested.

Miranda's brown eyes sparkled. "Or a glass of chardonnay?"

Barry frowned. He'd always made clear his stance that alcohol should not be part of a workday. Miranda said, "Oh, come on, Barry. One little glass won't do us in, will it?"

"Well, okay, but just one glass."

ON THAT SAME hot August day, Lila had been assigned the duty of taking an out-of-town client to lunch. Usually, this was a task she enjoyed but today she felt the way she often felt these days. Tired and out of sorts. So at the last minute she decided that an expensive lunch at The Eagle's Nest might be just the thing to perk her up. She knew her client would enjoy it. All the out-of-towners loved the drive over the Golden Gate Bridge and into the picturesque hills above Sausalito.

As she drove her green Porsche up the winding road toward the restaurant, she glanced now and then at the man beside her. He was much younger than most of their firm's clients. Better looking. A little wet behind the ears. A refreshing change from the jaded businessmen Lila dealt with every day. She smiled as she spotted him clinging to the armrest when she swung around a particularly sharp bend.

When they pulled up in front of the double doors of The Eagle's Nest, he said, "Wow, you're a great driver, Lila!"

She laughed out loud at his obvious relief at their safe arrival. "You get used to these roads when you live in California."

As they climbed out of the car, the young man gazed upwards at the terrace jutting out above them. They could see the tables of checkered green and white cloths shaded by green umbrellas. "Wow!" he said again. "Looks fabulous." But when they walked into the lobby, Lila directed him firmly toward the indoor dining room. His face fell. "We're not going to eat up there?"

"No, I'm sorry. I can't sit out in the sun. I have a skin condition. They serve the same great food downstairs." To appease him, she added, "After we've eaten, I promise we'll go upstairs and take a look at the view."

BY ONE-THIRTY, Barry and Miranda had finished their chicken pasta salads, two glasses of chardonnay apiece, and a discussion of the department retreat. The last item had not taken long, primarily because Miranda had left her notes and the contract behind in her office. She didn't, however, seem unduly worried by this. "As long as you promise to sign it as soon as we get back," she told Barry. "I'll get hold of Katie this afternoon and tell her she has the honor of co-moderating the retreat with me." She snickered.

Hearing Katie's name reminded Barry he was due to spend the day with her tomorrow. He leaned back in his chair, his eyes half closed in the warm sun, and said, "I'm off to Beresford tomorrow with Katie."

"What for?" Miranda looked startled.

"Oh, to observe her while she presents results of the employee survey to division management. So I'll have some input for you for her performance review."

"Ah, performance reviews!" Miranda looked cheerful again. "That's one thing I'm going to talk about at our retreat. My radical ideas about performance reviews."

Barry couldn't hide a grin at the thought of Miranda with radical ideas.

She said, "I'm going to propose some innovations that will shake up the old stick-in-the-muds in this department."

Barry yawned. "Better check it out first with this old stick-in-the-mud."

"Now, Barry, no need to be sarcastic. Since you made me assistant manager, I've been reading up on the latest ideas in creative management. Did you see that book by Norman Peters? Or Peter Norman? No, maybe that was another book. Anyway, the really hot idea in management right now is the concept of multi-skilling." She threw out the word and looked at him, mouth open in a breathless expression as though certain he'd be stunned at the news.

He yawned again. He was tired of hearing about the latest "best practices" with their accompanying buzzwords. And this idea wasn't new anyway. He said, "You mean in connection with assembly plants? Everyone on the team learns to do the job of everyone else so the team members are interchangeable. Supposedly."

"That's right. Only it's not just assembly plants, Barry." She leaned forward, her elbows on the table. "You can apply it to everyone in a department. For instance, take the management team in our department. Terry Lynch, Katie Carlisle. Me, too, of course. Oh, and you." She looked confused for a moment. "Anyway, the point is we all need to practice multi-skilling. This means that Terry would learn to handle Katie's job, and Katie would learn Terry's."

Barry looked at his watch. It was time they were going. He said, "Okay, slow down. Terry and Katie are experts in their fields. What would be the point of having them spend a lot of their time and company money learning to do each other's jobs? If Terry were to quit, we'd recruit someone with similar qualifications to take over. We wouldn't try to train someone who has no knowledge or interest in that kind of work. The same with Katie."

Miranda cried, "Barry, you're so wrong. So not up to speed."

He burst into laughter and pushed his elbows on the table toward her—aware, but not caring, that their arms were touching. "Oh, golly gee, Miranda, not up to speed, you say. Why, I'm devastated."

"No, Barry, listen. There's a seminar being given next month at some School of Management in Phoenix or somewhere. It's all about creative management and what all managers need to know to face the challenges of the nineties. In fact..." Her voice speeded up. "It's only twelve hundred dollars for three days. I was going to ask you if we have enough money in the budget for me to go. I think it would be well worth the cost."

Barry laughed again, leaning his head toward hers. She was so cute, he thought, with her earnest expression. "Ah, so this is what this is all about. A little jaunt to Phoenix."

"No, no, Barry." But she laughed too and for a moment her fingertips brushed his as she leaned forward also. "In fact, I think you should sign up too. It's always good to have two people go from the same company. We can talk it over afterwards and— Oh, Barry, stop laughing. I'm being quite serious here."

But it seemed she couldn't stop laughing either.

AFTER LILA AND HER CLIENT finished their lunch, Lila paid the check and then, true to her word, led the way upstairs to the outdoor dining area. The light outside was dazzling after the gloom indoors. Lila reached for her sunglasses as they wound their way through the tables toward the front of the terrace.

Her young client exclaimed, "Spectacular!" Which indeed it was. From the balustrade, they looked over the roofs and treetops of Sausalito tumbling downhill toward the bay. Lila pointed out the sights: Angel Island, Alcatraz, and, in the distance, the city itself—its ghostly contours looking like the backdrop for a stage setting.

Her companion leaned forward, hands on the rail, drinking it all in.

After a few minutes, she touched his arm and turned away, hoping he would follow. He didn't and, reluctant to rush him, she waited, letting her eyes wander around the still-crowded terrace.

And then she spotted them.

They were at a table at the farthest side of the terrace, tucked away in a corner. Lila recognized Miranda instantly. Barry's face was in profile, but there was no mistaking him either. From where she stood, Lila couldn't hear them but she could see they were laughing—hands touching, heads close together. There were even, she noticed with a surge of anger, wine glasses on the table. And Barry claimed never to drink during a workday.

A wave of nausea overcame her and she clapped a hand to her mouth, fearing she might be sick on the spot. Abruptly, she hurried to the stairs, quite forgetting about her guest until a plaintive voice called from somewhere behind her, "Oh, are we leaving?"

BARRY SIGNALED the waiter for the check. He said to Miranda, "Well, this is delightful but I think we'd better get back before you have me multi-skilling my way into the mailroom." Miranda excused herself and made off for the ladies' room. While he waited, Barry rose and stretched, looking down over the railing at the lushly landscaped entrance to the restaurant below.

For a couple of minutes, he gazed idly at the patrons arriving and departing. Then his eyes widened in surprise as a parking valet drove up in a vehicle that looked very much like Lila's green Porsche. A man and a woman who'd been standing under the overhang of the portico stepped forward. The valet jumped out and ushered the woman into the car. It was Lila.

Barry exclaimed out loud, "Good Lord! What a coincidence."

He guessed instantly what had happened. Lila, with her skin problems, had insisted on eating indoors. That's why he hadn't seen her before now. Then Barry chuckled as his eyes lit on his wife's companion. Lila's clientele sure was looking up. This youngster looked like a movie star.

He thought he mustn't forget to kid her about it tonight.

30

Katie Has a Bad Dream

THE SHRILL OF THE ALARM clock startled Katie into wakefulness. She sat up in bed, still in the grip of a disturbing dream. Today was Thursday, the day of her trip to Beresford with Barry. Her cats stretched lazily beside her and she stroked each furry stomach in turn, struggling to regain her composure.

It was ironic, she thought, how often she'd argued with Lorraine who seemed to regard dreams as oracles from the gods. "For Pete's sake, Lorraine, they just reflect random thoughts banging around in the corners of your mind. They don't mean anything." But, there were times, like now, that Katie felt shaken by the mood a dream could create.

She got out of bed and pulled on her robe and slippers. The cats were already marching, tails at full staff, into the kitchen.

As she prepared breakfast for them all, she thought about the day ahead. It would be an important day because Barry would be observing her and because he, in turn, would be reporting on her performance to Miranda. Miranda had claimed that this year she'd be giving "almost everyone" a C rating. This was bad news, if true, because only a rating better than a C was eligible for a salary raise. So today's visit might well be a pivotal one for Katie.

A short time later, when Katie sat down at the table with a bowl of cereal and a mug of coffee, her mind drifted back to her nightmare. She knew what had prompted it, of course—the upcoming trip today in a pint-sized plane.

In her dream, she was flying in such a plane, sitting in a single seat near the back. Suddenly Barry Bryce came hurtling down the aisle. To her terror, she saw that he was headed straight for her, his face contorted in fury. She opened her mouth to scream but no sound came. Then he threw himself upon her, grabbing her forearms and throwing one leg over her, straddling her. The next moment they were both on the floor and he was pushing down on her. She could feel his breath and the roughness of his chin as his mouth landed hard on hers.

And then the alarm went off.

Sipping her coffee, Katie reflected that the most disturbing thing about the dream was her reaction to it. She'd woken feeling frightened but also aroused. What on earth did that mean?

At this point, she got a glimpse of the clock and leapt to her feet. Today of all days, she'd allowed herself to lose track of the time.

OF COURSE, this had to be a day when traffic was backed up on the freeway. Katie felt herself sweating as the minutes moved forward faster than the traffic. Finally, she reached the airport turnoff, sped to the short-term lot to park the car, and ran into the terminal. The flight to Beresford left at 7:05. Katie reached the boarding area with exactly five minutes to spare.

At first, she didn't see Barry in the departure lounge and wondered if he'd already boarded. But he was in a chair facing out toward the windows, his face half-hidden in a newspaper. He noted as she slid into the seat beside him, "Nothing like cutting it fine, huh?" Before she had a chance to tell her prepared lie about the alarm not going off, he added, "They've just announced a delay anyway."

He put his newspaper down. "You'll have to remind me what today's program is. Things rather got away from me yesterday and I didn't have a chance to bone up."

Katie looked at him thoughtfully. Taking a two-hour lunch with Miranda yesterday had no doubt helped the process of things getting away from him. She said, "Well, we start by meeting with the division manager and his team—about twenty people—from nine till twelve."

"So we can leave at noon?"

"No, I'm afraid not. I'll present the survey results this morning, but this afternoon each supervisor will meet with the people who report to him to convey the results. I've told Mike Weston I'll be available to any group that would like help with their afternoon meeting."

"Hmm." Barry squinted into the distance. "And the kinds of results we're talking about? Satisfaction with pay, working conditions?"

"And a slew of other things. What the employees think about their supervisors, how much control they feel they have over their work. The questionnaire is ten pages long. I have a copy of it here."

She reached for her briefcase, but Barry shook his head. "No, I've seen it. I'd just forgotten." He added, "I take it the results of the survey are key in determining each supervisor's bonus for the year."

"Not at all. The survey was not designed to be a 'gotcha.' It's a tool to help managers improve their performance in a non-threatening way. If you start punishing people for poor results, they'll find ways to sabotage the survey."

Barry opened his mouth as if to argue but at that moment boarding for their flight was called. He stood up and said, "About time."

Saved by the bell, Katie thought. Saved from another Bryce harangue about how soft the company was on poor performers. Almost as if he were reading her mind, Barry turned to look at her as they moved side by side toward the gate. He smiled. In a purely knee jerk reaction, Katie smiled back and was immediately annoyed at herself. Especially in light of that silly dream.

AS IT HAPPENED, Barry's smile was no more than a sardonic reaction to what she'd just said. Trust Katie, he thought, to keep pushing the pathetic idea that people should not be punished for poor performance.

He wasn't as irritated with Katie, however, as he was with Miranda. Yesterday afternoon, Miranda had succeeded in undoing the good mood established during their lunch together. She'd marched into his office with the contract she wanted him to sign and then had screamed in protest when he'd told her he'd get it back to her at the end of the week. After a lot of *"but Barry you promised"* whining, he'd finally signed the damned thing. And then—he couldn't remember how—they'd got into a rehash of the multi-skilling discussion. His ensuing explosion had driven her out of his office in a sulk.

The rest of the afternoon had been taken up by a tedious staff managers' meeting. Finally, five o'clock rolled around and Barry went home to Lila.

ON THE PLANE, Katie sat by the window, Barry beside her in the aisle seat. He said, "I'd like to see a copy of your presentation, if you don't mind."

"Sure." Katie handed him the package containing her talk and copies of the handouts she planned to use. He put the package on his lap and waited for the plane to take off.

Katie had brought another document with her today. This was her manifesto, *A New Direction for Executive Support Services*. She wondered if there was any point in asking him to look at it, as Terry had suggested. But perhaps not now. From the look on his face, he had other things to think about.

LAST NIGHT, Barry and Lila had arrived home at the same time. He had commented on this unusual occurrence as they climbed out of their respective cars. Lila said nothing. In the house, she went into their bedroom to change. Barry went downstairs to the kitchen where he rummaged around for something to eat. Something light would do after lunch out today. He smiled, remembering Lila didn't yet know that he'd seen her at The Eagle's Nest.

When Lila came downstairs, she headed for the refrigerator and pulled out a bottle of Chablis. He said, "What do you think? Shall we just use up that leftover Chinese food?"

"Sure. Whatever."

"We could eat out, but I figured you wouldn't want to do that twice in one day." Lila turned toward him and handed him a glass of wine. He laughed at her expression. "I hope you enjoyed The Eagle's Nest."

She looked apprehensive, almost fearful. For a fleeting second, Barry wondered if maybe the young man with her today had not been a client after all. Lila with a lover? He dismissed the thought. He explained, "By an incredible coincidence, I had lunch there too."

"Yes, I know." Her hand shook as she lifted the glass to her mouth.

He frowned. "Oh? I didn't realize you'd seen me. I only saw you as you were getting into your car to leave."

Nursing her drink with both hands, Lila sat down on a dinette chair. "We ate indoors, but then we went upstairs for a couple of minutes so my client could look at the view."

"And that's when you saw me? Why didn't you come over and say hi?"

There was a long silence before Lila swung around to face him. Her eyes were full of tears. In a tremulous voice, she said, "I was only thankful my client had never met you so there was no need to talk to you." She put her head down to her drink.

Uh-oh.

Barry sensed he was in trouble but surely even Lila couldn't object to his having lunch with a colleague.

"Lila." She turned away, curling in on herself, clutching her drink. "You seem upset but I don't know why. It was just a business lunch."

She cried, "Business lunch? You and that woman were in each other's arms. You were practically kissing."

"*What*? Now you're being ridiculous. Do you really imagine I'd ever be that unprofessional with a subordinate, let alone in public?"

Lila screamed, "Yes. Because I saw it with my own eyes."

For Barry, the pent-up frustrations of the day were taking their toll. He said in the iciest tone he could muster, "Lila, there's something wrong with you. Your petty outbursts of jealousy are getting under my skin. For God's sake, get control of yourself."

Lila put down her drink and rose. As she made her way toward the door, he raised his voice. "Why don't you talk to your doctor? Go see a counselor?"

Now she was walking upstairs to her office where, he knew, she would close the door and not emerge all evening. In a burst of frustration, he went to the bottom of the stairs and shouted, "You know damn well there's absolutely nothing between Miranda and me. Nothing." Upstairs, the door slammed. He raised his voice still further. "But I swear there will be if you keep this up."

AS THE PLANE taxied down the runway, Katie said, "I hate small planes. They never seem safe to me." Barry said nothing. She glanced at him. He was staring past her out the window, looking into the distance. He looked a bit bleary-eyed, she thought with amusement. Too much carousing last night, perhaps? Not that Barry ever looked particularly engaged when he was around her. She was just one big nothing to this man.

A few minutes later, they were airborne, climbing their way through the overcast and into the sunshine above.

Barry said, "Have you ever worked with Public Relations?"

Surprised at the question, Katie answered, "Public Relations? Sure. I've done a couple of studies for them over the years. Why?"

"Miranda's just finished a study for them."

Katie's spirits brightened. She'd heard that PR had been less than satisfied with Miranda's efforts. Her delight was dampened, however, when Barry added. "I'd like you to see what help you can offer Miranda. Beretsky's giving her a hard time." He turned to her. "You know, she's such a babe in the woods when it comes to dealing with pushy characters like Beretsky."

Babe in the woods? Miranda? Katie asked, "What sort of help did you have in mind?"

"Well, I suspect the report she turned in to them was a bit too casual. You know how she hates writing reports. Maybe you could review what she wrote and perhaps write a stronger version that will satisfy Beretsky concerning her recommendations. Be tactful though. We don't want to upset Miranda."

For a few moments, Katie felt too angry to talk. Then she said, "You mean the way I wrote the final report on the Corporate Values Program? I seem to recall I got that assignment also because Miranda doesn't like writing reports."

Barry had the grace to look guilty. He muttered, "Something like that."

Katie's heart pounded but she pressed on. "I've often wondered what became of my report. I heard tell it eventually went out under your name, with all the parts that were critical of Miranda being taken out."

"I softened it down, yes. But it didn't go out under my name; it went out under yours."

"You can't mean that." She felt her voice rising. "I'd also heard not only did that report take out criticisms of Miranda but it also added criticisms about Chuck. Now you're telling me there's a document floating around this company that's disparaging of my former boss and with my name as the author."

She was almost spitting in her rage.

Barry shrugged. "For God's sake, don't let's rehash all that ancient history now." He settled back in his seat and opened up the folder on the Beresford questionnaire.

Katie looked out her window at the scene below. Sun and wisps of fog were playing hide and seek with the mountain peaks. She knew she had to be in a calm, confident mood to deal with the day ahead. But for a long time the knot of anger remained in her stomach.

The dream was starting to make sense to her. The anger, the violence, the kiss. Obviously a rape scenario. And that was what Barry, figuratively speaking, had been doing to her since he got here. Violating her, destroying her feeling of self-worth, her standing in the company, undermining and humiliating her.

Out of the corner of her eye, she could see him staring past her through her window. He had tuned out again, looking into space, making no attempt to review the material she'd given him.

OF COURSE, he'd regretted his harsh words. Not immediately though. For a time after Lila stormed out, Barry had remained leaning against the kitchen counter, flushed with self-righteous anger. He'd meant most of what he'd said. Lila was behaving unreasonably. She really did need to see a shrink.

But when the first flush of anger had lost its edge, he felt momentarily undone by a deep sense of loss and cradled his head in his hands. *Lila, please don't be this way.*

Later that evening, as he was reheating the Chinese food, it dawned on him just which particular moment of his lunch with Miranda his wife must have witnessed. It must have been that time when Miranda had made him laugh so hard that he'd leaned toward her. And hadn't their arms and hands touched? He sat at the table, eating slowly while he recreated the scene. Miranda had said something about a seminar she wanted to attend. Out of town. Then she'd suggested he go with her, her eyes dancing with blatant sexual innuendo. He'd been amused and flattered. So maybe this time Lila's "paranoia" was justified after all.

While he finished eating, he thought about the best way to proceed. First, he would fix something for her to eat. She had to be ravenous by now. He guessed she'd be too upset to eat a full meal but hot buttered toast and a cup of creamy cocoa might do the trick. And he'd have to come up with some kind of explanation—stopping short of the full truth, of course.

When he walked into her office a short time later, Lila was at her computer staring at the screen saver. He said cheerily, "Room service," and put down the food where she could see it. Then he pulled up a chair beside her.

She said, "I'm not hungry."

Her body tightened up as soon as he started to fondle her. First, he stroked the silky blonde hair, pushing it off her forehead and curling it around her ears. Then he slid his fingers up the hollow at the back of her neck—"the first erogenous zone I ever realized I had," she'd once told him.

He said softly, "My sweet baby. I'm such a bastard. How could I possibly talk to you the way I did?"

She kept looking at the computer screen. He went on, still stroking her, "I was so angry with you until it finally occurred to me what must have upset you." She turned then and looked at him. He said, "There was just one moment when I was laughing at Miranda and kind of leaning forward and touching her. That must be the exact moment you saw us. She'd just said something—I don't even remember what—that was so stupid I completely cracked up."

Lila looked skeptical but Barry could guess how much she wanted to believe him.

He broke off a small piece of toast and put it to her mouth with lip-smacking noises as if he were coaxing a small child. She ate the toast. He said, sighing, "Believe me, with Miranda, most of the time I don't know whether to laugh or cry. I spent much of our lunch today resisting the urge to strangle her."

He broke off another piece of toast and offered it to her again. And another piece. And then she took the slice from him and, still unsmiling, finished it. She ate so heartily the crumbs trailed down her chin. He laughed. "I should have brought a napkin." Not quite knowing what her reaction would be, he stuck out his tongue and licked some crumbs from her lips.

And then, overcome by feelings of tenderness, he put his hands either side of her small face and pulled her to him. Immediately, she relaxed and her mouth melted into his.

That night, they made love.

As usual after a quarrel, their lovemaking was ardent—a gratifying release of the tension between them. But in its aftermath, Barry lay awake for a long time, troubled by a sort of free-floating anxiety. It was like a foreboding of some kind. Some trouble about to overtake them? Something he couldn't predict or control.

But he'd had a busy day and was tired. Eventually, the heebie-jeebies receded and he fell asleep.

31

An Expedited Departure

MIKE WESTON was at the airport to meet them. "Katie, great to see you again," he enthused. He shook Barry's hand energetically when Katie introduced them. "Heard a lot about you," he said.

On the drive into town, Barry sat in the front seat and looked out the window while Mike pointed out the dramatic changes that had occurred in the Beresford area of late. "All of this is new," he proclaimed, waving an arm around. "Shopping malls, business parks, housing developments. Coupla years ago, this was all fields and feed lots." He ran a hand across his forehead as if wiping off the sweat. "I tell you, Barry, it's all we can do to keep ahead of new service demands."

In the back seat, Katie tuned him out. She knew that Mike's spiel was part boast but also part complaint that a division as busy as Beresford was forced to spend valuable time in carrying out head office programs.

After Mike had exhausted the subject of Beresford's growth, Katie could sense his searching around for another topic. She was dismayed by the one he chose. "Say, Katie, have you talked to Sherm lately?" He said to Barry, "You know Sherman Granger, Barry? He's a local businessman-cum-inventor. He's got a patent out on a real neat device, a cogen unit."

Barry said in a flat voice, "Yeah, I heard about that."

Mike persisted. "It's a pretty neat device. You got to see it, didn't you, Katie? That time you were at his house?"

This did get Barry's attention. While Katie mumbled a denial—after all, it was Dan, not she, who had actually examined the thing—Barry turned around and gave her a thoughtful look.

The three-hour meeting went more smoothly than Katie had dared to hope. At the end of it, Mike drew her aside and said, in Barry's hearing, "Great presentation, Katie." Katie glowed.

After, she accompanied the two men to Mike's office. "I expect you two could do with some lunch," Mike said. "We have a real nice little place nearby, Willie's Watering Hole." He nodded at Katie as if to acknowledge he'd taken her there in the past. "Yo, Maisie," he greeted his secretary. "How about giving Willie's a call. Three for lunch."

Maisie said, "Sure," then turned to Barry and handed him a slip of paper. "Excuse me, Mr. Bryce, a phone call just came in for you. They want you to call right back. There's an empty office over there if you'd like privacy."

While Barry went to make his call, Katie followed Mike into his office. She sat down across from him at the big corner desk. The painting of sailboats in a harbor faced her as it had the last awful time she'd visited Mike's office. Now, alone with her, Mike dropped the fawning façade he'd worn all morning and hurried to look through the stack of message slips on his desk. He glanced at his watch and clucked. She felt some sympathy. A busy division manager must indeed have a thousand more pressing things to do than spend his whole morning discussing a survey he hadn't even asked for. On the other hand, that survey, as she'd told Barry, was supposed to be a useful tool for people like Mike.

She ventured, "What do you think of the employee survey, Mike? Do you find it useful?"

He snapped, "About as useful as that dumb— whatever the stupid thing was—Values Program."

"Oh, dear, I'm sorry." Katie couldn't help chuckling at his vehemence.

Mike rocked back in his chair and regarded her with a solemn expression. He said, "Incidentally, it was good of you to try to help Sherm sell his invention to the company. It wasn't your fault you didn't succeed." She was about to smile at this unexpected approval, but then he added, "Someone at your level obviously doesn't have the right connections."

As he started again to talk about "poor old Sherm," Katie leaned forward and said in a low voice, "You know something, Mike. I'd really appreciate it if we didn't discuss this topic in front of Barry. In particular, I don't want him to know I've been trying to help Sherman."

Mike's eyes glittered. "Gee, I just assumed you and your boss were on the same page."

"I wish. I'm not sure we've ever been in the same book, let alone on the same page."

Mike pursed his lips. He put his elbows on the desk and formed his hands into a pyramid. "Well, now, Katie," he said, "let me be straight with you. I'm planning to have a heart-to-heart with Mr. Bryce today. To my mind, he's just the right person to take up Sherman's cause. He *does* have the right connections. From what I hear, he and our CEO are that close." He raised a hand, pinching together the thumb and forefinger.

Katie protested, "Mike, there's no point in pursuing this. The company's already turned Sherman down flat."

"Ah," Mike wagged a finger at her. "If you'd been with this company as long as I have, you'd know the right hand never knows what the left is doing. Just because some lackey in Worthington's office wrote that rejection letter doesn't mean someone else couldn't get the wheels rolling again."

"No, Mike, please listen to me."

At that moment, Barry walked into the office. Mike's fawning tone returned as he asked, "Everything okay?"

"No, it isn't," was the terse response. I have to get back to the city right away. What time is the next flight out?"

Mike's secretary had followed Barry in and answered his question. "The next flight is at five. That gets you to Oakland at six-fifteen."

"That's no good. That was my wife's office calling. She's..." he hesitated. "...been taken ill. I need to get back as soon as possible. There surely must be another flight before then."

Maisie said, "Sorry, there isn't. But, you know, it only takes a coupla hours to drive to the city. Maybe we could find a division car to lend you."

Maisie to the rescue, Katie thought. And what a great suggestion. It would eliminate the heart-to-heart Mike had planned, and Katie could have a Barry-free afternoon and flight home. Her satisfaction was short-lived on both scores. Mike and Barry had no sooner approved Maisie's suggestion than Barry said to Katie, "No point you hanging around here. You might as well drive back with me."

"Great idea," echoed a happy Mike Weston.

"But I promised I'd be available to work with your staff this afternoon."

"Nah, we'll manage," Mike said. "Okay, Maisie, one car needed at short notice. Work your magic, girl." As she left the room, he called out, "Also, why don't you get some sandwiches for these guys from the lunch room. Don't want 'em to starve." He beamed affably at Barry and settled back in his chair. "It'll take a half hour or so to get the car so you might as well relax for a while. In fact, there's something I'd like to raise with you, Barry."

Katie's heart sank. Mike assumed the hands-in-pyramid position. He said, "So, Barry, do you recall a while ago I mentioned my inventor friend?"

Barry's mind seemed to be elsewhere. His eyes were fixed on the painting hanging above Mike's head.

"Gloucester Harbor, I bet."

"You're right." Mike seemed delighted to be led off on this particular tangent. He launched into his story of how he'd found the painting—on a visit to Gloucester, no less—how much it had cost, about the yachts depicted therein.

When Maisie returned, she was cradling several packets in her arms and carrying a bottle of Pepsi in each hand. "Ham and cheese okay?" she chirped. "It had better be. It's all we have." She put the drinks on Mike's desk and handed Katie and Barry each a plastic-wrapped sandwich and packet of chips. She said to Mike, "You'll have to get after that vending machine company yourself. They take no notice of me. The guy hasn't been to check the machine in heaven knows how long."

Mike muttered, "Yeah, okay," and waved her away.

Katie looked suspiciously at the sandwich as she unwrapped it. She wondered how long ham and cheese stayed edible in a vending machine. She noticed Mike didn't have a sandwich. Saving himself for Willie's, no doubt.

Mike said, "Getting back to the painting. I keep it there because I have a passion for sailing. You like sailing, Barry?"

Barry shrugged. "Don't do much these days. At one time I crewed for some of the best. Like Harry Mellon. St. Francis Yacht Club."

As Barry spoke, Mike's jaw fell. Katie was surprised too. It was unlike Barry to boast about, or even talk about, anything he did outside of work. Mike said, "Wow! I've never been in that league." He looked again at his picture and said, "I do keep a pretty nice boat though. Thirty-footer."

He cast an anxious glance at Barry. "You have a boat, Barry?" Barry shook his head. Mike went on, "I keep mine berthed at my summer cabin at Lake Almanor."

Barry had taken a bite out of his sandwich and was chewing in a grim, purposeful way. Mike said with a modest laugh, "I shouldn't call it a cabin. It's a house. Twenty-five hundred square feet and..."

Barry swallowed and said in a flat voice, "Yes, I know all about it."

Katie had by now decided to take a pass on the sandwich. The plastic wrap had yellowed, the bread was curling at the edges. She'd stick with the potato chips. As she struggled to open the package without breaking a nail, she became conscious there was silence in the room. Had Mike already run out of things to say about his cabin? Was he going to start talking about Sherman again?

She looked at him and was taken aback at his demeanor. Mike's lips were compressed and his cheeks a fiery red. He glared at Barry who seemed too preoccupied with pulling his sandwich apart to notice. Then he muttered something, stood up, and marched out of the room. Katie's eyes followed his retreating back.

Beside her, Barry held a slice of cheese to his nose, and made a face. "Someone should call the health department. This stuff must have been in that vending machine for months."

"Oh, surely not." Katie shuddered.

Barry wiped his fingers with a napkin, wrapped up the remains of his lunch and tossed it into the wastebasket. He leaned back and squinted up at the painting. "Nice picture. Seems overkill for this place, doesn't it?" He looked around the room, seeming to notice for the first time that Mike was no longer there. "I guess Mr. Weston got tired of our company."

"Yes, I can't imagine why he walked off like that. Maybe he was upset we were so unappreciative of his sandwiches."

Barry said, "He was upset, all right. But I don't think the sandwiches had anything to do with it."

It was too late to ask what he meant. They could hear Mike and Maisie talking outside the office. Mike, jovial again, told them, "Good news, folks. Your wheels are here already. There's a car in the lot now that's available." He hovered in the doorway as Barry and Katie gathered their things together. "Now you will make sure, won't you, that you have someone from HO drive the car back to us as soon as possible. We don't have a big fleet of cars in the division like you do in the city." Barry ignored this.

Maisie walked them to the elevator. Katie said, "Maisie, thanks so much for getting the car and the lunch."

Barry muttered as the elevator doors closed behind them, "And for the bellyache and the ptomaine poisoning."

"Oh, Barry."

He leaned his head back and smiled. It was a weary smile that reminded Katie of the reason for their expedited departure. She said, "I'm sorry to hear about your wife, Barry. I do hope it's nothing serious."

In truth, she couldn't imagine there was anything much wrong with Barry's wife. From Terry's description of the woman—"pale, fragile looking"—Katie guessed she was a neurotic bundle of imaginary ailments. Perhaps not surprising, considering her marital situation.

Barry said, "She had a heart attack "

"A heart attack? Are you sure?"

She chided herself instantly for asking such a stupid question. The elevator bumped to a stop at the ground floor and the doors opened. A minute later they were in the parking lot standing beside an unwashed, bottom-of-the-line, white Chevrolet.

Their "wheels."

32

Katie and Barry Drive Home

"BARRY, I'M STUNNED to hear about your wife. Has she had heart trouble for long?" They were on the freeway headed toward home. Barry was a fast driver and Katie found herself gripping the seat on several occasions.

"No, she hasn't. She's been tired and lacking in energy for some time, but we've never suspected anything was wrong with her heart." He paused. "I had to leave extra early this morning to catch the plane. She was still in bed, but I didn't realize she was ill. It seems she got to work and then collapsed."

Katie said, "I'm really sorry. I sure hope everything turns out okay."

"Thank you." He seemed deep in thought. Suddenly he said, "Did you really go to Sherman Granger's house to see his machine?" As Katie struggled to think of a reply, he gave her an out. "Or was that a figment of Weston's imagination?"

Keeping her voice steady, Katie said, "I don't know where that man gets his ideas."

Barry nodded. "He's some wheeler-dealer, isn't he? Did you notice how several times today he tried to engage me on the subject of 'good old Sherm'?" Katie realized this was true. Barry told her, "The two of them have been buddies since high school and you can bet they're cooking up some scheme to swindle the company with this invention."

Katie drew a breath. "What makes you say that?"

"Because of what Weston is. Remember how upset he got when he was talking about his twenty-five hundred-square foot summer home and I said I already knew about it?"

"That's right." She remembered that was when Mike had abruptly stopped talking and left the room.

"I don't know if you're aware of this, but the company provided the labor and most of the construction materials for that house. At absolutely no cost to Mr. Weston." He flashed her a wry smile. "Of course, the company didn't know about it at the time."

"And you found out about it?"

"It was one of the first things I uncovered after I started working for Worthington. Mike was lucky he wasn't fired on the spot. His boss at the time covered up for him—mainly because he was on the take in a similar way."

Katie remembered that Mike's boss, the man who was division operations vice president at that time, had taken early retirement.

Barry said, "We struck a deal. The V.P. took early retirement and Mike got a warning. From the look on his face today, he'd forgotten that I knew about that business."

"Hmm." Katie thought that Barry undoubtedly also knew about Mike's other past transgressions like taking kickbacks during the division's undergrounding project. Mike was not only dishonest, she thought, he was downright dumb if he imagined he could recruit Barry to help Sherman.

But, right now, she felt she had to come to Sherman's defense. She said, "You know, Barry, I agree that Mike has a shady side. But I don't think the same thing is true of Sherman Granger. On the few occasions I've met him, he's struck me as being a straight and honorable man. I can't imagine he'd ever be involved in anything unethical."

"Oh, you can never tell with people," Barry assured her. "From what I've heard, the man's scraping the bottom of the barrel, money-wise. You couldn't blame him for doing whatever he can to make a few bucks."

Damn Barry, Katie thought. Now she felt disloyal to Sherman because she was afraid to defend him more vigorously.

Katie sought about for another subject of conversation. "I must say Mike was a lot more relaxed today than the last time I saw him."

"When was that?"

"In February. I went to Beresford to tell Mike and his team that Beresford was going to be the test site for the Corporate Values Program." She chuckled. "Talk about a hostile reaction."

"Well, I can't blame him for that. The man has a job to do—a real job. Getting electricity to customers. All these bloody HO programs do nothing but waste time."

Katie glanced at him. Was he actually describing Miranda's Values Program as "a bloody HO program"?

Barry went on, "I'm afraid people like your former boss Chuck are largely to blame for that. He was the one who got Worthington all enthusiastic about these damn-fool time and resource wasting programs."

"Hey, hold on. The Values Program was Miranda's creation, remember?"

"Regardless of that, it seems to me the mission of your entire department under Chuck's management was to carry out similar half-baked programs. Like, what was it last year, the MOO program? Gimme a break!"

"Actually, Market Oriented Organization wasn't a bad concept—in spite of the acronym."

Barry said firmly. "All these programs cost money and take people in the field away from their real job of serving customers."

"You know, Barry, it so happens I agree with you to a large extent." She drew a breath. "In fact, a while ago, I drafted a document called *A New Direction for Executive Support Services* that describes my suggestions for a different mission for our department. In fact, I have a copy with me now." She twisted around and nodded toward her briefcase on the back seat.

"Is that right? Well, we could sure do with a new direction. I'd like to see that copy." Katie's spirits soared until Barry went on, "I can't imagine that Chuck would ever have entertained any new direction if it conflicted with Worthington's wishes. Chuck was basically a yes-man. I don't know if he ever had an original idea himself."

Her anger at these words made Katie reckless. "I can't believe what you're saying. For God's sake, Barry, what else are you but a yes-man? Have you ever done anything other than what Worthington has ordered you to do?"

There was a long silence. Barry said, "My, you've been saving that up for a rainy day, haven't you?"

Katie clutched her trembling hands together her lap. During the rest of the journey back to the Bay Area, she kept berating herself for her stupidity.

There goes my performance review.

33

A Dumb Way to Run a Love Life

Lorraine called on Saturday morning. Katie, still in her nightclothes, was sitting at the kitchen table finishing a second cup of coffee. Lorraine and Peter had been in Costa Rica for a month.

"You're back," Katie said. "I sure have missed you."

"Missed you too, baby."

"So, how was the rain forest? How did your tummy hold up?"

A snort of disgust from Lorraine. "Predictable, to both questions."

Katie laughed. Peter, a biologist, more often than not, used his vacations as an excuse to do research, often in what Lorraine called "belly-unsettling" regions of the world. Lorraine grumbled, "Normal people lounge around at poolside, sipping margaritas. We go grubbing around the forest floor hot on the trail of frog spoor while all I can think about is how far the nearest bathroom might be."

Katie propped a leg on an adjoining chair and settled back for an entertaining listen. She suspected Lorraine was more tolerant of these expeditions than she let on—after all, why else would she go?—but her accounts of their misadventures in foreign lands were typically hilarious.

Today was no exception. Katie's sides were aching with laughter when, some time later, Lorraine concluded, "That's enough about me. How about you? How's your man? Or is it men? Are you branching out?"

Katie finished wiping the tears from her eyes. "Branching out?"

"Pete and I saw you in the parking lot at Oakland International. On Thursday, when we got back. We couldn't stop to talk because we were running like hell to catch the shuttle bus. You were climbing out of a white car being driven by a delicious man. Who wasn't Dan."

"I was? The only man driving me anywhere on Thursday was Barry Bryce. He took me back to the airport parking lot to get my car. You see, we flew to Beresford that day..."

"Barry Bryce? Are you saying that comely specimen of male pulchritude is your Simon Legree boss? I'd always pictured him as a sniveling little runt with a Hitler mustache."

Katie gave a shout of laughter. "He's a specimen of something all right."

Lorraine huffed. "I'm always telling you, Katie, handsome men are wasted on you. Remember, I had to beat you over the head to get you to pay attention to the divine Dan. Speaking of whom, any progress there?"

Katie drawled, savoring her words, "I think you'd call it that. We've been together the past three weekends."

"Sharing a bed?"

"Uh-huh."

Lorraine whooped with excitement. "Sweetie-pie, you must be floating on air. So how is he? Fabulous lover, I bet." Katie hesitated and Lorraine added, "Or not?"

"Oh, Lorraine, you know I find it hard to discuss stuff like this. It's complicated."

It was complicated. The truth was that the most exciting thing about being with Dan was not so much his behavior but the effect he had on hers. Since they'd become lovers, a kittenish—playful, bordering on brazen—aspect of Katie's nature had emerged that she found both exhilarating and a little scary.

Lorraine said, "I know you're bashful about revealing the gory details. Start at the beginning. How about the first time? How did things take off?"

"Well, let's see. We went on a trip to Merced to visit Dan's son. That went fine, but on the way home we got into this argument about Sherman Granger. In fact, we passed near his house and Dan insisted on dropping in and meeting him."

"For what reason?"

"A question that bothered me. Anyway, here he is, the naïve hunk, trying to persuade poor Sherman who's just been fired not to accept a job with his son-in-law, but instead to go into business with Dan. Well, on the way home, I—shall we say—remonstrated with him."

"And he didn't like that?"

"You've got that right. So we both got into a snit with each other, but somehow when we said goodnight at my door...well, we sort of forgot about Sherman."

"I would hope so. Katie, how wonderful!"

"But then," Katie said, "After we went to bed, I discovered a major problem with sleeping with Dan."

"Oh, no!"

"It's the cats. It turns out Dan hates cats. He says he's allergic to them. Which I simply don't believe but that's another issue. Anyway, they always sleep with me and that night I had to lock them out of the bedroom. You can imagine the caterwauling and scratching at the door that went on. They wouldn't stop."

Lorraine shrieked with delight. "I hope Dan has a sense of humor."

"He really doesn't. Not about cats anyway. In fact, it's amazing he didn't leave in a rage."

Lorraine shrieked again.

Katie knew—and Lorraine would undoubtedly guess—she and Dan had both been so hungry for sex that night that it would have taken a major conflagration to have kept them apart.

"And then," she told Lorraine, "much later, after Dan had fallen asleep, one of those little devils managed to get the door open by pawing at the latch. They both came rushing in and jumped onto the bed. I smuggled them out in the morning before Dan woke up."

"Oh, my," Lorraine gasped, "Your cats or your lover—what a choice."

Later, after Lorraine had hung up, Katie bent down to Kit at her feet and tickled the little chin. "It would be an easy choice for me to make, sweetie," she whispered. But it wasn't a choice she'd had to make as yet.

Over the past couple of weeks, the two cats and she had come to a sort of understanding. They refrained from making a noise until all was quiet in the bedroom. Katie always smiled at the mental image of furry ears pressed against the door, listening. Then, in the early hours, the door latch would be quietly manipulated until the door swung open. Katie, who was waiting for this moment, would move over closer to a sleeping Dan to clear space for them.

A classic case, Katie thought, of having your cake and eating it too. Or, more accurately, a dumb way to run a love life. Well, at least she had no intention of keeping this up for long.

34

Miranda Takes Charge

ON MONDAY MORNING, Barry called a staff meeting for nine o'clock. Miranda, Katie, Terry, and Dorothy sat down to join him at his conference table. He said briskly, "This is going to be brief. No doubt, you've all heard of my wife's illness..." He paused to acknowledge the murmurs of sympathy. "Thank you. I'll be taking some time off as a result, and while I'm away Miranda will be taking my place."

He opened a folder he had in front of him. "Let's see. HR sent me a note saying performance evaluations are due in a month's time. Katie and Terry, please take care of those for the people who report to you. Miranda will do the evaluations on the two of you."

Katie looked down at her lap. It would be best that she keep her mouth shut on the evaluation issue. After her stupid "yes-man" accusations last Friday, she couldn't imagine getting much support from Barry.

A lilting voice. "Oh, Barry."

"Yes, Miranda?"

"Just a couple of things. Remember the department retreat we've discussed. We've been sort of holding off until after the employee survey is finished. Do you think....?

"For God's sake! No offence, Miranda, but I have too much on my plate right now to even think about that."

Miranda looked appealingly at Katie. Katie felt a bit sorry for her. The poor woman had so little to do—but a retreat at this time would be a ridiculous waste of time and money. She refused to meet Miranda's eye.

Barry pushed back his chair. "Okay, if there's nothing else...." Suddenly, Miranda pushed a folder toward him. "What's this?"

Miranda's face brightened. "The flyer on the creative management seminar. Remember, we talked about it?" She turned to Katie and Terry. "We've got a bunch of unspent money in the budget and you know how that doesn't go over well with anyone? Well, there's this great seminar coming up in Phoenix next month and that seemed like a good way to spend some of it." She cast a kittenish look at Barry. "Barry may accompany me. If Lila is well enough by then."

Katie, Terry, and Dorothy all looked at Barry. "I haven't given it a single thought," he snapped and marched back to his desk.

LATER IN THE MORNING, Terry stopped by Katie's office. He closed the door. "Do you think that bitch will really stick to her threats of giving us a C rating?"

Katie thought a moment. "I've no idea what she'll do. But I'm telling you if she gives me any less than my customary A, I'll tender my resignation. I'll tell her that no one with less than an A deserves to hold a job like mine."

Terry sighed. Then he smiled. "Say, what do you think was behind that talk of the seminar in Phoenix? Did you see Barry's face? He was red as a beetroot."

"*Naughty* Miranda," Katie snickered. "Talking out of school. I bet she'll get her knuckles rapped over this."

"Or her bottom spanked."

They both roared with laughter.

35

Growing Suspicions

ONE OF DAN'S infuriating habits was that he always waited until the last minute before calling Katie for a date. She didn't like being taken for granted and every weekend resolved she'd speak to him about it. But when he called the Friday afternoon before Labor Day, she responded as usual, "Fine, see you at seven."

And then, also as usual, when she questioned him about where he'd like to go for dinner, he responded, "To the best place in town. Your house." She'd have to speak to him about this too.

Dan showed up on her doorstep promptly at seven o'clock. Katie stood for a moment drinking in the sight of him. He looked well-scrubbed, his blond hair damp from a recent shower, the azure patterning in his cotton shirt matching the blue of his eyes. He beamed with an air of happy anticipation.

"Hiya, beautiful!"

"Okay, Mister," the new kittenish Katie responded, "you'd better step inside right quick before I rip every shred of clothing off your luscious body, throw you to the ground, and ravish you."

"Yeah, yeah. I get the picture." He gave a melodramatic sigh as he stepped through the door. "You sex—crazed older women really scare me."

She pushed the door closed behind him. By the time it had slammed shut, his arms were around her and his soft mouth was working its magic. Katie loved Dan's kisses. To her mind, he kissed with the passion and spontaneity of a teenager.

When the kitchen timer dinged, she reluctantly drew away. "To be continued," she murmured and took off down the hall with Dan on her heels. At the stove, she checked the contents of the pot simmering on a back burner. "Hope you like beef bourguignon, Dan," she said.

He joined her in peering into the fragrant mix of meat and vegetables. "Can't say as I've ever had it. Or even heard of it. But, if you made it, I'm going to love it."

Katie reached for a bottle of burgundy and poured some into the pot. "Have a seat. It'll only be five minutes. I just have to heat up some biscuits."

Dan pulled out a kitchen chair, tipping it to displace its occupant. "Skedaddle," he said and a protesting bundle of fur hit the ground.

"Hey, take it easy."

"You know, kiddo," an unrepentant Dan told her, "if you didn't have these pesky critters hanging around, you'd be the world's most perfect lady friend. I might even consider marrying you."

He snickered and she bristled. She said, "For your information, I would never ever consider a non-cat lover to be marriage material."

Dan laughed so heartily, it was clear to Katie he didn't think she meant what she had said. Or maybe, it occurred to her a moment later, his hilarity came from the fact that he hadn't meant what he'd said.

A few minutes later, Katie took the brown-and-serve rolls from the oven, put them in a basket, and spooned the stew into two bowls. They sat down to eat. Whenever she watched him eat, Katie experienced twin feelings of delight and dismay. Delight at his hearty appreciation of her food; dismay at the way he ate. Dan was a shoveler. His mouth almost touched the bowl as he scooped up the food with his fork. She leaned over to the silverware drawer and pulled out a spoon, which she handed to him.

A while later, after Dan had finished a second helping, he licked his lips and smiled at Katie. "That was dee-lish-us. Now, for dessert, how about I treat you? We'll drop by that Baskin-Robbins round the corner."

Katie was about to point out she already had a store-bought apple pie ready to be heated. But he said, "Hot fudge sundae, Katie?" His blue eyes sparkled with friendly mischief. Immediately, Katie's mouth watered as she pictured the chocolaty topping spilling over a mound of creamy ice cream. Dan knew this particular soft spot well.

"Dan, stop it. Oh, and you can stop that too." For now he had picked up his empty bowl and was making a big show of licking a smidgen of gravy off the rim. She clucked with disapproval as she took the dish from him but it didn't fool Dan. As she passed by him, he grabbed her and planted a kiss between her breasts. She reacted by putting her face down and sliding her cheek across the top of his silky blond hair. Not for the first time, her swings in feeling toward him left Katie feeling off balance. A few minutes ago, she'd been disparaging his table manners. Now he could eat his food with his toes for all she cared.

LATER THAT EVENING, the two of them relaxed on her couch. Katie sighed. His arm snaked around her shoulders. "Anything wrong?"

"Right now, absolutely nothing. What could be better than relaxing with a glass of wine and not having to think about that damned office for three more days."

Dan chuckled. She knew he found her reports on life at RPC to be amusing and wished she could share his blithe attitude. She snuggled into his shoulder, rubbing her face against the soft fabric of his sweater.

If anything, it had been a somewhat less horrendous week than usual, at least partly because Miranda had left her alone. Even so, she couldn't shake off a feeling of apprehensiveness about the future. "You know, Dan, usually I can drum up enough inner reserves to carry me through rough times. But, right now, I feel my life is on hold. I have no idea what to do about it but I have the sickening feeling that whatever I'm doing is going to lead to disaster."

Sharply, he said, "Meaning what?"

"It's my damn job."

His expression relaxed. "It's that boss of yours, huh? Always getting up your nose?"

"Well, yes. Him and his sidekick, Miranda. I've promised myself I'll simply wait them out. Miranda should be leaving in a few months. Everyone says Barry's just rotating through our department on his way to bigger and better things. So I suppose I should just be patient for a year or so."

He stroked her hair back over her ear. "Don't sound too healthy to me, honeypot. A year can seem like a real long time if you're unhappy."

"You're right. I should be looking for something else. But then I'm sure that bloody woman will give me a poor performance rating. And how will I get a new job with a bad rating?"

"You worry too much."

Katie felt a flush of irritation. Now he sounded like Lorraine and it wasn't comforting. Idly, she ran her hand over his chin. It was always a surprise to feel the stubble on his face at the end of the day. He was so blond it could barely be seen.

He said, "Now if I was you, I'd find myself some nice little business of my own. That way you don't have to bother with bosses and performance ratings and such."

Having a nice little business of your own, Katie thought, seemed to be Dan's solution to all of life's woes. She said, "Oh, Dan, that's never been my dream. Besides, I have the same problem as Sherman. No capital to get going. You know, my company told him they're not interested in his cogen unit?"

Dan said, "Yeah, I know. And on top of that the poor guy got fired from his regular job. That Sierra company."

Startled, Katie said, "He did? How do you know that?"

"He told me. I give him a call sometimes."

Katie tried to fight down her feelings of alarm at this news. It seemed Dan and Sherman were keeping up with each other behind her back. But why should she care? She wasn't responsible for Sherman. Or for Dan. True, Sherman might be hoodwinked into thinking her enthusiastic, if clueless, lover could help him start a business. And true, if Barry could be believed, Dan might unwittingly be drawn by Sherman into some illicit scheme to defraud RPC. But they were both grown men and didn't need her help to live their lives.

Dan said, "You don't have Sherman's problem though, do you?"

"What do you mean?"

"Well, Sherm don't have any money at all. He don't even own his house. But you own this place free and clear." He squinted down at her. "From what I hear, anyways."

Katie pushed herself from him and sat upright. "You hear from whom?"

"Well...uh, never mind."

But Katie knew the answer to her question. The only person who could have imparted that information to Dan would have been Mildred—her next-door neighbor, Dan's employer, and, it would seem, neighborhood gossip.

She sputtered, "So Mildred has been telling you about my personal financial situation. How dare she!"

Dan reacted heatedly, "What are you so fired up about? Why, if I owned my home outright, I'd be shouting about it to everyone."

Katie twisted so sharply toward him that the cat jumped off her lap. "I'm sure you would. Not that the situation was ever likely to arise."

She glared at him. He glared back, his mouth set in a thin defiant line. Then he removed his arm from her shoulders and stared straight ahead. Katie realized she was holding her breath and made a deliberate attempt to exhale.

After a long, silent minute, Dan stood up, edged his way around the coffee table and walked down the hall to the front door. Katie was disbelieving. Was he really going to walk out without another word? How immature. But it was just what he did, closing the door firmly behind him. She listened, still in disbelief, to the sound of his car starting up and backing into the street. This did it. If he was so childish he could react to a small quarrel in this way, she wanted nothing more to do with him.

A long hour passed. Katie reached for the phone. These were moments that girlfriends were created for.

Lorraine said, "Hi, honeybunch. How's tricks?"

Suddenly, Katie felt reluctant to tell her sad tale. It would make everything seem so final. "Dan and I had a spat."

"Ah, lovers' quarrel. Tell Mommy all about it. Just a minute." There was a scuffling sound from Lorraine's end, followed by a shriek. "Cut it out, you pervert. No, not you, Katie."

A gravelly male voice interjected, "Hi, there, Katie, Pete the Perve here." There were more scuffles and giggles from Lorraine.

Katie said, "You two are hopeless. Wish my life were half so much fun."

"Okay, that's enough, Peter. My buddy's breaking heart calls." To Katie, Lorraine asked, "So what happened?"

"Dan came over. I was moaning away about work, and—now that I think about it—he was probably trying to cheer me up." It hadn't occurred to her until now that Dan was probably trying to do just that. "He said why didn't I quit my job and start up a little business of my own." She fell silent.

"Yes. So?"

"Well, what got me all wound up was he said I'd have no trouble raising money because I own my own house, free and clear. You see, Lorraine, I never told him that—about the house—he got that information from Mildred next door. She's a real blabbermouth."

She paused again. Lorraine said, "I'm sorry, I still don't get it. Why does this upset you? It's not a dirty little secret, is it? To own your own house."

Katie wailed. "But it's none of his business. It makes me feel that—oh, I don't know—maybe he's only hanging around me...."

"For your *money*?" Lorraine gave a bellow of laughter. "Katie, do you know how paranoid you sound? I'm telling you, you should call up that gorgeous beast right away and tell him you were stoned or premenstrual, or something. And now you have to excuse me. I have some man business of my own I have to take care of."

She hung up to the sounds of what sounded, Katie thought crossly, like hippos doing a mating dance.

Telling the story to Lorraine had made her reaction seem really petty. Too bad tonight was the start of a long weekend. Could she really face the prospect of three Dan-free days ahead of her? She picked up the phone—then put it down again. For God's sake, she was rapidly getting in too deep with Dan. This might be just the push she needed to break loose of him.

Mildred was something else. That old fool didn't realize how much havoc she was causing with her loose tongue. She reached for the phone but then withdrew her hand. A personal visit would be better. She put on shoes and a sweater, picked up her purse, and made for the front door. She opened it and ran headfirst into Dan.

"Hi." He looked uncertain as though he thought she might slam the door in his face. "Katie..."

Katie was so overcome with relief, her knees started to buckle. It dawned on her in that instant that maybe Dan had never meant to pry into her private business. Mildred had told him about the house just because the old woman loved to talk.

She opened her mouth to tell him but no words came. Instead, she leaned into his open arms and buried her face in his neck. And faced, yet again, the scary realization that no matter what Dan knew or did or was, she just wasn't ready to stop this quite unsuitable relationship. At least, not yet.

36

Dan Tries to Pin Sherman Down

ON A SUNDAY MORNING in mid-September, Sherman parked his car at the Beresford Airport, and took the five o'clock United Express flight to Oakland. Tomorrow, he was due to start work at George's company. This week, he was attending an orientation and training course in the Bay Area, all expenses paid.

In spite of his lingering nervousness about what this new job might entail, Sherman felt that a week of goofing off in a hotel would be a pleasant break. And, of course, today he had the opportunity to get together with Dan again. He'd phoned Dan yesterday to tell him of his plans and was pleased when Dan offered to meet his plane at the airport.

Dan was the flame that kept Sherman's dream alive. Dan was often inspirational—stressing the notion that their marketing should be expanded outside the state to the whole country—or even the world. Dan dismissed Sherman's concerns about other people stealing the patent. "We'll just have to build it better and cheaper than everyone else. And eventually we'll have to invent something else."

Sherman had noted the "we," but let it pass.

Soon after his plane touched down in Oakland, he spotted Dan's cheerful face in the waiting crowd. Dan was alone. He grabbed Sherman's bag and strode off with Sherman hurrying to keep up.

Outdoors, it was much cooler than the oppressive Valley. They walked across several lanes of traffic in front of the terminal, dodging taxis and shuttle buses, and then across a giant parking lot. Several minutes later, they arrived at a small red Toyota. Sherman was out of breath. "My God, Dan, you remind me I'm not young anymore."

Dan laughed. Sherman thought that much as he adored his daughter, it would be wonderful to have a son like this smiling, clean-cut young man. Dan unlocked the doors and put the suitcase in the trunk. As they climbed in, he said, "In case you're wondering, Katie couldn't make it today. She said to say hi."

Sherman wondered, as he had ever since first meeting Dan, just what Katie's relationship was to this golden boy. Was she really his girlfriend? She seemed too old. And why would Dan be attracted to her? He could surely have the pick of any woman around. Sherman suddenly felt disloyal. Katie was warm and sympathetic, but hardly a beauty.

The company had booked Sherman into the motel in San Ramon where the training sessions would be held. He was surprised when Dan pointed out that this was a fair distance from Oakland. "No problem," Dan said, "I'll drive you there. But how about we eat first? I know a nice little place."

La Dolce Vita, a small Italian café just off 44th Street, wasn't as pretentious as its name. It was, however, cozy and welcoming with its décor of hanging plants and shelves full of empty wine bottles.

As soon as they sat down, Dan said, "This is on me, incidentally." He added, "They have great spaghetti and meatballs."

"Sounds good."

After the waiter took their orders, Dan leaned forward. "Now, tell me, what's happening with your energy converter?"

Sherman paused. He helped himself to a breadstick, took a sip of water. He felt a little guilty accepting Dan's hospitality, knowing full well why Dan had been so eager to meet him today. "Well, Dan, as you know, I'm really strapped for cash these days."

Glancing at Dan, Sherman was struck by the intensity in the younger man's face. Dan, his elbows on the table, leaned toward Sherman. "Yes, but now you're starting a regular job. So you'll have a steady income."

"True, but also I have a slew of debts to pay off and all my savings, such as they were, are gone."

Dan's face hardened. "Debts?"

"When I left Sierra, I had to pay back advance commissions that I received but didn't earn. Also, I pretty well exhausted all my savings paying for the patent and three demo units. It'll be at least a couple of years before I can even think about getting back to my cogen project again."

Dan leaned back. "That's no good. With those demos out there, someone's going to copy your patent. You gotta get out in front."

Their salads arrived.

Dan said, "Did I ever tell you about my brother-in-law? My ex-brother-in-law, that is? He owns his own machine shop near Merced but they only operate during the week. I bet I can get him to let us use the shop nights and weekends."

"For what? A machine shop by itself is no good to us. We need money, Dan. Lots of money. For publicity, marketing, the cost of materials. We'll have to hire people."

"We won't have to hire people. I can do the machining."

"No, Dan, I'm sorry. I'd like to just let things rest for a year or two while I build my up savings again."

There was a long silence. They finished their salads. The waiter brought hot dishes of spaghetti and meatballs. It occurred to Sherman that Dan was taking this rather well. He was quiet but didn't appear devastated.

Suddenly, Dan, his eyes examining Sherman's face, said quietly, "Sherm, you wouldn't mind if I went ahead with this on my own, would you? With you acting as a kind of advisor?"

Sherman swallowed a mouthful of hot food. "What are you talking about? You're saying you'd steal my patent?"

Right away, Dan leaned across the table and grasped Sherman's arm. "Absolutely not. You'd be in on this deal, fifty-fifty. You provide the patent. I provide the marketing and labor and the machine shop and the capital."

"Dan, I hate to sound negative, but where would you get the capital?" He resisted emphasizing the *you*.

"I think I have a source. Of course, if I can't raise the money, the whole deal's off."

Sherman stopped eating and looked at his companion for a long moment. "And you plan to raise capital how? Robbing ATMs?" He snickered at his own joke and was dismayed to see a flush rise in Dan's face. "Hey, Dan, let me think about this, okay?" Sherman did not feel he needed to "think about it," but he also hated to squash the poor kid.

Dan's flush faded. He withdrew his arm and returned to his food. "Okay. Oh, and how about Thursday evening, Katie and I come get you in San Ramon? We'll all go out to dinner."

"Does Katie know about this scheme of yours?"

Dan response was almost inaudible. "No, but she will."

IT WAS PAST NINE when Dan got home and called Katie. "So," she asked, "Did you get Sherman settled into his hotel?"

"Yeah." Dan chuckled. "The poor guy was thinking his hotel was across from the airport or somethin'. He never realized he might need a car."

"Is he excited about his new job?"

"I don't know. We mainly talked about his converter. He seemed kinda reluctant to proceed right now. Said he wants to take a couple of years—*years*—to save some money."

"I'm not surprised. He's flat broke."

"I think I talked sense into him though."

"What do you mean?"

"Look, time's awastin'. Next I know, you'll be saying it's too late for me to come over. How's about we save the talking for after I get there?"

"It's already too late, lover-boy. By the time you get here, it'll be past ten—and it's a week day tomorrow."

"Okay, tomorrow then. I'll pick up some Chinese food and get to your place about six. Then we'll eat fast and I'll love you and leave you. How's that?"

She laughed. "You've twisted my arm again."

Katie loved Dan's lovemaking. Nestled close to his body, with his strong arms stroking her, she felt like the most desirable woman in the world. And, of course, Dan had to know how much she loved it. She wondered if he realized just how temporary she considered their relationship to be. He surely must.

It wasn't until after she got to bed that Katie thought about Sherman again. Once, Dan had asked, "You really care about him, don't you?" It was true. There was an emotional tug there.

As for the man of her dreams... she thought back to her conversation with Lorraine on this subject. Did such a creature exist? Would she know him if she found him? In the bed, two small, furry bodies stretched and purred as she moved. Well, she knew one thing for certain. Whoever he was, he'd have to accept these cuddly creatures into his life. Which, for sure, ruled out Dan.

37

Performance Evaluations

IT WAS A FRIDAY MORNING, some two weeks later. As she walked down the hall toward her office, Katie bumped into Terry. He made a face. "Have you seen what's awaiting you this morning? The long-awaited performance evaluation by Herself."

Katie stopped. "Have you seen yours?"

"Sure have. Just as she promised, a C. To be precise, I got a C plus. Not that the plus will help when it comes to a raise."

"Bitch," Katie muttered.

She saw the envelope lying on her chair as soon as she opened her office door but waited until she'd checked her phone messages and sorted through the contents of her briefcase before she opened it. She was stunned to find Miranda had rated her a C minus. Even lower than Terry.

As her eyes ran down the written comments, her sense of outrage grew. Miranda had dubbed her "uncooperative," "not a team player," "needing improvement in her attitude toward her work." She picked up the phone and dialed Miranda's number.

"Miranda."

"Why, I bet this is Katie." Miranda said sweetly. "I thought I might be hearing from you. Would you perhaps like to discuss your performance evaluation?"

Katie was too angry to speak. She slammed down the phone, and set off down the hall, evaluation in hand, for Miranda's office. There, Miranda sat looking for all the world, as Katie later told Terry, like a smirking spider awaiting the arrival of a juicy fly.

"Now, tell me," Katie said, waving the evaluation, "what every line of this garbage means."

Katie didn't close the door and over the next fifteen minutes many passers-by sneaked curious glances into the room. It certainly was unusual for there to be so much shouting on the eighth floor. Finally, Katie rose. "So what you're saying is that you feel this evaluation of me is fair. I'm going to take this up with Barry. If he agrees with you, there's no point whatever in my continuing to be employed here."

She walked out the door to the sound of Miranda's "Whatever."

Katie had noticed that Terry was one of those who'd passed by the door during the shouting. She made her way to his cubicle and flung herself into the chair opposite him. He turned away from his computer. "Well," he said, "I would suggest a cuppa coffee in the caff but I'm off to a meeting in a few minutes."

Katie spoke quietly. There was absolutely no privacy in these cubicles. "I think I should storm into Barry's office right this minute—while I'm still on the boil. What do you think?"

"Won't do you much good, kiddo. I stopped by to see him myself but he won't be available until Monday. He's at some meeting this morning and then he's taking off for a long weekend with his wife."

Katie looked down at her trembling hands. "Damn and blast."

Terry said gently, "Katie, the C wasn't really a surprise, was it? I mean, I'd already told you that's what I got."

She leaned forward and hissed. "It wasn't even a C. It was a C minus."

Terry raised his eyebrows. "That *is* strange."

"The bitch had a sheet filled with the most stupid and illogical crap you ever saw. For example, she said I was uncooperative because I refused to back her in insisting on a department retreat. You may remember it was Barry who nixed the idea. Now she's taking it out on me."

"That's ridiculous. Of course, you have to appeal to Barry."

At this point, one of Terry's programmers put his head over the partition. "Ready to go?"

Terry got to his feet. "Sorry, Katie. Why don't you ask Dorothy to set you up with an appointment with Barry." He whispered, "Obviously, Miranda isn't playing with a full deck."

Brushing past her as he left the cubicle, he patted her shoulder. "Hey, it'll turn out okay. You'll see."

Katie wished she felt as confident. If she could only undo that conversation with Barry in the car. She sat for a while, staring into space. This just couldn't be happening to her. But it was. And she had to face it.

She went to her office and called Dorothy to make an appointment.

38

Upsetting Revelations

Katie sipped her lemonade, not trusting herself to speak while the two men watched her face. Dan had a half-smile on his lips. Sherman looked anxious. It was the Sunday afternoon after Katie's confrontation with Miranda. The three of them were seated around the dining table in Sherman's house.

Dan had just made a suggestion that left Katie feeling she'd been kicked in the stomach. She wanted to tell him how offensive she found his idea, but, for Sherman's sake, she wanted to be tactful. And, for her own sake, she didn't want to launch into a hissy fit she might later regret.

That morning, Dan had picked her up for a trip to the Valley to visit Sherman. Katie was annoyed to see him drive up in his truck. She said, "What the heck?"

Dan explained, "I promised Sherm I'd help him move. He's going to move out of his rental house and go live with his daughter."

"Holy cow, he's agreed to live with George?" She grumbled, "Helping someone move is not how I planned to spend the day."

"It won't take that long. Some charity outfit is pickin' up most of the furniture but Sherm wants to keep some stuff and he has a ton of boxes. So I said I'd bring the truck. C'mon, you haven't seen ol' Sherm in ages."

"That's true."

IN PINE FLATS, several hours later, after they had loaded up the truck, Sherman called for a snack break. He produced some lemonade from the fridge, which was not being moved, and seated them at the dining table— also not being moved.

Dan flashed a mischievous grin at Katie and said, "Hey, Sherm, shall I tell her now?"

Katie's stomach tensed. "Oh, no, what?"

"It's good news, poppy-seed. Sherm and me, well, we're goin' into business together."

Sherman didn't take his eyes off Katie who listened silently while Dan talked.

"See, things've changed now that Sherm's moving in with his daughter. He'll be able to save a bundle of money on rent. And so..." Dan put a hand on Sherman's shoulder. "Okay, Sherm, you tell it."

Sherman said, "Well, Katie, I have patents on all kinds of devices, not just the converter. Also, Dan's brother-in-law in Merced has a machine shop he'll let us use for free on weekends. So we can get started manufacturing and selling things and build up capital that way."

Katie looked at Dan. "So you're planning to move to Merced?"

"Sure, I could hardly commute from here. But—hey, get that look offa your face."

To her annoyance, Katie couldn't help the look he was referring to—one of utter dismay. She felt tears sting her eyes.

Both men turned toward her, each putting out a hand to cover one of hers. Sherman said, "You're part of our plans, Katie, really you are."

She swallowed, "I don't see how."

Dan said, "Sherm and me want you to be a part of this business. You keep saying you hate your job. When we was driving here this morning, you said you got this stinkin' performance grade or whatever. Why not throw it in? We'd have lots of work for you to do in the office."

"Bookkeeping and stuff like that," Sherman added.

Katie pulled her hands loose and took out a tissue. "Really," she sniffed, "it warms my heart that you want to include me in your plans, but I've become used to a certain way of life. Will you be able to pay me enough to keep me in the style I'm accustomed to?" She tried to smile. Dan looked uncomfortable and glanced at Sherman who looked away.

And then Dan made the audacious suggestion that to Katie was the last straw. "Sugar," he said, "if you was to move with me, it'd make sense to sell your house, wouldn't it? That'd give you a whole bunch of cash to coast by on."

Katie inhaled sharply. Her suspicions about his motives had been true all along. She suddenly had a mental picture of Dan assuring Sherman that he, Dan, knew of a source of capital for their venture: the rich, older woman who was nuts about him.

Struggling to contain her anger, she dried her tears and finished her lemonade. Quietly, she said, "I'll have to do a lot of thinking about this and get back to you."

Of course, there was nothing to think about. After she had composed her thoughts sufficiently, she would tell that cowboy just what he could do with his preposterous suggestions. Then she'd tell Lorraine all about it and they could both have a good laugh. And then she would get on with her life.

AS THEY WERE driving home later that afternoon, Dan said, "So waddyer think of moving to the Valley with me?"

Katie hadn't had sufficient time alone to think through the inevitable break-up scene she'd been envisioning. But now she had to say something.

She sighed. "Dan, you have to see things from my point of view. In spite of all my complaining, I do have a very good job. I know my boss is aiming for a vice-presidency and he probably won't be our manager for too much longer. Who knows, if I play my cards right, maybe I can get his job when he leaves."

A strangled sound came from Dan's throat. Katie glanced at him. He was staring straight ahead through the windshield, scowling. He said, "You sure don't know your own mind, do you? You never said before that you wanted to be manager. Where did this come from?

Yesterday, you was bitchin' about how you hated the place, how you thought you was going to get fired."

"Oh, Dan, becoming manager of ESS has been my dream for years. You've no idea how much time I spend thinking about what I'd do, the changes I'd make. I've even written up a whole plan on a new direction for our department."

"Heck, I always thought your dream was marriage and kids, jes' like most women. I know I'd like to have another kid. I hardly feel Danny belongs to me at all." A whiney note crept into his voice. "Shoot, I thought the two of us was aiming right up that road."

"Dan. Of course, I enjoy being with you, but the thought of marrying you has never entered my mind."

Dan flashed her a glance. He looked stunned. "You don't say! The way you carry on with me—you mean women do that stuff even when they don't want to marry the guy?"

"My God, Dan! Are you serious?"

Dan, the prude! Lorraine would die laughing when she heard of this conversation. But Katie fancied she saw his lips trembling, and, gently, she ran her hand over his thigh. His lovely taut, jeans-clad thigh. She said, "Dan, never in a million years would I expect someone like you to consider marrying someone like me. You can have any woman you choose. For a start, have you considered the age difference between us?"

It pained Katie to mention this last factor. It was something she tried hard not to think about. Quietly, she added, "I'm sorry you misunderstood."

He snapped, "Let's drop it. If you're not interested in getting married, you're not interested. We've just been talking cross-wise all along. I always thought you was kind of a mind with me is all."

Katie felt sad to be hurting his feelings. She also felt flattered that he would seriously consider marrying her.

Their customary coffee shop loomed up and Dan pulled into a parking spot. It was four-thirty, too early for dinner. They ordered coffee and pie à la mode and spoke little as they ate. After she finished her pie, Katie looked at the downcast face across from her. "Dan, how long ago did you break up with your wife? I know you told me once, but I forget."

"It was ten—no, seven—years ago. Ten when it started and seven when she filed for divorce."

"But a guy like you must have had a bunch of lady friends in the intervening years? Yes? No?" She tried to sound joking.

To her surprise, his face tightened into an angry expression. He took a last mouthful of coffee, put down his cup, and said, "How come you're always so goddamn interested in my past?"

"What? Well, I'm sorry...."

"If you're done, let's make tracks. I'd kinda like to get home early tonight." He signaled the waitress for the check.

LATER THAT EVENING, Katie phoned Lorraine and told her about the new side of Dan she'd just witnessed. "He brought me home and dropped me off with not even a peck on the cheek. I felt as if I'd committed the most gross faux pas."

Lorraine murmured sympathetically. "Obviously, he's one of these unsophisticated types who can't conceive of love affairs other than being events that lead directly to the altar. And obviously he's deeply hurt you don't want to marry him."

"But why did he get so angry at me? No matter what he says, I'm not always prying into his past."

"Okay, sweetie, it's been a bad day. But of course you're doing the right thing. Have fun with him as long as you want but, of course, marriage would be ludicrous. As for giving up your career to be a bookkeeper in a ratty machine shop somewhere.... What an idea!"

"You sure do put things in perspective." She added ruefully, "Of course, if I turn down his proposition, our relationship will end right on the spot."

"Which would be a good thing, right? Handsome, sexy and all—but not someone you want to get stuck with for life, for Heaven's sake. You've already started agonizing over how to end it without hurting him too much. He's making it easy for you by moving away."

"You're right."

That night, Katie lay in bed brooding. Of course, she'd recover from Dan. If she could recover from Alan she sure could recover from Dan. She'd always known their breakup was inevitable—just hadn't expected it to come so abruptly. But she couldn't stop feeling hurt about his anger, his unkindness in dropping her off without a kiss.

39

Showdown with Barry

ON MONDAY MORNING, as Barry's staff meeting ended, Katie lingered by his desk. He said, "That's right. We have an appointment, don't we?" Katie's stomach churned as she sat down across from him. In retrospect, she wished she hadn't made this appointment. It seemed much too soon after their confrontation in the car.

She started, "I hope your wife is doing okay."

"What did you want to see me about?"

"My performance review." She pulled out her copy and placed it on the desk. "I found Miranda's review extremely upsetting. In fact, downright offensive in places."

Barry's expression was blank. Katie went on, "Miranda has been anything but objective in writing that review. She's totally ignored my clients' evaluations of me and my projects. Much of her report seems to focus on how disloyal I've been to her."

"I take it you discount loyalty as an admirable quality?"

Flustered, she said, "Have you actually read it? Like the part where she's angry that I didn't support her on having a departmental retreat. You were the one who wanted to cancel it, right?"

Barry put his arms behind his head and leaned back. He said, "Well, I had promised her that retreat."

"Canceling it was the right thing to do under the circumstances. The point is Miranda shouldn't have taken it out on me just because I happened to agree with you."

"So what would you like me to do about it?"

Katie swallowed. This meeting was going as badly as she'd feared it might. She pleaded, "Please read what she wrote very carefully. Then tell me if you honestly think her criticisms are justified. And tell me," Katie heard desperation in her voice, "if you believe I warrant a C-minus rating after all the excellent work I've done this past year. A rating like that is only ever given to someone whose performance is so bad they're on the point of being fired."

Again, he said nothing. She might as well give up, Katie thought. She pushed back her chair to leave.

Barry said, "Just a minute. There's something else." He opened a drawer and took out a letter, which he handed to her. "Have you seen this before?"

She hadn't. That is, she hadn't seen the actual document. Two pages of cream stock with Sherman Granger's name and address printed on the top page. But, as her eyes scanned the contents, she recognized her own words. "No," she said. "I haven't."

He pressed her. "Are you sure? Read it over."

As she pretended to read, she thought crossly that, at the least, Sherman might have rewritten her draft instead of copying it verbatim. In his own words, it might have had the flavor of something written by a small town salesman. This thing sounded so *corporate*, it was obviously penned by someone like herself.

Barry said, "Do you notice how he keeps referring to our corporate values—straight out of the Corporate Values Program? Do you think he had inside help in writing this letter?"

She looked up. Now was the time to bring out what Lorraine would call "obfuscating skills." "Oh, I don't know. Certainly, he's heard company people talk about the corporate values enough. For instance, when I visited Mike Weston that first time..."

"Exactly." Barry thumped a hand on the table. "Both Worthington's aide and Worthington himself are sure Mike Weston and Sherman Granger are in cahoots. Remember, I suggested that to you before. They're planning to foist something on the company and split the proceeds."

"Oh, surely not." Katie's voice sounded weak to her.

"Well, anyway, Weston's boss hauled him in and questioned him about it. I think I've mentioned to you that Weston is sort of on probation."

"Because of that house he built with company materials?"

"Exactly. If we can pin this Granger thing on him, they'll fire him for sure."

Katie felt sick. Barry took the offending letter from her and put it back in the drawer. He said, "I just wanted your word that you had nothing to do with writing this."

She had to ask. "What did Mike Weston say about it?"

Barry spoke slowly, looking into her eyes. "He denied having any part of it. In fact, he said that *you* were the one who wrote the letter. He says he's going to find proof, like emails you've sent Granger. Bluffing, would you say?"

As the peril of her situation sunk in, Katie continued to look back at him. Barry obviously had guessed all along that Weston had told the truth. He'd been stringing her along, allowing her to get entangled ever deeper into this morass by lying. He'd even allowed her to get to the point where another person was about to be fired for her actions.

"Right. That's all I have." He turned away to sort through his message slips.

Katie stood. She picked up her notebook and headed toward the door. After two paces, she turned back.

"Barry."

"Yes." He didn't look up.

"I—well, I didn't tell the complete truth just then."

Still not looking up, he said, "You don't say."

"You see, what happened is..."

"I know what happened, Katie." This time, he did look up and she was struck by his expression. It was one of deep disappointment, as though he'd been betrayed by a trusted colleague.

In a tone of exasperation, she demanded, "If you

know what happened, why not say so? Why are you deceiving me into thinking—"

He exploded. "Why am I deceiving *you*? That's rich."

Katie exploded too. "For God's sake, why is everyone making a federal case out of this? Sherman asked what sort of thing he should say in his letter. I sent him some notes without realizing he would copy them word for word. And it's ridiculous to think that Sherman and Mike are in cahoots to defraud the company. Mike is too stupid and Sherman is too much of a gentleman."

A humorless snort from Barry.

Katie continued, her voice rising, "And, tell me, how exactly does it damage our company to have someone write a letter to the CEO about an invention they have? The company can reject it, which they have done. You're all acting as if Sherman was planning to blow up head office."

"Katie, you seem to be missing the point." Barry's voice was icy. "I agree, this pathetic little letter can't possibly make a dent in our company's operations or fortunes. But you have been specifically instructed not to get involved in this. You've deliberately flouted that order and lied about it."

With a dramatic gesture, he again slammed his fist on the desk. "What's more, you have the temerity to complain about Miranda's evaluation of you. She didn't go far enough. Not only disloyalty, but also untrustworthiness and insubordination. You don't like a C minus? Neither do I. How does an F grab you?"

Katie had resolved long ago never to cry over anything in the workplace. Tears, she felt, were somehow the ultimate womanly weakness. So her eyes were dry as she shrilled, "You do realize that loyalty has to be earned and insubordination is an inevitable consequence of oppression."

Barry said, "Oh, get out. You make me sick." He turned away from her. Katie stood, frozen, until he looked up again. "I said, get out."

She did.

THE NEXT MORNING, Tuesday, Katie got to work at seven o'clock. She filled her coffee cup in the break room and carried it to her desk, where she sat staring unseeingly out the window. She hadn't told anyone about the meeting with Barry yesterday. Not Terry. Not even Lorraine.

Her unwillingness to unburden her unhappiness came mostly from feelings of shame. She no longer was certain about her motives in helping Sherman. Had she really been acting out of altruism? Or had she been trying to spite the company? Had she proved herself to be an untrustworthy and disloyal employee?

Halfway through her coffee, she heard footsteps in the hall. They stopped at her open door. She knew it was Barry. After a long moment, she turned away from the window toward the door. He said, "Got a minute?" She nodded. He looked at her cup and said, "Coffee. I'll be right back."

While she waited for him to return, Katie cleared off a chair for him to sit on. She felt numb. She had no idea what he'd say or how he'd be. His voice just now had seemed normal. At least, she reflected wryly, as normal as his usual menacing self would permit. She could hear Dorothy calling to him from down the hall. He called back, "Give me five, okay?"

So he needed five minutes to can someone?

When he came back, he closed the door behind him and sat down. Katie turned to look out the window again.

"Katie, I want to apologize for my behavior yesterday."

"You were angry."

In a level voice, he said, "I was and I still am. Extremely angry. But that's no excuse for losing my temper like that. I'm sorry."

She nodded. She could think of nothing to say. He sipped his coffee. Then he said, "Tell me about Sherman Granger. Is he a relative? A boyfriend?"

"Heavens, no." She almost smiled. "No, he's just a really nice man with a fantastic invention that this company would buy if it had any sense."

He said, "You talk as though you're in a position to evaluate its technical worth. Let me disabuse you. Granger's cogenerator unit has already been evaluated by our engineering and operations departments. Quite apart from the fact that it would be a hugely money-losing proposition for us—remember, it claims to cut electricity use by fifty percent—it is, in fact, incredibly expensive to manufacture and install. It's a completely un-business-like proposition."

Katie bowed her head. And those two idiots, Sherman and Dan, were throwing their all into the pursuit of this un-business-like proposition. And they wanted her to sell her house and throw those proceeds into the mix, too.

Barry continued. "Anyway, the merits or otherwise of this invention are neither here nor there. As I said yesterday, it is your behavior vis-à-vis the company that's been so disappointing."

Katie murmured, "Ah, yes, insubordination."

She looked up to meet his eyes. Green highlights sliding into brown. Hard to read. There was no mistaking his words. "Are you sure you still want to work for RPC, Katie?"

She shook her head and, to her annoyance, the long withheld tears pushed their way to the surface. She turned to the window again. There was a long silence. Barry stood up. He said, "Never mind. As we used to say when I was a kid, 'In a hundred years, we'll all be dead.'"

"My God, is that meant to be a comfort?" The words caught in her throat on top of a strangled laugh.

"What makes you think I want to comfort you?" Something playful in his tone made her look up. She caught a brief smile as he made his way out the door. None of this mattered anyway. Giving her an F was as good as firing her.

His question, "Are you sure you still want to work for RPC?" was unsettling enough. Even more unsettling was her growing conviction of what her honest answer might be.

LATER THAT MORNING, Barry checked over the list of performance ratings for departmental employees. He had to submit these to payroll so the raises for the following year could be calculated. No one with a rating of C or lower would be eligible for a raise. He stamped his automatic approval on the ratings Katie and Terry had given to the trainers, survey consultants, and programmers who reported to them.

Then he looked at the ratings Miranda had assigned to Katie and Terry. C minus and C plus. He himself had examined client evaluations of the work of his two supervisors and had observed much of it first hand. He knew these ratings were ridiculously low. At some point, he'd have to rewrite Miranda's evaluations.

Meantime, though, he could fix the ratings to be submitted to Payroll. For Terry, he changed the C to an A. He reflected a moment over Katie's rating. She had, after all, screwed up over that Granger business. But, what the hell, she no doubt thought she was doing the right thing. He changed her rating to an A also.

He added his signature to the end of the sheet and slid it into a *Confidential* envelope, which he sealed. No need to update anyone on this yet. First, he'd need to let Miranda know what he'd done. Then he could pass on the word to Terry. As for Katie, she deserved to be left swinging in the wind a bit longer.

40

Even More Upsetting Revelations

THE FOLLOWING SUNDAY, Katie stood with Sherman. They were leaning over the railing of a bridge in the Beresford Zoo, watching Dan and his son ride the zoo train. Danny waved to them as the train puffed by.

Sherman said, "Real shame he lost custody of the kid."

"Mmm, I'm not sure what happened there."

Sherman looked at her, a speculative look on his face. He said, "He very much wants to marry you, you know. Says you're not interested."

Katie gave a faint smile and said nothing. To her relief, Dan hadn't raised the subject of marriage since their spat last weekend. After a few moments, Sherman went on, "Dan says you're on vacation this week. Must be a nice break for you."

Katie sighed. "Not that nice. I had a huge showdown with my manager at work the other day and I'm sure I'm going to be fired any day."

He turned to her, his homely face displaying concern. "Oh dear. So is this really the best time to go on vacation?"

"Well, for a start, they owe me about six weeks. And I felt I just had to get out of there for a while."

Katie tried to speak lightly, but her stomach tensed, remembering Dorothy's reaction when she had called in. "Have you cleared this with Barry?" And Dorothy's shock at Katie's response. "No, and I don't intend to."

Sherman cleared his throat. "Katie, I can't tell you what to do, but if things don't work out for you at RPC, Dan and I would love to have you be a part of our team." He chuckled. "Our team! Now doesn't that sound good and corporate? Makes me think of a bunch of oxen yoked together."

They both waved as the little train passed by them again. Sherman said, "Of course, it would be a major change in lifestyle for you though, wouldn't it?"

Katie fell silent. It would be unthinkable. Scorching summers in the Central Valley. No more forays to theatres, ballets, concerts—to say nothing of trendy shops and restaurants. She'd be insane to even consider the proposition.

Sherman said, "Why don't you try it out during your vacation?"

"What do you mean?"

"Give it a trial run. Dan's found a room to rent in Merced, close to his brother-in-law's plant. He's moving there next weekend. Move in with him. See how you like it."

Suddenly her eyes lit up as his words sparked something she hadn't thought of before. "You've given me a great idea, Sherman. I could apply for a leave-of-absence. I can get up to six months without penalty. That would give me a chance to really explore other options. At the very least, it would be a wonderful break from the office."

"There you go." He seemed not to notice her dodging his suggestion about moving in with Dan.

AT FIVE O'CLOCK, they dropped Danny off at home. Then, Sherman insisted on treating them to a meal. He directed them to an air-conditioned coffee shop off the highway. "Nothing fancy," he told them, "just good wholesome food."

They all settled for burgers and fries. As they waited for the food, Dan said, " Hey, Sherm, Eddie says we can start using his plant anytime. Waddya say I take a crack at some of that garden equipment you was showing me?"

"Great." The two men exchanged grins and slapped hands.

Eddie was Dan's ex-brother-in-law. The garden equipment, Katie knew, was a watering system that Sherman also owned a patent on but had never developed. Katie said to Dan, "You're planning to move so soon. What about your customers? What about Mildred?"

"I'm talking to them all this week. Hey, I'm not irreplaceable." He and Sherman guffawed.

The "good, wholesome" burgers and fries arrived. There was continuing enthusiastic chatter between the two men of the new business they were about to start. Increasingly, Katie chided herself for not having thought of the leave-of-absence idea earlier. Now she had to hurry to get her application in to Employee Relations before Barry fired her.

Later, they drove Sherman to his daughter's home where he now lived.

He got out of the car, stuck his head into Katie's open window and gave her a kiss on the cheek.

He said, "Listen, you two. I don't know where y'all are headed. Marriage. Living together. Business partners. Whatever. It's not my business to give advice, but I do know one thing is critical. There should be no big secrets between two people. Otherwise, you're headed for a train wreck. Know what I mean?"

Katie frowned.

Sherman said, "Sorry for lecturing, but you're two of my favorite people. Dan, talk to you later." He waved as he left.

Dan was quiet as they drove away. After a while, Katie asked, "Big secrets? What was he talking about?"

Dan said, "Sherm knows something about me you don't."

Instantly, Katie wished she could retract her question. After what seemed like an endless silence, she asked, "What's that?"

"He knows where I was the last few years of my life. Well, the years between '82 and '88." He glanced at her. "I haven't told you before because I was sure you wouldn't want to see me no more." There was a question in his voice as though he were asking her to guarantee this wouldn't be her reaction.

Katie forced herself to ask, "So how *did* you spend the years between '82 and '88?"

"I'd 'a thought you coulda guessed. I was in prison."

"Oh, Dan." It was a whisper. "What happened?"

"It was right after me and Josie was married. I was out of work, and, like, we had the baby on the way." He glanced at her again. "Yeah, that's no excuse, right? Anyways, me and this other guy got in trouble. Armed robbery. He got twenty years, I got ten. They let me out early though."

Oh God! Katie felt physically sick.

Finally, she asked, "How come the other guy got so much more time?"

"Well, like, he had a gun and he—well, he shot the clerk in this gas station. We thought it was just a flesh wound but later the guy died."

"Oh, Dan!" she said again.

"I didn't even know he brought a gun. They believed me."

She turned to face his profile. Serious, but detached. As though he were talking about someone else.

"Dan, was that the only time you'd ever done anything like that?"

"Of course. The only time. And, man, have I learned my lesson."

"And Sherman knows about this?"

"Yeah. I figured I'd best tell him 'cause we're going to be business partners and all. He'd probably find out anyway."

She thought a moment. "But you weren't in any hurry to tell me?"

Dan said bitterly, "If I had my druthers, I'd never tell nobody. 'Specially not you. I wish I hadn't told you, but then Sherm probably would. Now you'll go stomping off and I'll never see you again." He paused. "I'n't that right?"

"Dan, this has come as a real shock. I'll have to think about it."

In the same bitter voice, he said, "Sure."

They didn't talk much during the rest of the journey home. Katie felt utterly at sea. There was no one she'd want to share this news with. Not even Lorraine. She'd never had to deal with such a situation and didn't know how to start. Should she ask him details about the crime, about how he'd been talked into it? Or had he talked the other guy into it? In truth, she wanted to forget the whole thing. She wished he hadn't told her. Which was, of course, the way Dan felt about it.

It was past nine when they pulled into her driveway. Late enough that she could claim work the next day to be the excuse for not inviting him in. He walked her to the door, waited until she unlocked it, and when she turned to him, said, "Katie, I'll understand if you don't want to see me no more."

She looked up at his handsome face. She noticed the deep frown lines that would probably become permanent in not too many years. He said, "I never shoulda told you. What would it matter if you never knew?"

For a crazy moment, she believed that.

"Damn. Honesty spoils everything." Her lips trembled as she spoke. She put her hands up to his face and pulled him down to her. He kissed her in his tender way and held her close. His lips brushing her ear, he whispered. "Katie, please don't stop lovin' me. I'll die if you do."

But all Katie could think about at this moment was that no matter how gently she tried to carry out the final inevitable breakup with him, he would be convinced that her sole reason would be the knowledge of his criminal past.

THAT NIGHT, in bed, Katie lay awake thinking about Dan. His news had initially horrified her and yet it was helpful too. For the first time, she was able to fit together all the pieces of Dan that she'd never quite been able to figure out before. Now she felt she really could understand the young man who had made a dreadful misstep early in life. His attempt to lessen the impact on the people he loved by encouraging them to build a life without him. His determination to make himself into someone he and others would respect—like becoming a successful businessman and marrying a successful woman.

Poor Dan. Her heart grieved for him. And for herself!

As for what she should do next--the more she thought about it, the more appealing the idea of a long leave from work seemed. Her career was washed up anyway and she was fed up with the office and the stress of dealing with Barry and Miranda and performance evaluations. But moving in with Dan, a long option to start with, was obviously completely out of the picture.

41

Leading up to the Big One

ON THE MORNING of Tuesday, October 17, Barry sat at his desk, trying to concentrate on the report in front of him. It was a proposal to re-staff head office departments. This was a topic that was dear to Barry's heart, too important by far to be rushed through as Worthington wanted him to do.

It had been a trying few days. Yesterday, Lila had taken a turn for the worse and had been rushed to the hospital for a second angioplasty. That had taken place this morning and Barry was to call on her later this afternoon.

And recently things in the office were going to pot. For some inexplicable reason, Katie had taken off on vacation—without consulting anyone. An angry Miranda had urged Barry to fire her, so Barry had been obliged to tell Miranda what he had not yet got around to telling her: that he'd raised the performance ratings of both Terry and Katie to an A. As he had told Miranda, "I can hardly fire someone I've just rated an A." A predictable brouhaha had followed and Miranda hadn't spoken to him since. But, shortly after nine this morning, Miranda phoned, apparently in a forgiving mood. "Bair-eee," she cooed. "So sorry to hear about Lila. How's she doing?"

"Okay, I think. I'm picking her up from the hospital later today. Thanks for asking."

"Can I stop by for a minute? There's a couple of things I'd like to go over with you."

"I'm sort of squeezed right now, Miranda. How about a late lunch?"

She giggled. "No can do, as it happens. I have another date. Guess who with?"

Barry yawned and looked at his watch. Miranda went on. "Terry Lynch. We're establishing goals and priorities for the coming year."

In spite of himself, Barry was curious. "Goals and priorities, huh? Any chance I'll get to hear what those are?"

"I've already told you about them. I'm establishing cross-training throughout the department. And I thought we could start by having Katie and Terry switch jobs for a while."

"What? Miranda, I thought I made it clear—"

Miranda spoke quickly. "The management courses kick off this week and Katie isn't here, so this is a perfect opportunity to get Terry up to speed in the management development end of things." She chuckled. "Teach Katie a lesson too. When she gets back, she'll realize she's not indispensable."

Miranda might have a point there, Barry thought. He said, "And, meantime, who runs Terry's section?"

"Oh, one of his programmers, I imagine. He has lots of them."

"And this is just for a week, right? Until Katie gets back?"

At this point, Dorothy tapped at Barry's door. "Excuse me, Barry. Mr. Worthington's secretary just called. He'd like to see you earlier than he'd said before. At ten o'clock."

"Oh, hell! Miranda, I'm in more of a rush than I realized. Look, we'll talk about your ideas later."

As soon as he hung up, he realized he should have stressed she was absolutely not to proceed with her cross-training ideas until they'd had that talk.

TERRY EXPLODED. "No, Miranda, I can't do what you're asking. I wouldn't dream of interfering with Katie's training programs without her express consent."

Miranda flushed. The two of them were eating lunch at Arturo's Cafeteria. "Terry, I'm not sure I appreciate your uncooperative attitude."

"Have you checked this out with Barry?"

The question angered her further. She still felt resentful at the way Barry had overridden her on the performance ratings for Terry and Katie.

She snapped. "I have, actually. This morning."

"You're saying Barry agreed I should kick off Katie's management development courses without even checking with Katie? What am I supposed to do with this kicking off stuff anyway? What does that mean? And who says I have the time to run around kicking things off?"

Miranda put down her fork. "Terry, I find your attitude to be both flippant and insubordinate." She saw the corners of his mouth turn up and said loudly, "What's more, I think we both know the reason for your reluctance to take on more work at this time." He looked surprised. She said, "Oh, yes. Don't think I haven't noticed the way you're taking extra time off. Leaving early nearly every day."

"I've cleared it with Barry. I've needed time off recently for personal reasons. To be with a sick friend."

"You need to clear it with me, not Barry. I'm your supervisor." A smirk crossed her face. "Yes, and I know all about your sick friend."

"What's that supposed to mean?"

"He's got AIDS, hasn't he? Your friend? And this is the guy you live with? You're lucky we continue to employ you."

Terry jumped to his feet. "How dare you, you stupid little trollop! You, of all people, think you have the right to lecture people on anything." His voice was loud and people at adjoining tables turned to look. Terry grabbed his jacket from the back of the chair and marched out without putting it on.

Miranda sat, open-mouthed, until she noticed the bemused stares coming her way. Her hand trembling, she downed the rest of her coffee and left the restaurant. She couldn't let him get away with this.

Back in her office, she picked up her phone and dialed his number. "Terry, I need to speak with you right away."

He said, "I'm at my desk."

Miranda put down the phone. Very well, if he wanted a showdown in his office where the whole world could hear, so be it. Two minutes later, she pushed her way into his cubicle and sat down. Terry jumped to his feet, picked up a thick file from the cabinet behind him, and threw it on his desk.

"These," he said, "are just some of the excellent client evaluations I've received this past year. I made certain Barry got copies."

"Feel-good sheets," she spat. "Those things aren't worth the paper they're written on, as well you know. Sit down, please."

"I know no such thing." He remained standing. "You're mad because Barry chose to raise my rating to an A."

So Terry already knew. She said coldly. "I said, sit down. Don't you dare stand there threatening me."

"Threatening you? You paranoid bitch..."

"How dare you swear at me. I'll call security if you keep this up. We need to get some things straight around here."

Miranda could hear people in adjacent cubicles murmuring.

Terry shouted, "What things straight? Me, for example? Miranda, you'll have to treat me very carefully indeed. Stress leads us queers to do all kinds of things. Like running to our attorneys."

"What are you talking about?" But Miranda's tone reflected her uncertainty.

He continued shouting. "I've been gathering evidence, you know. About your behavior toward me. All your homophobic comments."

"Homo... I don't know what you mean."

"You're trying to tell me you've never referred to me as 'that damn queer'?"

Miranda got to her feet. "I refuse to sit here and be insulted. I think your illness must have gone to your brain." She hurried out of the cubicle.

"Illness?" he taunted. "You mean, the queer disease?"

She walked through the maze of cubicles, refusing to meet anyone's eye, and shouted back, "Yes, that's what I mean."

Miranda's first thought was that Barry had to hear about this from her. It was a terrible situation, but Terry had goaded her to the breaking point. She stopped at Barry's office door, which was closed. She tapped and opened the door. He was at his desk, an intent look on his face as he pored through a document—underlining and scribbling notes. He glanced up. "Not now, Miranda."

"Barry, it's extremely urgent I speak with you."

"Later."

A shaky Miranda made her way back to her own office. She reflected that many people must have overheard Terry's incredible rudeness. They would back up her story.

BARRY'S MEETING with Worthington that morning was irritating, to say the least. Worthington did not like Barry's initial draft of the staffing report. "Far too drastic," he had declared. "I know we're over-heavy on staff positions but, Barry-boy, this would cause a revolt."

"Maybe that would be a good thing." Barry suggested. "Get half these deadbeats angry enough to quit."

"Okay, I gotta agree with you in theory. But not in practice. There's no way I'm going to present this thing to the executive committee. Sorry, but you'll have to come up with something more palatable."

As it happened, the task of revising the report wasn't as onerous as Barry had feared. He left in most of his recommendations, but proposed they be considered at some future date rather than today. The report was shaping up to look like an honest, but not immediately threatening, assessment.

At four-thirty, he put his head out his office door and beckoned Dorothy. "Dot, would you get these revisions made, ASAP. I didn't have any lunch today so I'm slipping down to the caff for a snack. I'll be back in twenty minutes."

Dorothy said, "Don't forget, Miranda really wants to see you. She came by a couple of times this afternoon while you had your door shut."

"Miranda. Of course." He smiled.

Dorothy smiled back.

42

Earthquake

IN THE CAFETERIA, Barry bought a muffin and coffee and sat at a table in the almost empty room. Someone from P.R., whose name Barry couldn't recall, greeted him. "Mind if I join you?" They chatted for a while.

The clock struck five. Barry said, "Time to make tracks. We're getting dirty looks from the cleaning staff." He stood up and took his tray to the station in the corner. The P.R. man followed.

A sudden enormous jolt shook the building. There were cries of distress from the people around. Barry grabbed a table for balance and looked across the room. Through the floor-to-ceiling windows, he could see buildings swaying across the street.

Earthquake.

The shaking stopped. Barry and the P.R. man exchanged glances. Barry said, "I'd better get back to the office."

This proved to be difficult. Outside the cafeteria, Barry pushed his way across the courtyard through a crowd of excited chattering employees who appeared to materialize out of nowhere. He looked up at the shattered windows of the Annex Building and carefully picked his way through the shards of glass on the ground. In the Annex lobby, he headed toward the elevator banks but was reminded by someone rushing by, "No elevators running."

Barry hesitated. It made sense to leave the building with everyone else, but he'd left his briefcase in his office, along with that damned staffing report for Worthington. He headed for the main staircase. It was packed with panicky employees making their way down.

As he tried to push his way up against the flow, he was stopped by a manager from another floor. "Don't go up there. It's too dangerous. Walls are bulging, windows shattering. We're all supposed to meet in the lobby."

Barry stopped and headed back into the lobby. He was glad he was wearing his jacket so at least had his wallet and keys with him. He would, he decided, try to go out the front doors and walk to the parking garage which had an entrance onto the street. Then he'd get his car and drive straight to the hospital to see Lila.

At least, he thought, he wouldn't have to bother with Miranda and whatever was ailing her today.

In the lobby, people were milling around in what seemed like a disorganized, noisy mass. In a corner near the door, a young woman was pinning up a chart with the words, "Executive Support Services Department" on it in large, thick letters. He faintly recognized her as one of their secretaries, and struggled toward her. "What's going on?"

"I'm the emergency response coordinator for ESS. Are you in ESS?"

Barry couldn't hold back a grin. "I'm the manager."

She regarded him for a second with suspicion. "Okay. Well, I'm in charge of emergency supplies. We have water and cots and blankets down here."

"Cots and blankets? You're expecting people to sleep here?"

"Could be. Some people might be scared to go outside with all the falling glass and bricks."

Barry cast his eyes upward in the lobby toward the giant chandeliers that hung above them. Who on earth had picked this as a gathering place after an earthquake? He left her and threaded his way to the entrance.

Almost instantly, he was assailed by a frantic, high-pitched voice that he hardly recognized. "Barry, Barry. Oh, thank heavens you're here." Miranda was at his side. "Barry, I've never been so scared. I don't know what to do."

He continued pushing toward the front door and tried to loosen her grip on his arm. "Well, see that woman over there? She's the emergency coordinator for our department. She says they have blankets and water and stuff so people can stay here if they can't get home."

Miranda's shrill voice in his ear made him jump. "Barry, I can't stay here." She pushed her body into his side, her face close to his, and whispered, "I'm scared to death. I had an awful meeting with Terry Lynch. He was so rude." Her eyes darted around as if she expected Terry to lunge at her with a knife.

"So what do you expect me to do?"

Her voice rose again. "Where are you going? Take me with you."

"Miranda, I'm sorry but there's no way. I'm going to the hospital to visit Lila. That is, if I can get my car out of the garage." He tried to pull free but she clung still, running her hand down his arm until she grasped his. He hoped that no one around them noticed this physical contact.

"Your car's in the garage? Oh, Barry, please let me come with you."

"But..." Barry glanced around. He felt that people were indeed watching. "Okay, we can try to find a hotel for you."

"I don't want a hotel." He didn't let her finish. Quickly, he walked to the door, half dragging Miranda who continued to cling to his hand.

He muttered aloud, "This is a huge mistake." Of that, he was convinced. But he didn't know what else to do.

AT FIVE O'CLOCK on that same afternoon, Katie and Dan lounged on the couch in his new apartment, discussing what to have for dinner. Dan had persuaded her to drive over to Merced that morning for an overnight stay. (*"C'mon, Katie, you gotta see this place. It's real nice."*)

It was, in fact, really nice. His rented rooms were on a sub-street level, stretching the length of the house. From where she lay, Katie could see out the large picture window at a pleasant view of the river and farmlands.

"I sure feel like eating some good red meat for dinner tonight," Dan said. "And you know what?" He raised himself on one elbow to look at Katie. "Mrs. Lopsided"—Dan's pet name for his landlady—"says I can use the barbecue any time I want. How's about we pick up a coupla steaks for tonight?"

"Sounds good." Katie suddenly felt hungry. "We'll get some salad fixings too and some crunchy bread."

"Way to go, pardner." He sat up and swung his legs off the couch.

Katie glanced at the clock. Almost six o'clock. "Let's check the news first." She reached for the radio.

Right away, it was obvious something strange was happening. There were two announcers, alternately making hysterical pronouncements about something that had just happened. "For Heaven's sake, what is it?" She turned up the volume. "An earthquake, it would seem. In the Bay Area."

Dan said, "I didn't feel anything, did you?"

"Shush, listen. This seems like a big one." They listened for a few minutes. A hard to figure out jumble concerning interrupted baseball games, fires, freeways falling down. "My God, the Bay Bridge has fallen down? I don't believe it. I hope the cats are okay. I'd better call Mildred." She struggled off the couch and went to the phone. A couple of minutes later, she hung up. "I guess all circuits are busy. I'll have to try again later." She thought for a minute. "You know, Dan, maybe I'd better head back home tonight."

"Aw, come on. That's too much driving in one day. You know these news guys always exaggerate. Another day won't make no difference."

Another day? Katie envisioned two terrified cats huddling in a house that had collapsed around them. A frantic Mildred. But Dan was right—the news was so

often exaggerated. It would be silly to set out before
getting through on the phone first.

43

Unexpected Consequences

BARRY RETRIEVED HIS CAR without difficulty. He and Miranda climbed in and he set a determined course for the hospital. Driving through the city was murder. There were traffic snarls at every intersection. The streets were littered with glass and fallen masonry. People drifted on and off the sidewalks, seemingly oblivious to traffic.

Barry commented, "There sure is a difference between the damage sustained by the older buildings compared with the newer ones. I guess they've been doing something right with the new earthquake standards."

Miranda had been silent until now. At his remark, she burst out, "RPC's buildings obviously didn't have any new standards."

"Well, they didn't fall down, did they? Even the chandeliers in the lobby were intact."

She curled forward into a ball, hugging her knees with her arms. "It was awful. The worst thing I've ever known."

"Yeah, earthquakes are pretty scary. Is this your first?"

She turned toward him angrily as she continued to rock back and forward. "Where were you anyway? I didn't see you when all the shaking was going on."

"I was in the cafeteria."

"The cafeteria? Barry, I had left word I urgently needed to see you. Didn't you get the message?"

"Yes, I did. I was planning to return to the office." She glared at him and he added, "Honest."

They were in the midst of yet another giant traffic snarl. With no signals operating, each intersection was a survival-of-the-fittest scene. "Know something, Miranda. I think I'll give up trying to reach the hospital and head for home instead. I'll call Lila from there."

Miranda relaxed back in her seat. As he wound his way across to the west side of the city, she started to talk. "It was horrible on our floor, Barry. All the walls started to bulge out and crack. The noise was horrendous. I thought the whole building was going to fall down."

"Mmm."

Miranda looked hard at him as though daring him to question her terror. "Everything was shaking like mad. We all got under our desks and were scared to move. Then people started shouting for us go down the stairs, but I was terrified. I couldn't move from under the desk."

After a silence, Barry asked, "So what happened?"

She said abruptly, "Someone sort of dragged me out."

He thought to himself that no doubt she had made a hell of a scene and got everyone mad. He said softly, "So you didn't exactly exercise leadership in this situation either?"

It was a nasty comment, calculated to arouse her ire. Which it did. "What do you mean, *either*? Are you implying there are other situations where I haven't exercised leadership? Barry, I've had it with you. Every time I try to use my initiative, you stomp on me. You undercut me, like with those performance ratings. I've just had a horrible experience and all you can do is make sarcastic jabs."

He slowed the car to a near standstill. "If you've had it with me, Miranda, no need for you to stay. Do you want out here?"

Miranda swung her eyes around to look through the windows at the unfamiliar neighborhood. She burst into tears. He said, "Okay, I'll stop being such a bastard if you stop acting like you're the only person in the world who's affected by this."

She slouched back in the seat and took a tissue from her purse. He felt some remorse at his cruelty but was also genuinely disgusted with her. As assistant department manager, she did bear some responsibility to act managerial once in a while.

He turned on the car radio as he speeded up again. All earthquake news, of course. It had been a big tremor. Reports ranged from 7.8 to 8.2 on the Richter scale. It was certainly a much bigger quake than he'd ever experienced.

Away from the city center, the traffic eased off. Barry was relieved to see relatively little damage as he drove toward his home neighborhood. It did strike him that there were no lights on anywhere. He'd probably have to entertain Miranda by candlelight. He felt increasingly annoyed that he'd not succeeded in escaping before she'd spotted him in the lobby.

Miranda sat up as they pulled into his driveway. "It's going to be candles and cold cereal tonight, Miranda." She said nothing but climbed out of the car, slammed the door, and stomped up to the front porch. It was almost, but not completely, dark inside the house. Barry found flashlights for each of them and guided Miranda downstairs to the bar in the living room. "Help yourself. I'm phoning the hospital."

The line was dead.

Miranda found the ice cubes and fixed herself tequila on the rocks. Barry got a beer and joined her on the couch, taking care not to sit too close. He said, "That should settle your nerves." She didn't reply. "Okay, how long are we going to keep up this sulking act?"

She slammed her drink down on the coffee table. "Never in my life have I come across anyone so insensitive to other people's feelings. I've had the most appalling day. You have no idea the scene I had with that faggot. I desperately wanted to talk to you about it but you wouldn't get back to me. Then the earthquake. I really think I'm in shock. I feel cold and shaky and all you can do is make snide remarks." She hugged her knees and shivered.

That faggot, Barry assumed, referred to Terry. He sighed. "I'll get you a blanket." He took the flashlight and made his way to the kitchen where he retrieved the candles they kept for blackouts. He lit three candles, cementing each one to a saucer with dripping wax. One for the kitchen, one for the living room where Miranda sat, and one for the hall outside the bathroom. Then he found the blanket.

When he returned to Miranda, she was pouring the last of the tequila into her glass. She returned to the couch, and he dropped the blanket onto her lap. She drank as though slaking her thirst with water. At this rate, she'd soon be out cold and there'd be no way he'd be able to unload her anywhere else.

She said, "I'm hungry. Is there anything to eat?"

"Just cold stuff. I'll go take a look."

He took his beer into the kitchen and started foraging. In the end, he fixed what he thought was a pretty decent meal. He defrosted a package of cooked jumbo shrimp, fixed a salad of lettuce and tomatoes, and added bread and butter and cold milk. He called her to the kitchen table to eat. "Voila!" he said, pointing to his feast. "We even have chocolate chip ice cream for dessert. Might as well eat it before it melts."

After they'd eaten, they returned to the couch. Miranda said, "How long do you think the power will be out?"

"I've no idea, but with an earthquake this big it might be a very long time."

"Oh, my God. I hope nothing's happened to my house."

Barry added dryly, "Or your husband, for that matter."

She burst into a fit of giggles. Barry was surprised at how his own mood lifted with her laughter. He really didn't like being on the outs with her. He spoke warmly to compensate for his earlier harshness. "How about another drink? There's no more tequila, I'm afraid. How about Scotch, or gin?"

"Sure, anything." He fixed them both Scotch with ice. He turned on his Walkman battery radio and they listened to the news on and off throughout the evening. It wasn't good. A major fire was raging in the Marina District. Part of the Bay Bridge had fallen down. A whole freeway structure had collapsed in the East Bay. Many people had been killed. Scores of downtown workers were stranded in the city overnight. By morning, one report said, they hoped to get ferries working to take people across the Bay.

Sometime after ten o'clock, Barry felt Miranda lean close to him. Somehow, she'd ended up at his end of the couch. "Barry, I'm so glad you rescued me. I'd have been sleeping on the streets tonight."

He scoffed, "I don't think so. Remember, they had cots in the lobby at RPC?"

She pouted, moving her face up close to his. "That's an even worse prospect than sleeping in the streets."

Barry laughed loudly. Too loudly. Miranda's voice was becoming slurred, and he felt somewhat out of control himself. Her right hand holding the glass was propped on the back of the sofa. She brought her left hand around to cup his chin and then his cheek, and gently pulled him toward her. He thought, *No, I don't want to do this*, but as she started kissing him it really did feel good. He removed the waving glass from her hand and got on with the serious business of kissing.

They were there a long time. The candle sputtered and finally drowned in its own pool of wax. Gently, he removed her clothing and then his own, stroking and exploring while he continued to kiss her. Just like a couple of necking teenagers, he thought. She melted into him, responsive and tender, till finally he laid her back on the couch and lowered his body onto her.

Strangely, at this moment, she seemed to tense up. He thought he heard her whisper, "No, Barry." But that couldn't be. Because wasn't he giving her what she had wanted from him all along, from the moment they first met? Besides, there was no way he could back up now. In fact, her barely perceptible resistance lent an exciting fillip to the whole thing. He enjoyed it immensely.

Afterwards, he lay beside her, tired. He hadn't really drunk very much—not compared to Miranda certainly—but it was enough to make him feel sleepy. Now, all he wanted was to get into his own comfortable bed. He wondered if it would be too callous to just leave her here on the couch. Cautiously, he extracted himself from clothing and limbs. He whispered, "Miranda, are you okay?" But she was asleep, or pretended to be. He covered her with the blanket and tiptoed off with his flashlight. First, to the bathroom for a quick shower, and then to the California King bed he and Lila shared.

44

The Morning After

BARRY AWOKE THE MORNING after the earthquake, knowing that something was wrong. It was getting light outside and the alarm hadn't gone off. He stretched out an arm toward Lila's side of the bed before remembering she wasn't here. Then it all came back to him. No alarm. No power. Earthquake. Miranda.

There was a spooky silence in the house. No motors running. No fridge, no water heater or furnace. No sound from Miranda either. He made his way quietly to the bathroom. Better not take another shower. He'd leave whatever hot water was left for Miranda. He brushed his teeth, slipped on a shirt and jeans and went in search of his guest.

She was crouched in a half-lying, half-sitting position on the couch with the blanket pulled around her. He could see she had put back on the cream two-piece suit he had removed last night. He said, "Good morning. How are you?"

"I'm freezing."

"I'm sorry. We have no heat." She shivered dramatically. He said, "Look, why don't you climb into my bed upstairs and I'll fix us both a nice hot cup of coffee."

He hoped she'd ask how he'd manage this because then he could tell her about his amazing brainwave. He would use the barbecue to boil water and cook food. But she said nothing. He put an arm around her shoulders to help her off the couch and steered her up the stairs and into his bedroom where she snuggled into the rumpled bed. Barry donned a sweater and sneakers. "I'll go light the barbecue and make us breakfast."

It was very quiet outside. He got the barbecue fired up and then bustled around the kitchen getting things ready. He told himself he wouldn't think too hard about last night. After all, men had extramarital adventures all the time. Lila was lucky that he was such a faithful stick-in-the-mud.

First, he found a pan of water to boil for instant coffee. They had a griddle on which he could fry bacon and eggs. If they had bacon and eggs. He looked in the refrigerator. Yup, there they were. Toast. That stumped him for a moment, but he found a wire rack in a cupboard. Perfect. He could put the bread on the rack and the rack on the grill. He felt proud of his ingenuity. For one forgetful second, he even pictured himself boasting about all this to Lila. Whoops!

He noticed his houseguest was being extremely quiet. He heard the toilet flush so he knew she was awake. He called out, "Miranda, how do you take your coffee?" She didn't answer so he returned to the bedroom where she was climbing back into bed again. "Miranda..."

"I don't want any coffee."

"Sure you do. What's wrong?"

She leaned against the pillow, staring glassy-eyed across the room. She did look white, although that might be her usual early morning, makeup-free, face. "I don't feel good."

He walked over and sat on the edge of the bed. "You had quite a bit to drink last night. It's probably a hangover. Coffee might be just what you need."

"Okay, then. Just black."

In the kitchen, he poured the coffee and assembled the breakfast. Orange juice. Bacon, eggs, toast. Did she want this upstairs, he wondered, or could he persuade her to come down here? He went to the bottom of the stairs to call her, but the sound of vomiting from the bathroom stopped him in his tracks.

Oh, hell! He was damned if he was going to let all this good food go to waste. And yet, he supposed he'd better check on her. He went back up the stairs and stopped at the bathroom door. "Miranda, are you okay?"

In a strangled voice, she replied, "No, I'm not. Get me some water please."

He got a glass of water and cautiously pushed open the bathroom door. She was huddled on the floor by the toilet looking as abjectly miserable as any human being he could recall seeing. She said, "No breakfast for me, Barry."

"Obviously not. Call if you need anything. I'll be in the kitchen." He hastened out of the sour-smelling bathroom and went back to the kitchen. Once he started eating, his hungry stomach responded appreciatively. He ate all of Miranda's share too.

She appeared as he was rinsing the dishes in the sink. She was wearing a coffee-colored silk slip, and carrying her two-piece cream suit over her arm. "I'd like to iron this."

Without thinking, he said, "Okay." Then he remembered. "Oh, no, you know what?"

She wailed, "No electricity. Now how on earth am I to go out with these crumpled clothes. This is awful."

"You won't look any worse than the people who slept in the Annex lobby last night."

She wailed again and made her way back upstairs, still carrying her suit. Barry followed and watched as she woefully contemplated herself in the mirror. It seemed to him that her clothes were the least of her problems. She looked dirty and disheveled. He said, "Why don't you take a shower? We have a spare toothbrush somewhere." He glanced at her tangled hair. "Probably a hairbrush too."

Suddenly, Miranda turned and glared at him. "We had unprotected sex last night."

Her accusatory tone caught him by surprise. "Have you only just realized that?" He couldn't resist sounding sarcastic. After all, there'd been no talk of protection last night while she'd been throwing herself at him with such abandon. He added, "As it happens, I had a vasectomy years ago so you needn't worry about pregnancy."

Miranda, still clutching her suit, paced around the bed. "Pregnancy isn't the only thing to worry about, is it?"

"You think I'd give you a *disease*? I'll have you know I haven't been with anyone except Lila for over ten years. It's more likely I'd get a disease from you."

To his surprise, she didn't argue.

"Well, do you want this shower or not?" He marched into the bathroom without waiting for an answer and got out towels and soap, which he dumped on the bed. He walked out, leaving her to it.

A few minutes later, he heard her footsteps dragging down the stairs. "Did you shower already?"

"Are you going to drive me to the ferry?"

"Yes, we'll go see if they're running. Then I'll make for the hospital."

They left the house at ten o'clock. Barry hadn't quite figured out what his story would be if he met one of his neighbors. As luck would have it, no one was around. Miranda was quiet and sullen. He supposed she was still miffed at his lack of sympathy for her yesterday.

He asked, "So, what happened with you and Terry yesterday? I heard some yelling going on."

Angrily, Miranda said, "He was doing the yelling. He was swearing at me, calling me a paranoid bitch."

"Good heavens, what did you say to provoke that?"

Her voice rose. "I didn't say anything. Why do you assume it must have been my fault? I tell you he'd lost his mind, screaming hysterically...."

"You mean, like you're doing now."

Abruptly, she turned away and muttered, "I don't believe this." He glanced at her. Her face was red, her mouth downturned. He thought this was a fine way to carry on for two people who only a few hours before had made love. If you could call it that.

Getting to the Ferry Building was not as difficult as Barry had feared. Some streets were blocked off but there was little traffic. At the Ferry Plaza, Miranda released her seat belt and grabbed her purse before he'd come to a full stop. She said curtly, "Thanks for the ride," and opened the door.

"Shall I wait for you? In case there are no ferries?"

She got out and closed the door without replying. He waited a few moments anyway, watching her walk across the sidewalk and down the side of the Ferry Building toward the dock. She walked upright with dignity. Barry thought with some admiration that she didn't look too bad really, given her disheveled appearance.

But what a funny woman she was. Barry chuckled. Unprotected sex, indeed.

THE FERRIES were running. A young married couple who worked in the city were returning on the same ferry as Miranda. They had, they told her, left their car parked at the Oakland ferry terminal the day before and were planning to drive back to Walnut Creek from there. They were strangers to her but she seized the opportunity.

"Could you possibly give me a ride back to my car? I left it at the station in Walnut Creek." They readily agreed.

On the drive from Oakland to Walnut Creek, the young couple chatted. He said, "They told us we could sleep in RPC's lobby but that didn't appeal to us. Can you imagine having those huge chandeliers come down on top of you?"

The wife said, "So a whole bunch of us camped out by the Ferry Building. It was kind of fun really. We built a fire to keep warm."

Miranda was silent. The wife asked, "What about you? How did you spend the night?"

Miranda said, "I was raped."

"Excuse me?" The young man raised startled eyes to seek hers in the rear view mirror.

"I was raped."

The wife turned around to face Miranda. "My God, I'm so sorry. Is there something we can do? Go to a police station or something? What on earth happened?"

"I don't want to talk about it. I just want to go home."

She said no more during the rest of the journey. They dropped her off by her car and drove away looking—Miranda thought—heartily relieved to be rid of her. She didn't blame them; she was probably beginning to smell and was longing to take a bath. But, before going home, she needed to do something first. She got into her car and sat for a few moments, plotting her next steps.

45

Miranda's in Trouble

TWO DAYS AFTER THE EARTHQUAKE, Barry got a call from the director of emergency services. "We're calling all Head Office employees telling them to report to work tomorrow."

Barry was surprised. "Even those in the Annex? That was pretty badly damaged. Is it really safe?"

"Yeah," the director acknowledged, "I know they've been talking of earthquake-proofing that for years but, you know...." Yes, Barry knew. True to the company's standard mode of operating, such action had been postponed from year to year.

The director went on, "We've identified the most affected floors, including yours—the eighth. We've already found new quarters for you so, tomorrow, you guys can start packing up your things."

When Barry groaned, he added, "You're lucky being among the first to relocate because we've found you empty space in the Tower Building—nice modern offices. They've been renovated for someone else, but you have priority."

The next day, Friday, Barry got to work at eight o'clock. Most employees had heeded the call to return to duty and were already tackling the formidable task of gathering up their belongings from the wreckage and filling up the cardboard boxes provided by the building department for the moving process.

There was the inevitable confusion but on the whole people were cheerful and cooperative. After a while, it occurred to Barry that something—or, rather, some people—were missing. He told Dorothy, "I don't recall seeing any of my senior staff. Would you round up

Miranda, Katie and Terry. We'll meet in my office in half an hour."

Dorothy responded. "No one's around, Barry. Miranda left word she won't be in. Katie still hasn't returned from vacation. And then a while ago Terry went over to Employee Relations."

"Oh, for God's sake! Just the time I most need my management team and they're all gone. So why isn't Miranda coming in?"

"She said she won't come back until the building's fixed." Dorothy hesitated. "I know she was pretty traumatized when the earthquake hit."

Barry sighed. "I'd forgotten about Katie and her damned vacation. Give her a call and tell her I need her to come in today. In fact, I'll call her myself."

"No, Barry, she's not at home. She's in Merced right now."

"Merced? Doing what?"

"Staying with her boyfriend, Terry says."

Barry screwed up his face. Katie with a boyfriend! "And what is Terry doing in Employee Relations? No, of course you have no idea. Well, ask him to come see me when he gets back."

Terry didn't show up that morning. But at noon Barry got a call from Worthington's secretary. "Barry, Everett needs to see you in his office right away. Something urgent has come up."

"Did he say what?"

"No, although he did request that you bring Terry Lynch's personnel file with you. Also, Miranda's, if you would."

"Got it."

Barry's curiosity was aroused. He took the two confidential files from a cabinet in his office, put on his jacket, and walked to the elevator. The doors opened and Terry Lynch emerged. His eyes widened at the sight of Barry but he hurried away without a greeting. Barry made his way to the Tower Building, up to the fortieth floor.

There were already three people sitting around the desk in Worthington's office. Besides Worthington, there were Joe Fenniman, the vice president of human resources, and a company attorney Barry knew only as Jake. "Sit down, m'boy," from Worthington. He handed Barry a folder. "A little matter here that requires your attention."

There was a sheet of notes inside the folder. Joe Fenniman leaned toward Barry. "These are just rough notes, you understand, jotted down this morning by the employee relations rep."

Barry ran his eyes over the handwritten notes, while simultaneously listening to Worthington's explanation. "The gist of the matter, Barry, is that one of your supervisors, Terry Lynch, is accusing Miranda Peabody of engaging in discriminatory behavior and language, causing him deep distress. He says she has not only made homophobic remarks to him, but also gave him a poor performance rating this year in spite of excellent evaluations by clients."

The young attorney spoke up. "He claims to have retained the services of a law firm specializing in these matters."

Worthington spoke again, "Furthermore, Barry, Lynch says he may bring charges against you also because you have been aware of this behavior on Peabody's part and have done nothing to stop it."

Barry closed the folder and placed it on the desk. "For Pete's sake." He turned to Fenniman. "Miranda gave C ratings to both Terry Lynch and Katie Carlisle. I thought she was being too harsh and changed both those ratings to A's. Miranda knows that. And Terry knows that. As for homophobic remarks, I haven't heard them."

Worthington rocked back in his chair. "I'm relieved to hear that. In the meantime though, I'm very concerned about Miranda. What's she doing handing out performance ratings anyhow? In fact, what does she do all day, period?"

"It's true," Barry admitted. "It's hard to keep her occupied, and that's no doubt why she gets her nose into things she shouldn't."

Fenniman said, "That's another thing the ER Rep reported. Peabody told Lynch she was instituting a policy of job exchange, or some such." He turned to Worthington. "Apparently, she asked him to trade jobs with the management development supervisor."

"Get outta here." Worthington shouted. "Barry, you're letting this woman run amok. Get rid of her ASAP. I'm serious. What are you waiting for?"

As the others at the table flashed accusatory looks at him, Barry felt a flash of anger. "She had some idea of cross-training. It wasn't supposed to be a permanent exchange of jobs."

From Worthington, "You mean you approved this ridiculous scheme?"

Barry spoke in his coldest voice. "Everett, may I remind you it wasn't my idea to put Miranda on our department's payroll. In fact, I was under the impression I was doing you a favor by, to quote you, finding a place for her until her contract expires."

Barry had never spoken to Worthington so boldly before. His present anger had driven him to do so. Now, looking at the matching anger in Worthington's face, Barry wished he could have withdrawn his words.

"I don't give a goddamn why she was put on your payroll. I'm telling you *now* to remove her. Do you think you can manage that?"

For a long moment, Barry met the eye of the man across the desk glaring at him with such contempt. Could it really be, Barry wondered, that Miranda had engaged in some sort of sexual relationship with this aging hunk of blubber? Maybe even his own Lila...he'd never quite sorted out what her relationship with Worthington had been before he himself had entered her life. He said slowly, "You're saying you're no longer concerned about keeping Miranda on the payroll until her contract time expires?"

Fenniman broke in, "Now, Barry, don't worry about that. We can work out a severance package for her that doesn't leave her short one penny in terms of the original contract."

Worthington said, "That's great, Joe, you do that."

The attorney, addressing Barry, said, "You don't have to worry about the process of severing her either. We'll help you write up a letter, and we'll make sure you have a witness with you when you discuss the issue with her."

"That's fantastic, gentlemen." Worthington rose. "I'm glad we've settled this." He turned to Fenniman and Jake in turn and shook their hands. He didn't shake Barry's hand.

Barry asked, "And what happens next with Terry Lynch?"

Jake said, "Don't worry about that. If he asks you, just say it's being handled. I'll get in touch with him today and try and talk him out of this litigation nonsense."

Barry left to the sound of continued expressions of gratitude from Worthington directed toward the two other men.

"YOU KNOW HOW that made me feel?" Barry grumbled to Lila later that evening. "I felt like an incompetent nincompoop who was being bailed out by my betters."

They were lying side by side on their bed. Lila reached up to stroke his hair. "I'm sure no one has ever thought of you as an incompetent nincompoop."

"Not until now maybe." Barry's tone was bitter. "All the rest of the day, I kept mulling over nasty things to say to the SOB, like *Next time you get involved with a woman, you horny old goat, don't expect me to help you out.*"

Lila laughed but she looked anxious.

He said, "It's okay. I wouldn't be quite that stupid."

BARRY HAD PICKED Lila up from the hospital two days earlier, shortly after dropping Miranda off at the Ferry Building. It had been a happy reunion. Far from being annoyed at his not having shown up the previous night, Lila had been overjoyed to see him. He told her, "Just spoke to the doctor in the hall. He says all went well."

"Thank God you're here." She had put her arms around him, hugging him as though she'd feared she'd never see him again. Barry, for his part, had been temporarily overwhelmed by feelings of intense love and protectiveness. Now, he raised himself on one elbow to look at her. "You really are looking much better, sweetheart. It's good to see some color in your face again. Next step, a vacation for us both."

Lila was silent for a few moments. Then she said, "Barry, how do you feel about Miranda getting the push?"

"Why, it's the best news I've heard in a long time. I'm just annoyed at the way Ev's presented it. As if I were the one who wanted to keep her in the first place. I've been telling him all along she's nothing but trouble."

"And you're the one who'll have to tell her? Won't that be awkward?"

"Why should it be?"

She looked up at him, her gray eyes solemn. He said, "Oh, please. You're not still concocting some mad love affair between Miranda and me, are you? I tell you, I can't stand the woman."

Lila looked away again. "No. I just thought you might find it awkward."

"You mean, because I'm so unused to firing people?" He joined in her laughter.

MIRANDA TURNED OUT to be an elusive target. Barry left a couple of messages for her at her home over the weekend, but she didn't reply.

On Monday, Barry phoned Jake, the attorney. "So do I just wait until she decides to turn up?"

"No," Jake told him, "I've already prepared a letter of dismissal. I'll bring it to your office this morning. After you sign it, we'll send it to her by certified mail."

Barry's first feeling was relief at avoiding a personal confrontation with Miranda. His second feeling was uneasiness. Somehow, this all seemed way too easy.

46

Katie Catches Up

Katie drove back to Alameda on Monday afternoon. With a feeling approaching dread, she turned into Alara Way. The houses on both sides of the street appeared to be in good shape. Pulling into her own driveway, however, she noticed a large crack in the asphalt running from side to side. That hadn't been there before. Inside the house, the two cats greeted her with joy. She was relieved to see there were remnants of food in their dishes so clearly Mildred had been feeding them.

She made a brief tour of inspection of the house. Nothing broken although the English bone china tea set that she kept in a glass-fronted cabinet in the living room had been tossed around.

Next, she checked her mail and phone messages. The leave-of-absence form she'd requested was there. No letter of dismissal—yet. There were a couple of predictable, pre-earthquake phone messages from Barry and Miranda wanting to know when she was coming back to the office. And there was one from Terry left on the day of the earthquake. "Katie, sure do miss you." Pause. "I just had a horrible fight with Miranda." Another pause. "I really would like to talk to you. Please call."

She felt mean at not having been here to get his call but also relieved because they'd probably sorted it all out by now.

At three o'clock, Katie picked up the phone and called Dorothy.

"Katie, how are you? Where are you? We've all been worried about you."

"I'm just fine. I was in Merced yesterday. I really didn't feel the quake. I'm the one who should be worried about you."

"Yeah, things are sure a mess around here. And the earthquake is only one of the shakeups we've had since you've been gone." Dorothy lowered her voice. "There've been real fireworks between Miranda and Terry. He's threatening lawsuits and goodness knows what."

Probably, Katie guessed, they had come to blows over his performance evaluation. "Oh, my! Does Barry know?"

"He sure does. This morning, he was called to a meeting in Mr. Worthington's office, and this afternoon he was locked up with Terry for a while."

"And Miranda?"

"She isn't here. She hasn't been back to the office since the earthquake."

Interesting. Well, Dorothy, the reason I called was to say I'm planning to take this week off too."

"Oh, no! Katie, you ought to talk to Barry first. He keeps asking when you'll be back. I think he feels abandoned by his management team."

"There's no point in coming in. I bet all our training programs have been placed on hold for now. Also, do I even have an office to come back to?"

"Good question. Our floor has been condemned by the building department; it's in a terrible state. But they've found us temporary offices in the Tower. Right now, we're all packing up to move."

"Makes me feel like a rat not being there to help you. But...there are things I need to do first."

Katie was looking forward to her day of reckoning with Barry—the day on which she would tell him what he and Miranda could do with their lousy performance rating. But she didn't want to face him until she'd arranged for her six-month leave of absence. Now, she opened the envelope from H.R. and glanced over the application. Her heart sank as she realized that Barry had to approve the wretched thing.

At five o'clock, she fixed canned tomato soup and toast for her dinner. Afterwards, she went to her desk and pulled out her copy of *A New Direction for the Executive Support Services Department* and settled down on the couch with the cats. She wondered if Barry had ever looked at the copy she'd left with him. He'd never mentioned it, but perhaps that was understandable given that was right after she had taken it into her head to lecture him on his incompetence as a manager. She sure knew how to screw things up.

She pulled the document out of its brown envelope and read the pages over again. She was struck at how good her proposal sounded—and how wistful the words made her feel. With all that had happened of late, she now knew she would never be the manager of ESS. She might as well toss this thing in the trash, but given the hours of careful work she'd put into it, she couldn't bear to do that just yet. She placed the pages back into the envelope.

THE NEXT DAY, she called Terry. "Terry, it's me. I've been meaning and meaning to call you but there's been so much going on."

"Tell me about it," he said. "I hope you're getting back to the office soon. We need some sanity around here."

"That's what Dorothy said. What's happening?"

"Well," he said, "where to start? First off, the day of the earthquake, I had a huge blowup with Miranda. But it was good, Katie. You know how she was always making snide remarks about my sexual orientation? Well, that day, she started screaming dreadful things at me, all within the hearing of people around in the cubicles."

"God, she's stupid," Katie commented.

"You can say that again. Anyway, with that ammunition, I marched into employee relations and told them I had hired an attorney and would be filing suit against the company. Also, I charged Miranda with discriminatory behavior, like rating me a C to ensure I got no raise this year. Well, that sure stirred the pot."

Terry sounded happy.

"Yes, I heard something of that from Dorothy. She hinted that Barry had become involved and Miranda hasn't been into the office since."

"She hasn't been into the office since the earthquake. And, yes, Barry is involved. He met with Worthington, Fenniman, and a guy from the law department. Then later he called me into his office. He reminded me that the C rating was a mistake."

"What does that mean?"

"Oh, I guess I didn't tell you he changed my rating to an A? But that didn't make Miranda's behavior any better. He said the company would send me an official apology and hinted that Miranda would not be with us much longer."

After a pause, Katie asked, "I suppose you don't know what happened to my rating?"

"Don't worry. If Barry raised mine, I'm sure he raised yours too."

Katie didn't feel so sure of this, remembering back to her unpleasant interchange with Barry the week she left on vacation.

"In the meantime," Terry continued, "things have been a bit strange in the office with you and Miranda not here. And Barry seems to be preoccupied with various things—like his wife, I suppose."

"Terry, let me tell you about a decision I've made since I've been away."

"Oh, no."

"The past week or so has been heavenly, just escaping from that charged atmosphere. You know, the whole sick-making Barry-Miranda thing."

"Katie, remember the department will be a much pleasanter place for all of us if Miranda leaves. And I really think she will. I'm sure we can all forge a better relationship with Barry if she goes."

Katie said firmly, "Terry, there are issues between Barry and me you don't know about. I'd need for both of them to leave before I could feel comfortable continuing to work there. Anyway, no matter, I'm applying for an immediate six-month leave of absence. In that time, I'll decide on my future. At the very least, I should organize a serious job search."

After a silence, Terry said, "I'm really sorry to hear you say that, Katie. This place won't be worth working in without you."

"I'll miss you too. But you're the only person I'll miss. Right now, I feel I just have to take care of myself for a while."

Another silence. Terry asked, "How's the hunk?"

She laughed. "You mean Dan? Another part of my life I have to sort out."

"What's he doing now?"

"He's working with Sherman Granger. They're manufacturing garden equipment at his brother-in-law's plant near Merced. He and Sherman use the place nights and weekends. They want me to work with them part-time, help tidy up, do bookkeeping and stuff."

"Wow!"

"No, Terry, seriously, it might be kind of fun, just for a few weeks. It'd certainly be a complete change of pace."

"You know, you should be careful about getting too involved there." His voice quickened as she chuckled. "Really, I'm sure Dan's okay in his way, but he isn't right for you. You deserve someone a big, big step up from Dan." After a moment, he added, "I know, you're thinking 'What the hell business is it of yours?' and you're right. But I care about you, Katie. I often think you don't realize just how great you are."

"Terry, please stop. You'll have me crying." She did indeed feel close to tears. "Anyway, I'll let you go now. Please give me a call if any juicy Barry-Miranda type developments occur."

"Sure will. Take care."

After Terry hung up, Katie realized she hadn't asked about his partner Stefano. How uncaring of her.

47

Lila Gets a Phone Call

Barry left work early on Thursday and was home by four o'clock. He had heard nothing from Miranda all week, although she had signed for her letter of dismissal on Monday afternoon.

Lila was resting in the backyard in the lowering sun. "Hi, babe," he greeted her. "Guess what? I cleared the decks so I can stay home tomorrow. We can take a little drive if you feel up to it." He leaned down to give her a peck on the forehead, and tapped the glass she was drinking from. "What you got? Lemonade? I think I'll find me something stronger."

She murmured something and he went into the kitchen to get himself a beer. When he re-emerged, he lowered himself into the chaise beside her. "This fall weather is great, isn't it? A bit cool but that sun just hits the spot." Lila, he thought, seemed quieter than usual. "So how are you, cutie-pie?"

Lila put her glass down. She said, "I got an odd phone call this afternoon."

"Oh?"

"Your friend, Miranda."

Barry sat up, swinging his legs over the side of the chaise onto the ground. "She wanted to talk to me, I suppose. Why on earth did she call here?"

"No, she didn't want to talk to you. She wanted to talk to me."

The uneasy feeling Barry had any time he'd thought of Miranda this week came over him stronger than ever. He waited, feeling suddenly that one of his worst fears had come true. A fear he'd told himself over and over was completely irrational. The bloody woman surely wouldn't tell Lila.

Lila went on, her voice unsteady. "She said that on the night of the earthquake she came home with you. Home to this house here." Lila's eyes looked up to meet his with reproach. "She says she spent the night with you. You got her drunk. And then you raped her."

The last sentence came as such a surprise that Barry burst into a laughing shout. "I did *what*?" Lila's eyes widened at his reaction. "The woman has lost her marbles. Lila, you know earlier this week I sent her a letter dismissing her? I haven't been able to reach her on the phone. She hasn't called in. This is evidently her revenge. My God! You don't believe her, do you?"

Lila looked uncertain. "I'm not sure what I believe," she said finally.

Barry leaned forward, holding his sides in a gesture of amusement. "So I'm a rapist!"

Lila said slowly, "Did she come to this house with you after the earthquake?"

"Yes, she did. And she did stay overnight, although that wasn't the original plan. She was in such a hysterical state, begging me to rescue her from the crumbling building downtown. So I agreed to take her out of there and find her a hotel after I'd visited you in the hospital."

"But you didn't find a hotel?"

"No, didn't get to the hospital, didn't find a hotel. The city was one horrific traffic jam so we came back here. I got us some food to eat. Only Miranda hardly ate a thing. She drank just about the whole contents of our liquor cabinet. By ten o'clock she was out cold. I left her on the couch in the family room. I just put a blanket around her and went to bed myself. In our bed upstairs. By myself."

His mind raced. Miranda had actually been in that bed in the morning for a short while. But he'd changed the sheets since then. There was no way her presence could be detected now. Was there?

Lila was watching him. He knew she wanted to believe him but felt skeptical. "In the morning, she had a giant-sized hangover. I got her some coffee and then I drove her to the Ferry Building to get a ferry back across the Bay." Lila's silence continued. Barry went on,

"She was in a foul sulk. In fact, she'd been sulking at me all evening because she wanted to complain to me about Terry Lynch and her fight with him. She was pissed off that I didn't want to hear about it."

He glanced at Lila. She looked sad. And thoughtful. She said, "And when were you going to tell me about this incident?"

Best to stick to the truth as far as possible. Barry said, "Never, if at all possible. I couldn't imagine you'd relish hearing about it. Only now my hand has been forced, to put it mildly. But please, Lila," he leaned over to cover her hand with his. "Please don't read more into this than you should. There most assuredly was no physical contact between us, let alone rape." He laughed again to underscore just how ridiculous an assertion that was.

Lila withdrew her hand from his and picked up her glass again. "Barry, obviously I want to believe you. And I guess for now, I must." She paused and looked into his eyes intently. "But if I find out you've been lying about any of this, I'll never trust you again. I mean that with all my heart."

He breathed an inner sigh of relief. If it came to a showdown, it was his word against Miranda's. And he hoped that Miranda, with her accusation of rape, had made herself look ridiculous.

He said stiffly, "I'm sorry you still have doubts. Personally, I don't know if I could stand to be around a man who's raped a woman. I can't believe you could think I'd be capable of such a thing."

She said quietly, "You know, one person might define as rape what another might call consensual sex."

"Oh, for God's sake." He rose, putting as much indignation into his tone as he could to shut off further debate.

It worked. Lila said, "Okay, please let's forget it. Know what? Let's go out to eat tonight. How about that Persian place you told me you'd seen off Market Street?"

Barry went through the motions. He went into the house to look up the Persian restaurant in the phone book. He phoned them to make sure they were open. He got washed up and changed for their meal out.

Only now he didn't have an appetite.

48

Barry's in Trouble

ON THE FRIDAY he was planning to take off work, Barry awoke feeling tense. Lila was acting cheerful enough but he could feel the lie hanging out there between them like an invisible bogeyman. One part of him ached to confess the truth but he knew that if he did his marriage was doomed.

After breakfast, he donned his oldest jeans and a plaid shirt. Lila watched him put on his boots at the patio door. "What have we here? Farmer John?"

"I had a sudden urge. I thought I'd dig up that patch beyond the lawn. Then maybe next spring, I'll plant tomatoes again."

"I thought we were going to take a drive somewhere."

"That too. We can drive over to the coast for lunch." The phone rang. Hastily, Barry made his way out the door. "Whoever it is, I'm not in."

From the potting shed at the far end of the patio, he tried to find the right tools. He grumbled to himself about the way spades and shovels seemed to vanish between his gardening bouts. Finally, he found a spade and tested the handle to make sure it was secure. Out of the corner of his eye, he could see Lila in the kitchen, phone in one hand. As she talked, she walked toward the patio door.

She slid open the door and called, "Barry. It's Ev."

Reluctantly, Barry put down the spade and made his way indoors to the phone. Worthington said, "Sorry to interrupt you on your day off. Something urgent's come up and we need you here."

Barry strove to hide his annoyance. He hoped the "something" wasn't Miranda, but feared that it was.

"That's okay. I knew being home on a Friday was too good to be true."

Worthington said, "How soon can you get down here?"

"Well, I have to get changed, shave..."

"By eleven?"

"I guess so."

"See you at eleven then."

WHEN BARRY got to the CEO's office, the door was open and he walked in. He had half-expected to find Miranda there and was prepared for a blazing confrontation with her. But there was no Miranda. Instead, Worthington was accompanied by the human resources VP Joe Fenniman and Jake the attorney. They rose when Barry walked in.

"So we meet again," Barry said cheerily.

Worthington remained seated. He said to Joe, "How about you fill him in."

Joe sat back and crossed his legs. He looked uncomfortable—yet Barry had the feeling he was relishing this. "Barry, as you know, we've been waiting for some reaction from Miranda Peabody with respect to her dismissal. Well, we sure got it."

Both he and Jake snickered. Worthington stared at Barry, his face sober. Joe continued, "The good lady tells us she has retained a firm of attorneys and is planning to bring not one, but two, lawsuits against us. The first one is based on a charge of wrongful dismissal. Breach of contract."

Jake quickly said, "We can easily refute this. She doesn't have a legal leg to stand on. Our offer has made her whole from a financial point of view and—"

Worthington interrupted, "Never mind that." He nodded to Joe, "Go on."

Joe said, "The other lawsuit is more, er, difficult." He turned to Barry. "She's bringing a suit against you personally for having sexually assaulted her."

Barry groaned but he was prepared. "Don't tell me. I abducted her the night of the earthquake, got her drunk, and then raped her."

Looks of astonishment from around the table. Worthington said, "You've heard this before?"

"I sure have. She phoned my wife with this story. And I can tell you," Barry leaned forward, speaking in his firmest voice, "To say I am pissed off is putting it mildly. It started with my doing her a favor. She was in hysterics that day."

"The day of the earthquake?" Worthington interjected.

"Yes. I was trying to leave to get to Lila in the hospital. Miranda stuck to me like a clam and begged me to help her because she was afraid she wouldn't be able to get home."

Fenniman turned to Worthington. "She was right. It ended up all East Bay employees were stuck in the city."

Worthington nodded and turned back to Barry.

Barry continued. "I agreed to try to find a hotel for her. Well, we drove around in circles for hours. All the streets downtown seemed to be blocked. In the end, I took her to my home, thinking I could phone hotels from there. But of course the phone wasn't working."

He gave a deep sigh. "All this time, Miranda was screaming at me because of the earthquake. She seemed to think it was my fault. She was also angry with me because she felt I hadn't sympathized sufficiently with her over a fight she'd had with Terry Lynch." He paused to glance at Worthington, whose steely look Barry thought had softened.

Barry went on. "At the house, all she wanted to do was drink. I fixed us some cold food, but she just proceeded to drink through all the liquor we had in the house. And the drunker she got, the more affectionate she got. And the more I fought her off, the angrier she got." Barry noted Worthington was nodding. "By about ten o'clock, she'd passed out cold. She was on the couch in our family room, so I put a blanket around her, and left her there. I went upstairs to my own bed. By *myself*, I should stress."

Barry felt cheered. The more he talked, the more convincing his performance sounded to his ears, and the more sympathetic Worthington looked.

"And in the morning?" Fenniman asked.

"In the morning, she was hung-over as hell, grumpy as all get-out, and very angry because my iron didn't work so she couldn't iron her crumpled clothes." Barry laughed and they all joined in.

Jake asked, "But why would she concoct the rape story?"

"Sheer spite, I would think. Because she thinks I had something to do with her being fired. Or at least thinks I didn't do enough to prevent it."

Worthington mumbled in what sounded to Barry like agreement.

Worthington said, "Well, Barry, things sure look different now we've got your side of things. Miranda is pretty good at putting on an act though. What was it she said, Jake, about seeing a doctor?"

"She said she didn't shower after the alleged attack so as to preserve, quote-unquote, physical evidence. And that before she went home the next day she went to a hospital to have a doctor examine her."

Barry's stomach turned to ice.

Fenniman asked, "What did the doctor say?"

Jake replied. "I don't know. She says her attorney has the results."

"Sounds like a bunch more bluff to me," Worthington said. "We all know she's real good at that. Well, gentlemen, thank you so much for meeting at the last minute like this. But, Barry," the blue eyes that turned to Barry were friendly, "it's a good idea for you to retain an attorney anyhow. You can obviously refute her story and if it comes to physical evidence, why, that's sure to sink her case."

He stood. This time, he shook Barry's hand.

Fenniman stayed to discuss other issues with Worthington. Jake and Barry took the express elevator down to the lobby. Jake chatted about his lunch plans. But his words went over Barry's head.

This was the deepest trouble he had ever been in. He interrupted Jake to ask, "Jake, do you think it's likely I'll be asked to provide a semen sample?"

Jake was reassuring. "I very much doubt it. As soon as Miranda hears you're denying her story, she'll know there's no point in pursuing it. We all know she's trying to bluff us."

Barry looked down at the floor. The elevator arrived in the lobby and the doors opened. Jake said, "Of course, if she keeps insisting that she has physical evidence, then you would have to do it."

They stood for a moment in the middle of the big lobby. It was almost lunchtime and they were surrounded by employees scurrying from the elevators and out to the street. Jake's expression had turned thoughtful. Barry wondered if his question had aroused the attorney's suspicion and how much their conversation was protected by attorney-client privilege. Jake said, "I think you should engage your own attorney, as Everett suggested. I'd be glad to refer you."

"Yes, thank you. I'll give you a call."

Barry watched Jake head across the lobby. The blood was thundering in his head. The sound, he thought, of his world collapsing around him. He could see absolutely no way out of this mess.

A FEW MINUTES LATER, when Barry was back in his new third floor office, the phone rang. It was Worthington. "Barry," he boomed. "I've been talking to Larry about our—or rather, your—little problem with Miranda." Larry was Larry_Atchison, Jake's boss. "He suggested, and I agreed, that your very best strategy is to cut Miranda off at the pass, as it were. Don't wait for her attorneys to request anything of you. Instead, you should immediately make yourself available to provide whatever they might require. I told Larry he should give instructions to his staff to notify Miranda's attorneys to this effect. They'll be making the call this afternoon."

In the silence that followed, Barry's indignation grew. You'd think that Worthington of all people, who thought nothing of having a fling with any pretty face that struck his fancy, would be more understanding of a fellow male with woman trouble.

"Okay with you?"

Barry said coldly, "I appreciate your efforts on my behalf, Ev, but I'd really have to think about this. Let me talk it over with Lila."

"Now why would that be a good idea?" Worthington sounded aggrieved. "Poor Lila has enough to contend with right now, what with her illness and the partners in her company sneaking around behind her back. You do know, don't you, that the lead partner has gone ahead with bringing his nephew on board despite her objections?"

Barry sighed. "Yes, I knew that."

"In fairness to Lila, you need to dispose of this whole Miranda business ASAP without getting her involved. I suggest you call Larry or Jake right now and figure out a time when you'll be available to give this sample. Specimen. Whatever."

"Ev, I'm increasingly getting the impression that my word on this matter isn't good enough for you. The more I think about it, the more I do *not* intend to provide specimens of anything to anyone."

Another silence. Worthington cleared his throat. "Barry, if that's your final word on the subject, I'm going to have to ask for your resignation. Because I'm afraid your refusal sounds to me like a clear admission of guilt."

"If that's how you feel, I'll be glad to resign. I'm sorry, but whether or not I provide this sample, there's no way I could continue to work with you knowing that you distrust me."

Worthington said, "That's too bad," and hung up.

For a while, Barry sat thinking of his shattered life. Now, he thought with a flash of wry humor, he'd have to get a real job. Not this sham fill-your-day-with-meetings-and-unneeded-reports type of existence, the aim of which was to please the boss rather than the customers.

He picked up the phone and called Joe Fenniman. "Joe, how do I go about resigning?"

Joe sounded shocked and also wary, as though fearful to ask too many questions. "How soon do you want to resign?"

"How about, right away?"

Joe made clucking noises. "Barry, I hate to sound crass, but have you given any thought as to who will run your department? I mean, obviously Miranda's out of the picture too, isn't she?"

Barry snorted. "Believe me, she was never in the picture. The perfect person to run our department is Katie Carlisle. In fact, you should seriously consider her as a candidate for manager. She has some really good ideas for reshaping the department."

Fenniman hesitated. "Barry, have you talked this over with Everett?"

"About resigning? Oh, yes."

Fenniman, still sounding stunned, said, "Okay. I'll come by your office this afternoon with the necessary paperwork. About two, okay?"

"Fine."

After he hung up, Barry looked at the piles of material on his desk. There was a bunch of stuff in his "To be signed" folder, a bigger bunch in his "To be read" folder, several pink slips of phone calls to be returned, a couple of proposals from staff members to review. He'd do as much as he could by five o'clock. Then he'd head home for a sober conversation with Lila about their suddenly altered future.

WHEN BARRY got home just after six, no one responded to his greeting from the front door. It was dark indoors. He set off down the stairs toward the kitchen without turning on a light. Not until he'd tripped over it did he see the laundry basket that lay at the foot of the stairs. A white-hot pain shot through his right ankle. Angrily, he shouted, "How the hell did that get there?" No one answered. He staggered, hopping, into the kitchen. When he turned on the light, he saw the sheet of paper attached to the front of the fridge.

Barry

I'm on my way to Palm Springs. I'll be staying with my mother for a few days. Ev called and told me about Miranda's lawsuit and his conversation with you. Maybe I'm overreacting but I do need time to think things over. Please don't try to get in touch.

Lila

Barry laughed out loud. That lousy bastard. So concerned with not upsetting Lila and the first to get on the horn to let her know all about it. Okay, so now he was at the very bottom of the pit. From now on, there was nothing anyone could do to him that mattered.

He hopped over to the liquor cabinet and poured himself a bourbon and soda. Then, moving with difficulty with the drink in his hand, he made his way to the living room. He sat down on the couch—the same couch where for the only time in his life he had cheated on his wife. And, gingerly, he proceeded to examine his ankle.

49

A Career Ends

KATIE RETURNED TO WORK on Monday, October 30. By now, the disoriented occupants of the Annex had been moved to temporary accommodations in various downtown locations. ESS had moved to the third floor of the Tower.

As Katie crossed the street in front of the RPC block, she looked with sorrow toward the old Annex before making her way to the elevators in the Tower. From a distance, the building looked little changed save for some boarded-up windows and some missing gargoyles.

Their new quarters in the Tower were stark: grayish-blue walls with white modular furniture. She found her office by the paper sign on the door but stayed only for seconds. It was too depressing. She took her leave-of-application form out of her briefcase, and put her briefcase and purse in a drawer. Then, form in hand, she made her way to the manager's office, which she assumed would be in a corner of the floor. She was right. Barry's new office was a spacious corner one with nice views of the waterfront. Dorothy sat alone in the vestibule outside. She broke into a smile on seeing Katie. "Thank goodness you're back. It's wonderful to see you. Did you find your new office?"

"Sure did. A soul-less box. Like the whole floor, I guess."

"Oh, this is so different from the Annex. It's going to be a huge adjustment. Katie, I have so much to tell you..."

Katie interrupted. "First, Dorothy, there's one very important thing I must do today. I must have Barry sign this form for me."

Dorothy hesitated. Katie was surprised to note she was actually wringing her hands. "Katie, he isn't here. Oh, I don't know where to start. Have you talked to anyone recently? About everything that's been going on?"

Katie sat down in the chair beside Dorothy's desk. "You mean, about Miranda? Miranda fighting with Terry? Yes, I've heard about that."

From Dorothy's expression, it was clear there was something else. "Well, there is that. Miranda's been gone since the earthquake. All week, we'd been hearing about her getting fired and stuff because Terry is suing for discrimination or something. But there's more than that."

Dorothy paused, glanced at Katie and then turned away, looking more distressed than Katie could ever remember seeing her. "Well, last Friday she called me to say she wanted someone to pack up her things and send them to her." Dorothy's mouth trembled. "Then she started to make all kinds of wild accusations about Barry. She said the real reason she was being fired was that Barry was being spiteful."

"Spiteful?"

"She said that on the night of the earthquake, he got her to go home with him. His wife was in the hospital that day, you know. And then, according to Miranda, he proceeded to ply her with drink and rape her. *Rape her!* She fought him off and she says that's why he got her fired."

Katie gasped. "That's one hell of a story. Surely no one believes it."

There was a pause. Dorothy fiddled with a pencil. Then she said, "Barry didn't come in today. He didn't even call. That's not like him." Finally, she looked up to meet Katie's eye. "A few minutes ago, Mr. Worthington called and asked to speak to him. So I contacted him at his house. He said he was staying home today because he'd fallen down and sprained his ankle."

For a long moment, Dorothy's eyes searched Katie's face. "It's kind of a weird excuse, isn't it? What's weirder is that when I called Mr. Worthington back and told him, he said, 'You tell Barry to get down here. I want to see him in my office this morning.'"

Katie felt her throat tighten. Dorothy said plaintively, "Sounds like he's in trouble, doesn't it?"

Katie got to her feet. "Okay, so he's coming in this morning?"

"Well, no." Dorothy resumed her handwringing. "When I gave him Worthington's message, he said this morning wouldn't be convenient and that he might come in later this afternoon. I left that message with Worthington's secretary." She shuddered. "I can't imagine the two of them duking it out."

Katie couldn't imagine this either. Could it be that Worthington actually believed the rape story? Whatever, she just had to get Barry's signature on her leave-of-absence application.

She said, "Dorothy, I don't have time to wait for him to come in. What's his home address? I'll get a company pool car and drive over there this morning. Would you please call him and let him know I'm coming."

AN HOUR LATER, Katie drove along the street where Barry lived. Nice neighborhood. Tree-lined avenues, large houses with manicured lawns and shrubs. No evidence of earthquake damage that Katie could see. She found his house and pulled into the driveway. As she stood at the door and rang the bell, she could see inside a room at the front of the house. A sort of den. Barry was visible, lounging in a recliner and holding a glass. He saw her through the window and shouted, "Come in. The door's unlocked."

He didn't get up when she entered the room, pointing to his bandaged right leg which was resting on an ottoman. "I apologize for not rising to greet you. It is literally a pain to do so." His voice was slurred.

"I'm really sorry to barge in on you like this. How'd this happen?"

"On Friday, I came home to find my wife gone. Gone to stay with her mother in Palm Springs, or so her note said." Now Katie felt sure he was drunk. "Anyhoo, when I went downstairs to the kitchen I tripped over a laundry hamper at the bottom of the stairs." He waved his glass at her. "Ha! Can you imagine? She'd left the damned thing just where I'd fall over it."

"Oh, no, Barry. I'm sure it was an accident."

"Sure. You're welcome to a drink, but you'll have to get it yourself. Downstairs, in the living room cabinet."

"No, I don't need anything, thanks. I've come by to ask you to sign a form for me." She pulled the application from her briefcase. "I know you planned to be at the office later today but I wanted to hand this in this morning."

She carried the form over to him. He put down his glass and took it from her. Katie went back to her seat and held her breath as he went through each page. Then he looked up. "What's all this about?"

Katie spoke quickly. "Barry, to put it simply, my work life has become pretty well untenable of late. I've always worked hard and done well for my clients. And my client evaluations are consistently excellent, not that you or Miranda ever bother to read them. And with all this, I get a C-minus performance rating. In fact, I recall your threatening me with an F."

He smiled.

She continued, "So I've decided to take a few months off to think things over. And relax for a while."

"With your boyfriend in Merced?" He laughed aloud at Katie's astonished expression. "You can't hide much from the office grapevine. Is this the infamous inventor?"

"No, no." She hesitated, wondering how much to tell him. "My friend Dan and Sherman have set up a business together. But I'll have you know they are not planning to cheat the company in any way. Sherman has patents on lots of things and they've set up a machine shop to manufacture them."

"And you're going in with them?"

"I'm just helping them set up the books and stuff."

"Wow! Sounds exciting!" He looked at her with amusement. Then he asked, "So is marriage in the works?"

"That's none of your business." Her retort brought another burst of laughter from him.

"Well, I certainly don't intend to stand in your way." He turned back to the document in his hand. "Where do I sign?" After he signed the form and handed it to her, he added nonchalantly, "Incidentally, I changed your rating to an A. Just as I did Terry's. Didn't you know that?"

"I knew about Terry's but I didn't know you'd changed mine."

"I decided not to tell you about it too soon. I thought you deserved to be kept dangling for a while. I guess I kept you dangling a bit too long, huh?"

"I guess you did."

She gathered her things and made toward the door. He struggled to his feet, pulled his crutches under his arms, and followed her. At the door, he said, "When is this leave of absence due to start?"

"I've been told I have to give two weeks' notice, so I guess I'll spend that time getting my projects in shape to hand on to someone else."

A bird sang in a clump of blue plumbago near the door. Barry's eyes drifted over to it. With a dreamy expression on his face, he said, "I may not be seeing you again, so I guess this is goodbye."

"I'll be around for two weeks at least."

"Yes, but I doubt that I will."

His words were not really a surprise given what Dorothy had said this morning. Katie watched him, as he rested on his crutches, a vacant look on his face, his clothing and hair uncharacteristically disheveled. She was now sure her opponent was about to leave the ring. Not that this would make any difference to her now. But she should be feeling happy about it, shouldn't she? Somehow, she didn't.

She said, "Barry, things seem to have gone very wrong for you."

His brown-green eyes clicked into focus as he turned to her. "More wrong than they've ever been before in my life."

She looked at his unshaven face and felt a sudden desire to comfort him. She even felt her hand moving forward to touch his face. But, quickly, she recovered herself, and turned away. As she climbed into her car, she looked back toward the door. He was still standing there. She waved, and he waved back.

IT WAS ELEVEN O'CLOCK when Katie got back to RPC. She went straight to Employee Relations to hand in her form. The ER rep—a bespectacled, prematurely bald young man—took her into his cubicle and invited her to sit down while he perused her leave-of-absence application. "So Barry signed this? I must say I'm surprised—given the circumstances."

"What circumstances?"

He looked at her owlishly over his glasses. "Didn't he explain to you that he's resigning from the company? In fact, I think his resignation takes effect today."

"He didn't, but I sort of guessed something was up. I wanted to get that form signed to avoid having to deal with a replacement."

As the owlish one scribbled on the form, Katie asked, "Do they know yet who'll be replacing him?"

The rep took off his glasses and regarded her solemnly. "No, but I know Joe Fenniman asked him if he wanted to recommend anyone." He raised his eyebrows.

Katie raised hers too. "And?"

"He recommended you."

A STUNNED KATIE made her way back to her third floor office. Everything was moving so fast and in such unexpected ways. She called in on Terry. He was busy with two of his survey design people, papers spread out on his desk. He looked up as Katie put her head around the partition.

"My God, Katie, I thought you'd vanished down a dark hole somewhere. We need to talk. How about your office?" He excused himself from his colleagues. As they walked down the hall, he said, "Things have been jumping around here and I wanted to catch you up on the latest dirt."

In her office, he closed the door behind them and they both sat down. She said, "I went to see Barry this morning. At his home."

"Really?"

"I had him sign my leave-of-absence application form."

"How did he seem?"

"A bit drunk, to tell the truth. Pretty upset. He's sprained his ankle or something. And then the ER rep told me he's resigning. Surely not over this cockamamie story Miranda is spreading around?"

"So you did hear that? Yeah, that's around the whole department. None of us believed it for a minute. But then, the weirdest thing. On Friday afternoon, I was talking to Worthington's private aide who was eavesdropping where he shouldn't have been. This part is all confidential, incidentally. It seems that Miranda claims to have physical proof that Barry raped her, or at least had relations with her. She went to a doctor apparently. So, again according to Miranda, her lawyers said he'd have to submit a—you know—a specimen."

"So what happened?"

"According to my source, Worthington got hold of Barry, said he'd have to provide this specimen, and Barry refused!"

"Oh, my, that sort of implies..."

"It sure does. So, to make matters worse, Worthington—a real bastard, if you ask me—called Barry's wife who's just recovering from heart surgery. Told her she had to talk him into this if she wanted her husband to hold onto his job. And I don't know what happened next."

"I think I do," said Katie. "She took off for a stay with her mother in Palm Springs. Barry fell over coming down the stairs and is now in the house alone with a sprained ankle." She sighed. "Poor Barry."

Terry gave a burst of laughter. "*Poor Barry*! My, Katie, you've changed your tune."

They sat in silence for a few seconds. Terry said, "He wasn't all bad, was he?"

"No, he wasn't."

BACK AT HIS HOUSE, Barry dressed for his meeting with Everett Worthington. Not being able to put any weight on his right foot made this a hellishly difficult task. In fact, on Friday he'd had to call a neighbor to take him to the emergency room. It had been embarrassing explaining Lila's sudden departure and listening to his neighbor's condolences. At the hospital, they'd diagnosed a torn ligament. Lots of rest and ice packs.

He called for a taxi. Damn Everett, anyway. Fennniman already had his resignation letter. Why did the stupid old man require his physical presence?

He arrived at RPC about three o'clock and went straight to Worthington's office. Worthington wasn't there. Instead, Eileen said apologetically, "Please sit down. I have to make a call."

Apparently, the call was to security because a few minutes later two men arrived to escort Barry to his own office. "We have to supervise the packing up of your belongings and make sure you leave the premises," they told him.

In his office, a distressed Dorothy helped him pack. He said, "Remember the day I arrived at the department, you told me I traveled light? Aren't you glad?" She started crying. When they'd finished, the security men loaded his boxes onto a trolley. They phoned for a cab, and then escorted Barry and his belongings out of the building and into the cab.

This treatment for departing executives was the utmost humiliation, usually reserved for people who had been fired for such dastardly deeds as embezzlement. Barry struggled into the taxi. Before closing the door, he looked up at the windows of the Tower Building, now glinting in the afternoon sun. He called aloud, "And screw you too, RPC."

But then, as he settled back in his seat, a thought occurred to him that brought a moment of pure spiteful pleasure. He would not be the last victim of this ridiculous brouhaha. Not by a long shot.

50

A Career Begins

LORRAINE BEAMED across the table at Katie. "Sure is great to see you, sweetie. And on such a beautiful day. And it's even a Friday!"

They were sitting in a crowded student-laden coffee shop near the Berkeley campus. Lorraine's choice. An unfortunate one, Katie thought. Not conducive to the cozy chat Katie had been hoping to have. However, it was the best Lorraine could manage at short notice, and Katie urgently needed to talk. She and Lorraine had exchanged only brief phone calls since the earthquake and so much had happened in Katie's life since then.

Lorraine tore apart her sandwich and removed the cheese. "Keep forgetting to tell 'em to skip the cheese. So what on earth have you been doing all this while? And how come you haven't been letting Auntie Lorraine in on all the details?" She smiled, but Katie caught a trace of rebuke in her voice.

"Lorraine, I'm so sorry. I've been lousy at keeping in touch of late. But things have been just frantic."

"I can imagine," Lorraine countered dryly. "It's all go for you, isn't it? If not earthquakes, then running off into the hinterlands with lover boy. And how was it back at the office?"

"A mess. In fact, the building department has pretty well condemned the Annex. They've moved us all to the Tower Building."

"Nice offices?"

Katie made a face. "Sterile is the word, I guess. Anyway, Lorraine, the reason I asked you to meet me today is because this afternoon I am going to make the most momentous decision in my life."

But Lorraine's attention was distracted by some other ingredient in her sandwich. Hot chiles. Katie's heart fell. This obviously wasn't the right venue for sharing her news. But she so longed to get reassurance from someone dear to her that she was doing the right thing. Which, of course, she was.

She said, "Lorraine, forget the sandwich. Don't talk, okay. Just listen to me. I have so much to say and it's all so unbelievable." She glanced at the clock. "And you have to get back to work in an hour."

Lorraine said, "Half an hour."

"I'll talk really fast."

Katie did talk fast. In just ten minutes, she summarized the news concerning Miranda and Terry, Miranda and Barry, and the accompanying lawsuits and potential lawsuits.

When she paused, Lorraine said, "Whew! Sounds like it's not just the San Andreas Fault that's been rattling and rolling."

"I haven't even started on the best part yet. The part I really wanted to tell you about." Katie gulped down some coffee and took a bite of her sandwich. She was hungry and needed to be fortified for her meeting this afternoon. She summoned up a grave tone as she continued. "What I haven't told you yet is that as a result of all this brouhaha Barry has resigned. Worthington insisted on it."

Lorraine gasped. "Oh, my! Your CEO really thinks Barry is a rapist."

"Who knows? Regardless, they asked Barry to recommend someone to take his place. And guess who he recommended?"

Solemnly, she stared across the table into her friend's eyes. Lorraine said, "Katie Carlisle?"

Katie exclaimed, "How did you guess?"

"Why wouldn't he? You're the best there is."

"Oh, sure. Joe Fenniman, who's our V.P. of Human Resources, called me yesterday. He said he's spoken to Worthington and they're thinking of making me a formal offer to be manager of ESS. A permanent appointment. I'm meeting with Fenniman this afternoon to talk about it. Three o'clock."

Lorraine squealed, "That's fabulous. Your wildest dream come true, right? Oh, Katie, I'm so happy for you." She put down her sandwich and reached out a slightly greasy hand to stroke Katie's. And then, "What? What is it, for God's sake?"

Katie, to her annoyance, couldn't keep her lower lip from trembling. "Lorraine, I'm so excited, it has me both laughing and crying. Also, of course, it would mean the final inevitable breakup with Dan. As you've said before, just the push I need to make that happen."

Lorraine looked thoughtful. After a moment, she said, "Of course, if you wanted to, you could keep going with Dan a while longer. You know, at weekends...."

Katie remembered that Lorraine didn't know the worst thing about Dan—his prison record. "Well, not often. He'll be occupied at evenings and weekends because that's when they get to use his ex-brother-in-law's machine shop." She added slowly, "Remember, Lorraine, Dan was just a stopgap thing for me. It really is time I finished it."

The two women looked at each other across the table for a few long seconds. Lorraine said sadly, "Yeah, that's true."

"Look, this is a win-win for both of us. He feels this business venture is his break of a lifetime. I feel this manager job is what I've always wanted. So we've both got what we've always wanted."

Lorraine glanced up at the clock over the counter. "God, Katie, you might have picked a less rushed time to tell me about all this. We have a faculty meeting at one-thirty. I was late for the last one. I have to be on time today."

"Yes, I'm sorry. But this was the soonest you could meet, remember? And I did want to let you know about this huge change coming up in my life."

Lorraine wrapped up the remains of her food and placed it in an adjoining garbage bin. She wiped her fingers and mouth on a paper napkin. "What can I say but 'Congratulations!' Heaven knows, you've clung to your dream with the tenacity of a bulldog. Most, including me, would have quit the stupid company years ago." She stood to leave. "Meanwhile, you might as well stay and finish eating."

Katie nodded and leaned toward her friend for a kiss on the cheek. Then Lorraine gathered up her voluminous handbag, tossed a scarf around her neck, and stood. As she made her way toward the door, she looked, Katie thought fondly, just like the scatter-brained university professor that she was. A wonderful friend.

As she finished her lunch, Katie mused about friends. A friend was a valuable being. Someone to gripe to when things went wrong, someone who was on your side, who gave you caring if not necessarily useful advice. And soon she planned to give one friend his walking papers.

No matter. She knew she had made the right decision.

AT SIX O'CLOCK that evening, Katie got onto the elevator on her way back to her office. It had been an exhausting afternoon. She'd spent well over an hour with Fenniman, and another hour with Employee Relations doing endless paperwork.

The final package she'd been offered had exceeded her wildest expectations. However, Fenniman had not given way on Katie's request that she postpone starting her new job for a couple of weeks in order to take care of personal business. "You must start right away," Fenniman had insisted. "For the sake of department morale and to reassure your clients that things are being taken care of." Finally, he'd agreed that after one month in her new job, she could take a week of vacation.

When all was settled, Fenniman had accompanied her to Worthington's office. Worthington had warmly grasped her hand in both of his. "Katie, I've always thought most highly of you and your work ever since the days when you were Chuck's right-hand gal. Welcome to the ranks of new managers."

Now that everything was settled, Katie felt strangely unafraid. She felt not only buoyed by optimism, but also triumphant. For assuredly, she had triumphed. It was her turn for a place in the sun.

As Katie stepped off the elevator on the third floor, she became aware that not everyone had gone home yet. In fact, someone—one of Terry's programmers—was leaning against the wall in the elevator lobby. He didn't greet her but on seeing her hastened down the hall. Curious, she followed him right down to the big corner manager's office, the office that was about to become hers.

There, she was surprised to find Dorothy, Terry, and several other staff members—all smiling brightly. Dorothy said, "Here she is."

And, from Terry, "Congratulations, Madam Manager!"

Katie had not said a word to anyone about her meeting with Fenniman this afternoon. She said, "How on earth did you know?"

Terry snickered. "We knew they were going to offer you the job. We knew that this afternoon you accepted it." In a fake German accent, he added, "Ve 'ave our spies every-vare."

Katie felt the tears course down her cheeks and put out her arms to hug everyone within reach. It might all seem different in the morning but at this moment she couldn't remember ever loving them all so much and feeling so happy.

51

One Year Later

It was October 1990, a year after the earthquake. On a Monday morning, shortly before noon, Katie returned to her office on the third floor of the Tower Building. She had just had a heck of a meeting with the new CEO and could hardly contain her excitement.

As Barry had guessed a year earlier, there had been another victim of the Miranda rape accusation, and that was Everett Worthington. The Board of Directors had been shocked at what it saw as Worthington's mismanagement of some key employees and before long he had been pressured to resign. His successor was Harry Bosworth whom many had noted had had his eye on the Chief's position for a while.

Some anxious times had followed while Bosworth and the company at large had sounded each other out. Katie, in particular, had felt threatened by Bosworth's occasional question to her, "Tell me again, what exactly does your department do?" This morning, he'd asked for a private meeting with her. At 10 o'clock, she'd arrived in his office and sat down at his desk, prepared for the worst. The first thing she noticed, to her surprise, was a copy of her Manifesto on the blotter in front of him. She'd given him a copy of this at their first meeting, but he hadn't referred to it since.

Bosworth had a solemn expression and wore thick horn-rimmed glasses that he wore far down his nose. After a polite greeting, he looked up at her over the glasses. "Katie, this weekend, I've been studying this document of yours."

Katie's heart raced. "Oh, yes?"

He turned away from her and seemed to be searching for words. For a moment, she tried to guess what he would say next—"It's great" or "It's a pile of garbage." Finally, he looked back. "Do you think you'd be able to rewrite this to apply to the whole human resources organization?"

She was so surprised, she found herself at a loss for words. He continued, "I know it'd be a big job but would you be willing to take it on?"

She recovered her voice. "Of course. I'd be happy to do it." Although, she thought, this would be something of an impossible task with Joe Fenniman, the V.P. of H.R., hovering over her shoulder. Joe was always most resistant to outsiders poking their noses into the affairs of his organization.

Bosworth leaned back in his chair. "Good, good."

There was a long silence. Katie ventured, "Is this something Joe has requested?" She couldn't imagine this was the case. Joe was pretty unadventurous, probably just marking time until his retirement in two years.

Bosworth's reaction was emphatic. "No, no, nothing like that. In fact, Katie, I was rather hoping you might play a key role in convincing him his organization needs a 'new direction' as you put it here." He tapped the Manifesto.

Now, Katie felt uncomfortable. "Er, Harry, I'm not sure I'm the best person to do that."

And that's when he dropped his bombshell.

"Well, Katie, he may come around after I explain to him that I have you under serious consideration to replace him as vice president of human resources when he retires. So your recommendations would be most relevant."

Her face must have registered the shock of his words because for the first time his face relaxed into a smile. "Of course, we're talking a couple of years off. But I don't mind admitting I've been most impressed with you. You're smart, plain-speaking, and enthusiastic. And you really understand the company." He nodded, and pushed his chair back. "We'll talk further. Meanwhile, you start thinking about ways to approach this task."

As she left, a dazed Katie mumbled, "Yes. Thank you."

WHEN SHE got back to her office, Dorothy greeted her with the news that her luncheon appointment that day had been cancelled. "That's great," Katie said. "A nice quiet lunch is just what I need."

A few minutes later, she walked out of the building into the sunshine. It was a lovely fall day. Several downtown eateries had closed up after the earthquake but others had sprung up in their place. Katie made her way to one small place she enjoyed, in a quiet alley. It was undiscovered so far by most company people, and served a great Caesar salad.

Stepping inside the open front door, there was one person ahead of her waiting to be seated. The hostess was asking him, "Table for one, sir?" Then, catching sight of Katie, "Oh, are you together?"

Katie recognized him the split second before he turned around. "Hullo, Barry."

"Katie!" He looked at the hostess and back at Katie. "Would you like to share a table?"

"Sure, I'd love to."

A ripple of excitement had run through Katie at the sight of Barry. She hadn't seen him since his ignominious exit from RPC last year, and had heard little news about him.

As soon as they sat down, he said, "You look great."

"So do you." She meant this. He looked fit and tanned. "Do you work in the city? I heard a rumor you'd moved to Southern California."

"That's right. I'm up here on business for a few days. So what's good to eat?"

Katie turned to the menu. Barry showed no interest at her mention of Caesar salad, and chose the grilled salmon instead. He said, "So how do you enjoy being manager of ESS? More than I did, I hope."

"I'm loving it. Though it is one damn challenge after another." She wrinkled her nose and he laughed. "Did you hear that Worthington resigned? We have a new CEO, Harry Bosworth."

"Indeed, I did hear. That must have been quite a shocker. How are you coping with the new regime?"

"So far, so good." She couldn't resist adding, "In fact, Bosworth's one person who's actually enthusiastic about my Manifesto. Remember that?"

"Sure do. Well, good for you." Katie was longing to share her morning's news—but not with Barry. Not with anyone, yet. Barry continued, "And how's Terry?"

"Oh, sad news there. His partner Stefano died of AIDS last Christmas. Terry left the company shortly after that and moved back to Wisconsin where his family lives. I really miss him."

"That's too bad. Terry was a good guy. He must have been hard to replace."

"Well, actually, I've outsourced most of the work his section used to do. Surveys and so forth."

Barry frowned. "But you still have a viable department? Reporting directly to Bosworth?"

"Oh, yes. They're not thinking of getting rid of me yet. So, how's it going with you, Barry?"

"Pretty well. Things were rough for a while but then I found a job with a firm of efficiency experts. We show our clients how to tighten up operations so they can sell more products and make more money."

"You'd be good at that."

He smiled. She remembered that she'd always found his smile attractive—except when he was being sarcastic. He added, "Some day I'd like to go into business for myself." He smiled again. "I like to be in control, you know."

"Yes, I remember."

There was a brief silence. Katie thought there was so much she'd like to ask him but feared being too intrusive. He probably felt the same way. Finally, he asked, "So, what else are you up to? Married, I bet." She shook her head. "No? But wasn't there some boyfriend you mentioned? Let's see, what was the story? You said he was going into business with that inventor? That's right..." He sat up straight and looked across the table at her. Katie could see the glint of mischief in his eyes. "They were planning to sell cogen units all over the state. Put RPC out of business." He chuckled. "Not yet, huh?"

"Lucky for me. Well, Dan and Sherman haven't sold any cogen units yet, but that idea isn't dead. So far, they've been making a go of it doing other things. Sherman owns all kinds of patents—on gardening equipment, kitchen tools. Heaven knows what else."

Barry looked amused.

She said, "To start with, they were borrowing someone else's machine shop, just using it evenings and weekends, but a few days ago I heard from Dan they've done so well that they've recently acquired their own place. Near Pleasanton. In fact, they've managed to get another investor interested in the cogen machine."

"Really. So RPC had better still keep alert?"

Katie murmured, "Mmm." She wanted to get off the subject of Dan.

A YEAR AGO, on the evening after she was appointed manager, she'd phoned Dan with the news. He'd been disbelieving. "What about your leave of absence? I thought you was comin' to live with me for a while—try things out."

She'd rebutted, "I never said that, Dan."

And then, "This is all because I told you about the prison thing, right?"

They'd been on the phone for over an hour—he'd pleaded; she'd tried to explain her decision. Finally, "I can't believe you'd choose your career before me," he'd said. "Your career won't keep you warm at night."

Their interaction had been so harsh she hadn't even brought up the idea of the one-week vacation she'd got Fenniman to agree to.

After that, they did see each other a couple more times—unsatisfactory dates that invariably ended in bitter recriminations on the part of Dan. But it had been months now without any contact. Until his call the other night.

THEIR FOOD ARRIVED. Katie asked, "So how do you enjoy living in Southern California?"

"I don't mind it," he said, "But Lila is itching to get back to the Bay Area."

Katie's fork stopped en route to her mouth. "Lila?"

"My wife. We sold the house in the city. That arrangement with the kitchen downstairs drove us crazy anyway. We bought a nice little place in Ojai. Have you heard of it?"

Katie had. Barry talked more about his house in Ojai, but Katie found it hard to concentrate. All the rumors floating around the office a year ago had been that Barry and his wife had split up over the Miranda affair.

When he paused, she asked, "How is Lila anyway?"

Barry, between mouthfuls, said, "She's doing really well. For a start, she gave up that cutthroat partnership she was in. Now she works independently from home—putting together investment portfolios for clients but picking and choosing her projects." He stopped. "What is it?"

Katie knew her surprise was showing on her face. She said, "Silly the rumors that fly around. I heard that you'd divorced."

"Good God, no." But his flickering eyes belied his offhand tone. He ate for a while before continuing. "We went through a rough patch. But things got better after I found a job."

"I'm glad it's all worked out well for you." Katie looked at him across the table. "The last time I saw you is when I went to your house to get you to sign my leave application. On that day, you seemed so depressed, what with your sprained ankle and Lila gone. Did she come right back when she heard of your fall?"

"No, I followed her down to Palm Springs."

"At which time, she welcomed you with open arms."

"Not quite, but my mother-in-law did." He added, with a sly smile, "She's a great woman, my mother-in-law."

Trust Barry, Katie thought, to charm some woman to being on his side. But she couldn't resist asking. "What about Miranda? And all the lawsuits?"

Not meeting her eye, Barry said abruptly, "It all got settled. Miranda backed down on some things." His tone didn't invite more probing.

When they'd finished eating, Barry ordered coffee. The waiter brought the cups, cream and sugar, and poured the coffee. Barry said—and Katie had a sense that this was payback because of her impertinent questions about Lila and Miranda—"So, now that the boyfriend lives closer, will you be getting back with him again?"

It was none of his business and Katie wasn't sure why she felt compelled to reply. "Look, he's not my boyfriend. For a start, he's many years younger than I am." As soon as she said this, she remembered that Barry himself was several years younger than his wife. She went on quickly, "Also, Dan wouldn't make a good corporate husband. I just couldn't imagine him at, say, some company function."

"Like the executive Christmas parties?"

Katie nodded, but his question had shaken loose a memory. The party at Lorraine's that she'd been so hesitant to take Dan to because she'd feared all those academics would make fun of him. And then, she remembered ruefully, he'd turned out to be the beau of the ball.

Barry said, "I used to feel that way sometimes about Lila."

"Oh?"

"Because of the age difference. When we were first married, no one could tell. But as she got older...well, I felt a bit self-conscious at times taking her to corporate events." He looked down, seemingly embarrassed to have revealed so much. "But, believe me, after I nearly lost her, I realized there's no way I would want to live life without her."

Lila probably realized that too, Katie thought. Why would any woman, let alone someone several years older, want to kick this guy out of her bed?

Katie said, "Also, Dan doesn't like cats."

Barry laughed, "Ah, now there's a fatal flaw."

When the waiter brought the check, he placed it in front of Barry. Katie said. "They still tend to do that, don't they? Actually, I'd like to pay for this because I owe you one."

"You do?"

Katie met his eyes across the table. She wasn't sure if he actually realized that she knew he had recommended her for the job of manager. She said, "For raising my rating to an A. I couldn't have gotten that promotion with a C." She got out her credit card and placed it on the tray.

He said solemnly, "Thank you. Now we're even."

As they walked slowly back toward her office, Barry commented on the earthquake damage still evident along the way. Boarded up buildings, gaping holes where demolition had occurred. "It's taking a long time for the city to recover, isn't it?" he commented. "That earthquake sure shook up a lot of things."

Yes, Katie thought, *buildings, lives.*

On their way to the Tower, they paused outside the Annex Building. Barry asked, "So what's happening with this old wreck?"

"It's still partly occupied on the less damaged floors. They haven't yet decided whether to earthquake-proof it and keep it, or tear it down and build something else in its place."

He said, "I'm guessing you'd like them to rebuild it? And move back in?"

"Mmm. One part of me would love that." And, she thought, if she ever became VP of Human Resources she could push to have this charming old building turned into a HR headquarters.

They moved on across the courtyard and into the Tower's giant lobby. There, they stood for a moment and looked at each other. With a solemn expression, he said, "Katie, I'm sure you have a wonderful career in front of you. But don't make your career your whole life."

"I know," she said, "but, at the same time, you must admit sometimes you have to make choices. You can't get everything you want all the time."

"No, but you can get a whole lot if you want it enough."

She wondered how to say goodbye to him. For most people in this situation, a hug would be appropriate. But she had never hugged him, and the thought of it made her feel uncomfortable. She held out her hand and he took it. She remembered the first and last time they'd shaken hands. It was in her office the first time they'd met. She'd never touched him since. Although, she remembered, she had almost touched his cheek when she was at his house a year ago.

Her eyes wandered to his cheek now. He seemed to read her thoughts for suddenly he smiled broadly as though they shared a joke. He gave her hand a final squeeze before releasing it. "Go get 'em, Katie," he said and turned to walk out of her life again. Maybe forever. Maybe not.

THAT NIGHT, as she rode home on the bus, Katie stared into space and thought about Barry. She genuinely felt she was a better manager of ESS than Barry had ever been. This was because she loved the department and wanted it to thrive. And possibly that love was something that Bosworth could sense and that made him think her worthy of promotion.

She thought about Dan. They hadn't had any contact since Christmas until last week when he'd called her.

He'd sounded upbeat. "Everything's jest rollin' along," he'd enthused. "We got a real lucky break. Remember George, the son-in-law Sherm couldn't stand? Well, he started to get interested in the whole idea of the cogen units, and you know he's a real sharp corporate type. Part of his job is acquiring companies for their company to run."

"I didn't know that."

"Me, neither. Jes' thought of him as a real stuffed shirt. Anyways, Sherm didn't work out too well in that office manager job George got for him so he quit that, and then George got involved in our little outfit. And, guess what, he's found out there might be a good market for Sherm's cogen units outside the country in third world countries—Africa and stuff."

"No kidding. That's pretty exciting." Katie had always felt guilty that when she dropped Dan she had of necessity dropped Sherman too. She was genuinely happy that things were looking up for both of them.

"Yeah, ol' Sherm's ridin' high these days. He's even got himself a lady friend—a widow he met at some seniors' function. Can you believe it?" Dan chuckled but Katie though she detected some envy there. "Anyways, what I wanted to tell you is we got our own buildin' now near Pleasanton. George helped set us up in this. George has gotten us a bank loan and he's hiring a new guy as a salesman."

"Really? That's wonderful."

"Yeah. And they've made me production manager. I'm in charge of all the shop work."

Katie repeated, "That's wonderful," although she now detected an uncertain note in Dan's voice.

"Yeah, well, we'll have to see how it all works out. Seems to me George is gearing up to take over the company at some point and then I don't know. I sort of liked it when it was just Sherm and me in the old machine shop." Abruptly, he changed the subject. "Why I was callin' was to tell you next weekend I'll be in the Bay Area looking for an apartment. Now we've moved the business to Pleasanton it makes sense for me to move close to there."

Katie said nothing.

He went on, " Maybe we could get together for dinner or somethin'?"

Katie didn't know what to say or how she felt. She said, "I'm not sure of my plans that weekend, Dan. I'll call you."

He said, "I have a new cell phone number." She reached for a pencil and wrote the number on the newspaper she was reading, later tearing out the piece of paper and sticking it under her phone.

AT HOME, Katie went through her customary steps of unwinding. She hung up her coat, kicked off her shoes, checked the mail and phone recorder. Then it was on to feeding the cats, and then herself. Meals alone on weeknights were pretty simple. Tonight, she fixed scrambled eggs.

After eating, she went to the phone. The scrap of paper with Dan's number was still under the phone where she had left it. She picked it up and looked at it for a long moment. She'd told Barry that you can't get everything you want all the time. But maybe she was settling for less than she'd like.

When she had accepted her promotion a year ago, she had, of course, not written off the idea of romance in her life. Somehow, she had fantasized that somewhere on her way up the ladder she would be bound to run into a suitable mate. No need to rush things.

But looking across the table today into Barry's green-brown eyes had made her suddenly feel impatient for a man. Someone to laugh with, grumble with, boast to, keep her warm in bed at night. And more than that: someone who cared for her opinion, whom she could help and encourage, who needed her. Dan sure wasn't ideal but he had filled a niche in her heart she had barely realized was there.

If she were to call him now, she might be starting something that might last for one date, or for a lifetime. She reached for the phone.

Dan sounded surprised to hear her voice. "Katie? Hi."

"Are you still planning to visit the Bay Area this weekend?"

"Yeah, sure. Why, would you like to get together?" She caught the familiar hopefulness in his voice.

"Yes, I was thinking maybe it would be fun to catch up."

"Hey, Katie, that's great. Just great. Let's see, how 'bout Saturday night. That okay? Y'know, you'll have to come up with a place to have dinner. I'm sorta outa touch with places in your neck of the woods."

"Well, I was thinking maybe we could eat at the best place in town."

There was such a long pause she wondered if maybe he didn't get it. But finally he said, "Will we be having beef bergins, or whatever it was?'

"Beef bourguignon. Sure, if you like. But you must promise me a hot fudge sundae afterwards at Baskin-Robbins."

"Oh, Katie."

After a long moment, he said, "Katie, don't get mad at me for asking. Is there anyone else in your life right now?"

She said, "Not in particular. Oh, but I still have my cats and nothing will part me from them."

His voice took on a philosophical tone. "I've decided there's a lot worse things in life than cats. Maybe I could even learn to like the pesky critters."

"Or even love them?" she teased.

"Hey, anything's possible."

THE END

Acknowledgments

Many people have helped me with their comments and suggestions in the writing of this book. They include Diane Jacobson, Nilda Chong, Amy Kelm, Diane Warner, Winifred McCaffrey and Teresa LeYung Ryan. My thanks to all of them.

Biography

Margaret Davis received a doctorate in Sociology from Stanford University with specialized study in the sociology of the family and formal organizations. She worked for many years as a management consultant in a large California corporation. She is the author of two works of non-fiction (*Families in a Working World* and *Organization Design.*)

The Miranda Affair is her second novel. The first, *Straight Down the Middle*, was published in 2009. She is also the author of several short stories.

Margaret lives in Northern California. Please visit margaretdavisbooks.com for more information.

www.SandHillReviewPress.com